Bernd Braßel

Implementing Functional Logic Programs

Bernd Braßel

Implementing Functional Logic Programs
by Translation into Purely Functional Programs

Südwestdeutscher Verlag für Hochschulschriften

Impressum / Imprint
Bibliografische Information der Deutschen Nationalbibliothek: Die Deutsche Nationalbibliothek verzeichnet diese Publikation in der Deutschen Nationalbibliografie; detaillierte bibliografische Daten sind im Internet über http://dnb.d-nb.de abrufbar.
Alle in diesem Buch genannten Marken und Produktnamen unterliegen warenzeichen-, marken- oder patentrechtlichem Schutz bzw. sind Warenzeichen oder eingetragene Warenzeichen der jeweiligen Inhaber. Die Wiedergabe von Marken, Produktnamen, Gebrauchsnamen, Handelsnamen, Warenbezeichnungen u.s.w. in diesem Werk berechtigt auch ohne besondere Kennzeichnung nicht zu der Annahme, dass solche Namen im Sinne der Warenzeichen- und Markenschutzgesetzgebung als frei zu betrachten wären und daher von jedermann benutzt werden dürften.

Bibliographic information published by the Deutsche Nationalbibliothek: The Deutsche Nationalbibliothek lists this publication in the Deutsche Nationalbibliografie; detailed bibliographic data are available in the Internet at http://dnb.d-nb.de.
Any brand names and product names mentioned in this book are subject to trademark, brand or patent protection and are trademarks or registered trademarks of their respective holders. The use of brand names, product names, common names, trade names, product descriptions etc. even without a particular marking in this works is in no way to be construed to mean that such names may be regarded as unrestricted in respect of trademark and brand protection legislation and could thus be used by anyone.

Coverbild / Cover image: www.ingimage.com

Verlag / Publisher:
Südwestdeutscher Verlag für Hochschulschriften
ist ein Imprint der / is a trademark of
AV Akademikerverlag GmbH & Co. KG
Heinrich-Böcking-Str. 6-8, 66121 Saarbrücken, Deutschland / Germany
Email: info@svh-verlag.de

Herstellung: siehe letzte Seite /
Printed at: see last page
ISBN: 978-3-8381-3275-4

Zugl. / Approved by: Kiel, CAU, Diss., 2011

Copyright © 2012 AV Akademikerverlag GmbH & Co. KG
Alle Rechte vorbehalten. / All rights reserved. Saarbrücken 2012

für Silvi

Contents

1 Introduction and Motivation   **9**
   1.1 Declarative Programming languages 9
       1.1.1 Functional Programming Languages 10
           1.1.1.1 Abstract Data Types and Pattern Matching . . 10
           1.1.1.2 Higher Order 13
           1.1.1.3 Call by Value, Name and Need 16
       1.1.2 Functional Logic Languages 19
           1.1.2.1 Non-Deterministic Operations 19
           1.1.2.2 Free Variables and Narrowing 20
           1.1.2.3 Call-Time and Run-Time Choice 22
           1.1.2.4 Controlling Search 25
   1.2 Implementing Functional Logic Languages 27
       1.2.1 Transformation to Functional Languages 29
   1.3 Debugging Functional Logic Programs 31
       1.3.1 Related Work 31
       1.3.2 The Approach Presented in this Work 33
   1.4 Content of this Work 34

2 Functional Logic Programs   **35**
   2.1 Signatures, Expressions and Programs 35
   2.2 Natural Semantics of Case-Based Programs 38
       2.2.1 Flat Expressions 39
       2.2.2 Heaps and Configurations 40
       2.2.3 Statements and their Derivation 40
       2.2.4 Correspondence to the Original Approach 43
       2.2.5 A More Abstract Notion of Semantics 45
   2.3 Modifications of the Semantics 47
       2.3.1 Changing Rule (VarExp) 47
       2.3.2 Elimination of (VarCons) 48

3 Elimination of Free Variables   **51**
   3.1 Treatment of Variable Chains 52
   3.2 Elimination of Free Variables 56
       3.2.1 Keeping Track of Generator Updates 57

CONTENTS

		3.2.2 Replacing Free Variables by Generators	59
		3.2.3 Reintroduction of Free Variables	64
	3.3	Summary	69

4 Uniform Programs — **75**
- 4.1 Case Lifting 75
- 4.2 Introduction of Uniform Programs 82
- 4.3 Flat Uniform Programs 85
- 4.4 Excursus Term-Graph Rewriting 86
- 4.5 Proving Soundness 90
  - 4.5.1 From Uniform to Flat Uniform 91
  - 4.5.2 From Flat Uniform to Uniform 93
- 4.6 Summary 95

5 Eliminating Non-Determinism — **99**
- 5.1 Informal Presentation of the Transformation 100
  - 5.1.1 Naive Functional Encoding of Non-Determinism 100
  - 5.1.2 Combining Laziness and Call-Time Choice 101
- 5.2 Formal Definition of Transformation 105
  - 5.2.1 Head Normal Forms and Transformation of Goals 112
- 5.3 Proof of Soundness 114
  - 5.3.1 Correctness 115
  - 5.3.2 Completeness 120
- 5.4 Summary 125

6 Advanced Topics and Benchmarks — **127**
- 6.1 Functional Programs 129
  - 6.1.1 First-Order Programs 129
  - 6.1.2 Higher-Order Programs 129
- 6.2 Collecting Sets of Choices 132
  - 6.2.1 Depth-First Search 136
  - 6.2.2 Breadth-First Search 136
  - 6.2.3 Iterative Depth-First Search 138
  - 6.2.4 Parallel Search 139
- 6.3 Failing Computations 140
- 6.4 Sharing Across Non-Determinism 142
- 6.5 Recursive let bindings 145
- 6.6 Encapsulated Search 149
  - 6.6.1 Primitives to Provide Encapsulated Search 150
  - 6.6.2 Set Functions 153
- 6.7 Free Variables Revisited 160
- 6.8 Adding Constraints 162
  - 6.8.1 Unifying Simple Data Types 162
  - 6.8.2 Complex Data Types 167
- 6.9 Drawbacks of the Presented Approach 170
- 6.10 Debugging 171

CONTENTS

    6.10.1 Debugging Functional Programs with Oracle 172
    6.10.2 Debugging Functional Logic Programs with Oracle 177
    6.10.3 Related Work for Debugging 180

7 Conclusion   183

Chapter 1

Introduction and Motivation

1.1 Declarative Programming languages

The structure and components of the first programming languages were dictated by the architecture of computers. It was the human mind which had to bend to the peculiarities of the machine. When basic technical problems were solved a reverse current began to get stronger. It was no longer the machine which was hardly able to do as commanded, but more and more it was the human mind that refused to be wrapped around the complex systems to be realized. There began a search for formalisms which would allow to program computers on a high and expressive level of abstraction. Especially, this included abstraction from tedious details such as the exact order in which commands would be issued and abstraction from the exact way in which complex data structures were distributed in the machine's memory. And finally abstraction from the concept of sequential computation at all. In theory the same high-level specification could be the source to derive e cient low level programs for sequential or parallel machines alike.

One eect of the search was the birth of those programming languages which we call *declarative*. In a declarative language, the programmer does not state how to compute the solution to his problem step by step. He does not dictate which part of that solution is to be stored how and where. Rather, he gives an abstract definition of the problem itself and leaves the derivation of e cient machine code to the compiler. Currently, the automatic generation of e cient code for *parallel* machines is still the subject of research. Nevertheless, substantial progress has been achieved in the field of high level declarative programming languages, and these days we can make use of systems that have every right to be attributed as *industrial strength* compilers.

From the beginning there have been two main streams in the field of declarative programming: *functional* programming and *logic* programming. A third stream tried to unify these paradigms and we will call this latter stream *functional logic* programming. It is this stream that the presented work is part of. Before we narrow down the subject of the presented work in Section 1.4, we first give a short introduction to the various basic concepts functional logic programming languages consist of.

1.1.1 Functional Programming Languages

Historically, functional programming languages are considered to be based on the λ-calculus [Church, 1941] which in turn can be seen as a variant of combinatory logic [Schönfinkel, 1924]. Both were introduced as abstract models to capture the basic aspects of computation. Especially, the resulting models should not depend on the operational conception of a concrete machine and its set of instructions. The goal was to approximate the tools humans have been using for centuries when aiming for precision: the formal concepts of mathematics and logic.

For any transfer of mathematical concepts to computer science there is a trade o between expressiveness and algorithmic complexity. In order to achieve a compilation into e cient machine code, one has to find suitable restrictions on the mathematical constructs allowed. Functional programming is one set of restrictions found suitable for practice. We will consider this set of restrictions by example in this section.

Historically, the first functional language to note was LISP [McCarthy, 1978] whose most popular successor today is Scheme [Dybvig, 2002]. Apart from Scheme there are several functional languages in current use, most noteworthy Erlang [Armstrong et al., 1996], ML [Milner et al., 1990] and its successors, and last but not least Clean [Koopman et al., 2001] and Haskell [Peyton Jones, 2003].

From the above languages, both Clean and Haskell support all of the features we would like to see included in the functional subset of a declarative programming logic language: *static type systems*, *pattern matching*, *higher-order functions*, and *lazy evaluation*. We will first give some introductory examples which reflect these general concepts of functional programming languages. Then we will give a short discussion of those features. For our examples we will use the syntax of Haskell.

1.1.1.1 Abstract Data Types and Pattern Matching

The first thing to note about modern functional languages is that they mostly operate on *abstract data types*[1], see, e.g., [Wirsing, 1990] for a survey of the according theory.

---

[1] Note that current compilation systems for functional programming languages m ay differ considerably in the possible definitions of data types. Indeed type (inference) systems can be considered to be one of the most active research areas in the field. W e will only consider very basic definitions and refer the interested reader to [Pierce, 2002] for an introductory survey of the topic.

1.1. DECLARATIVE PROGRAMMING LANGUAGES 11

Informally, an abstract data type has three parts: 1) the name of the type 2) a set of operations used on elements of the type and 3) a set of equations defining the most important properties of the operations. Most often, a subset of the operations can be identified called the *constructors* and *selectors* of the type.

The functional languages considered here do not support the declaration of equations for the operations on algebraic data types.[2] There has been, however, some work in testing equational properties at run-time in Haskell, e.g., by random data [Claessen and Hughes, 2000] or by reporting the violation of so called *assertions* [Chitil and Huch, 2007].

All the canonical constructors and selectors of an abstract data type in the functional programming language Haskell are introduced in a single *data declaration*. The resulting type is the sum of different constructors. Each constructor may constitute a product of different types, including the one it is constructing (type recursion), including variables for arbitrary types (polymorphism) and including functional types (higher order).

Example 1.1.1 (Data Declarations in Haskell) *The simplest data declaration possible contains only a single constructor which has no arguments.*

    data Success = Success

Note that the declaration introduces two *names which are part of different name spaces: the name of the type* Success *and the name of its only constructor* Success. *In Haskell it is mandatory that the elements of both name spaces are capitalized.*

An example for a type constituted by a sum of constructors is:

    data Bool = True | False

Both constructors, True *and* False, *are without argument (also called constants), and together they constitute all of the possibilities for type* Bool.

The following type has a constructor which constitutes a product of other types (whose declarations are omitted):

    data Date = Date Day Month Year

Each Date *consists of three independent components. For types with only a single constructor Haskell supports a light weight approach called* tuples, *i.e., there is no need for a declaration. For example, instead of* (Date 1 May 2008) *we could use a tuple* (1,May,2008) *and instead of* Success *we could employ the empty tuple denoted by* ().

An example for a type which features sum, product and both recursion and polymorphism is:

---

[2] There are, however, compilation systems for this purpose which go beyond mere toy implementations, see for instance the Maude programming language [Clavel et al., 2007]. The underlying paradigm of Maude is neither functional nor logic programming in the classic sense but *algebraic specification*. It is, however, beyond the scope of this work to go into the details of how this paradigm is related to functional logic programming.

```
data List a = Nil | Cons a (List a)
```

The "a" in this declaration denotes that (List a) *is defined for all types, e.g., there are lists of Boolean values* (List Bool) *and lists of dates* (List Date). *Moreover, the second argument of* Cons *is again a list – the type is recursive. This has the eect that, e.g.,* (Cons True Nil) *and* (Cons True (Cons False Nil)) *are both legitimate values of type* (List Bool). *Lists can therefore be of arbitrary length.*

Lists are a central data structure in functional programming. (The name LISP was derived from "List Processing Language".) Haskell therefore supports syntactic sugar for lists, i.e., the constructor Nil *is written as* [], (Cons x y) *is written as* x:y *and complete lists like* (True:(False:[])) *can be written as* [True,False]. *Likewise, the type of a list of Boolean values can be written as* [Bool].

Finally, a type with a higher-order argument is:

```
data Set a = Finite [a] | Infinite (a    Bool)
```

With this data type we could implement finite sets with lists but could also provide the characteristic function defining a set. We will describe higher order in more detail in Section 1.1.1.2.

There are many more possibilities to define data structures in current versions of Haskell, for example records and existential types [Peyton Jones, 2003], generalized algebraic data types (GADTs) [Jones et al., 2006], higher rank polymorphism [Jones et al., 2007]. The language Clean extends the setting with uniqueness typing [Koopman et al., 2001]. We will not consider any such extensions in this work. Indeed we will not consider types at all as far as possible.

For any operation definable in Haskell one can also declare on which type the operation is defined. This is done by a so called *type signature*. Such a signature consists of the name of an operation and the key symbol ":˙:" followed by a functional type expression.

Example 1.1.2 (Type Signatures) *The Boolean negation has the signature:*

```
not :: Bool    Bool
```

The first element and the rest of a list are retrieved by the operations head *and* tail, *respectively, which are of the type:*

```
head :: [a]    a
tail :: [a]    [a]
```

Functions with more than one argument, e.g., the Boolean "if and only if" have a type like this:

```
iff :: Bool    Bool    Bool
```

Type signatures may be omitted and can in most cases be inferred by the compilation system.

1.1. DECLARATIVE PROGRAMMING LANGUAGES

Operations are defined by *rules* of the form "f p_1 ... p_n = e" where f is a *function symbol* and the $p_1, \ldots, p_n$ form a *pattern*. A pattern consists only of constructor symbols and variables and an important restriction is that each variable may appear only once in a pattern. During evaluation the patterns are considered to choose among the dierent rules for a given function symbol. This choice of rules is called *pattern matching*. The right-hand side e of a rule may contain constructor as well as function symbols and also those variables which were introduced in the pattern.

Example 1.1.3 (Pattern Matching for Boolean Functions) *Functions on the type* Bool *(Example 1.1.1) like Boolean negation and* xor *could be written in Haskell as follows:*

```
not :: Bool    Bool
not True  = False
not False = True

xor :: Bool    Bool    Bool
xor True  x = not x
xor False x = x
```

When, e.g., the function xor *is applied to the values* True *and* False*, as in the expression* (xor True False)*, due to pattern matching the first rule of* xor *is chosen. According to that rule's definition the result is* (not False)*, which further evaluates to* True *due to pattern matching for the rules of* not*.*

Instead of the various loop constructs known from non-declarative programming languages, functional languages employ the concept of *recursion*.

Example 1.1.4 (Pattern Matching and Recursive Function) *As lists are of arbitrary length, cf. Example 1.1.1, two lists are concatenated by first recursively stepping through the first list until a final constructor* [] *is found.*

```
app []     ys = ys
app (x:xs) ys = x : (app xs ys)
```

A simple example for recursive evaluation in accordance with pattern matching is the following evaluation. (Remember that [1,2] *is a shortcut for* (1:(2:[]))*).*

```
  app [1,2] [3,4]
= 1 : app [2] [3,4]
= 1 : 2 : app [] [3,4]
= 1 : 2 : [3,4]
```

As expected, the result is equal to [1,2,3,4]*.*

1.1.1.2 Higher Order

An important feature of functional languages is the possibility to define functions which take another function as argument or, likewise, compute a new function as result. This possibility was the main idea behind combinatory logic

[Schönfinkel, 1924] and the λ-calculus [Church, 1941]. Accordingly, almost all of the functional languages introduced in Section 1.1.1 feature higher-order functions with the exception of Erlang [Armstrong et al., 1996].

Example 1.1.5 (Higher-Order Operation)
Two standard examples for higher-order functions on lists are `map` *and* `foldr`. *The function* `map` *applies the given function to each element of the given list and can be defined in Haskell as follows:*

```
map :: (a      b)    [a]      [b]
map _ []       = []
map f (x:xs) = f x : map f xs
```

For example, for the expression (`map not [True,False]`) *we have:*

```
map not [True,False] = [not True,not False] = [False,True]
```

The declaration of function `foldr` *looks very abstract at first glance and its type seems not to convey much information:*

```
foldr :: (a      b      b)    b      [a]      b
foldr _ e []       = e
foldr f e (x:xs) = f x (foldr f e xs)
```

However, there is a close correspondence between the structure of lists and the definition of `foldr` *that is best seen when using the list definition by* `Cons` *and* `Nil`:

```
foldr _ e Nil          = e
foldr f e (Cons x xs) = f x (foldr f e xs)
```

Each constructor `Cons` *is replaced with the first argument, each* `Nil` *is replaced by the second. Therefore, we have for the application of* `foldr` *on the arguments* `xor`, `True` *and the list* (`Cons True (Cons False Nil)`):

```
foldr xor True (Cons True (Cons False Nil)) =
               (xor   True (xor   False True)) = False
```

In the above examples there is the use of "_", e.g., in the left-hand side of the rule `map _ [] =[]`. This is a sign for an anonymous variable in Haskell. In other words, an equivalent formulation for the rule is `map x [] =[]` and the _ is an explication of the fact that the variable x does not appear on the right-hand side of the rule. Haskell supports another kind of anonymous declaration: lambda expressions. A lambda expression declares a function without giving it an explicit name. This is especially useful for higher-order programming, for example the rule "`reverse=foldr (λx y   app y [x]) []`" defines a function which computes the reversed list of the given argument. Depending on the point of view you can either replace all lambda expression by named functions (a procedure called lambda lifting [Johnsson, 1985]) or eliminate all named functions by lambda expressions (as required to operate in the pure lambda calculus). In the following we will take the first approach and will thereafter not regard lambda expressions any longer.

1.1. DECLARATIVE PROGRAMMING LANGUAGES

Example 1.1.6 (Lambda Lifting) *Instead of the program*

```
reverse :: [a]    [a]
reverse = foldr (λ x y    app y [x]) []
```

an equivalent "lambda-lifted" program would be:

```
reverse :: [a]    [a]
reverse = foldr addBehind []

addBehind :: [a]    [a]    [a]
addBehind x y = app y [x]
```

Because of the possibility to eliminate lambda expressions, we may use them in examples but not include them in the formal definitions of programs in Chapter 2. For the same reason we will not introduce constructs like "list comprehension", "do notation", the anonymous "_" patterns and other forms of syntactic extensions of Haskell, see [Peyton Jones, 2003] for a definition of these terms.

But we will go even further than eliminating lambda in the following. Most of the time we will assume higher-order features eliminated altogether. The according process is called *defunctionalization* as introduced in [Reynolds, 1972]. In this process new constructors are introduced for each function symbol which may appear as higher-order arguments to other functions. Such arguments are called "partially applied" as will be understandable when considering the following example.

Example 1.1.7 (Partial Application) *Reconsider the programs from examples 1.1.5 and 1.1.6. In the definition of* `reverse` *the function* `addBehind` *is partially applied. Indeed, it is applied to zero arguments when passed as an argument to the higher-order function* `foldr`. *But – a bit less obvious –* `foldr` *is also partially applied to only two of its required three arguments.*

In addition to new constructors for partially applied functions, defunctionalization also involves the introduction of a new function `apply`.

Example 1.1.8 (Defunctionalization) *For the collected programs of examples 1.1.5-1.1.6 the result of defunctionalization looks as follows.*

```
foldr _ e []     = e
foldr f e (x:xs) = apply (apply f x) (foldr f e xs)

reverse = Foldr2 AddBehind0 []

apply AddBehind0 x     = AddBehind1 x
apply (AddBehind1 x) y = addBehind x y
apply (Foldr2 x y) z   = foldr x y z
```

As an example derivation consider (`reverse [True]`*), first in the context of the original higher-order program:*

CHAPTER 1. INTRODUCTION AND MOTIVATION

```
reverse [True] = foldr addBehind [] [True]
              = addBehind True (foldr addBehind [] [])
              = addBehind True []
              = ...
              = [True]
```

In the transformed program, the expression to be evaluated does also have to be transformed and we get:

```
  apply reverse [True]
= apply (Foldr2 AddBehind0 []) [True]
= foldr AddBehind0 [] [True]
= apply (apply AddBehind0 True) (foldr AddBehind0 [] [])
= apply (AddBehind1 True) (foldr AddBehind0 [] [])
= addBehind True (foldr AddBehind0 [] [])
= addBehind True []
= ...
= [True]
```

The astute reader might have noticed that we have left out type signatures in the transformed program above. This is no coincidence, as the resulting program is not well typed with regard to Haskell's type system.[3] But as we have mentioned in Section 1.1.1.1, we will not be concerned with types in this work. Indeed, we will from now on be concerned with first order programs, with the understanding that this is not a principle restriction because of the possibility to transform higher to first order by defunctionalization.

Like the aforementioned transformation, lambda-lifting, the possible elimination goes two ways: On the one hand, one can eliminate higher order by the introduction of suitable data structures for the representation of partial applications. On the other hand, one can replace all data structures by suitable higher-order functions; a principle called the *Church encoding* of data [Barendregt, 1984]. We will not discuss Church encoding in this work but the interested reader is referred to a work of O. Danvy and L. Nielsen [Danvy and Nielsen, 2001] for some interesting insights into defunctionalization and its relation to Church encoding.

1.1.1.3 Call by Value, Name and Need

Concerning the semantics of functional programming languages there is one principle approach that distinguishes the languages LISP [McCarthy, 1978], Scheme [Dybvig, 2002], Erlang [Armstrong et al., 1996], ML [Milner et al., 1990] on the one hand and Clean [Koopman et al., 2001], Haskell [Peyton Jones, 2003] on the other hand. It is the distinction between call-by-value and call-by-need semantics, also called strict and lazy evaluation, respectively.

Example 1.1.9 (Evaluation Strategies) *Consider the following program.*

---

[3] See, however, [Pottier and Gauthier, 2004] for approaches to type the result of defunctionalization.

1.1. DECLARATIVE PROGRAMMING LANGUAGES

```
ones :: [Int]
ones = 1 : ones

head :: [a]     a
head (x:_) = x

tail :: [a]     [a]
tail (_:xs) = xs
```

There are different possibilities to evaluate the expression (head (ones 1)) *in the context of this program, e.g.:*

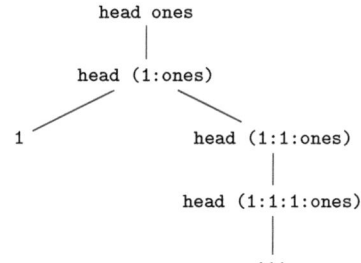

For the expression (head (1:ones)) *there is the choice of either applying the rule for* head *or the rule defining* ones. *Note that the same choice was not yet given for the expression* (head ones) *since it was not yet established that the rule for* head *is applicable. (For all we know at that point* ones *could evaluate to* [] *and then the rule for* head *would not have been applicable.)*

As you can see by the example, different *strategies* for the evaluation of the expressions are imaginable. The strategy known as *call-by-value* will always apply the rule of the left-most function symbol of an expression, whose arguments are all *values*, i.e., an expression not containing function symbols. For example, in the expression (head (1:ones)) head is further left than ones, but the argument of head (the expression (1:ones)) is not a value. All arguments of ones, however, are values (it has no arguments) and therefore the (sub) expression ones is chosen for evaluation. The rightmost derivation in the picture is a call-by-value derivation.

The *call-by-name* strategy, in contrast, applies rules "as soon as possible" also preferring rules for function symbols which are further left in the expression whenever they are applicable. For example, in the expression (head (1:ones)) head is further left than ones and the rule for head is applicable. Hence, the leftmost derivation of the picture illustrates call-by-name.

The example also illustrates that there are expressions for which call-by-value might lead to an infinite derivation whereas call-by-name can find a value in finitely many steps. It is well known that this is true in general, i.e., the number of expressions for which call-by-name finds a value is a proper superset of the expressions which can be evaluated by call-by-value [Barendregt, 1984].

18   CHAPTER 1. INTRODUCTION AND MOTIVATION

The next example illustrates, however, that call-by-name might duplicate work.

Example 1.1.10 (Call-By-Name and Call-By-Value) *The following definition is a slight variant of a standard example for the comparison of call-by-value and call-by-name.*

```
double :: [a]    [a]
double x = app x x
```

The evaluation of the expression (double (tail [1])) *can be depicted as follows, where call-by-name is on the left and call-by-value on the right.*

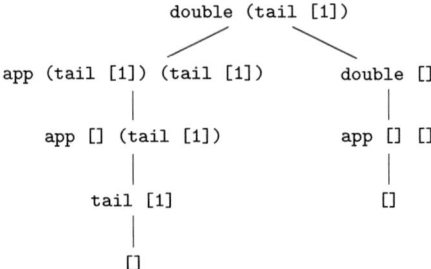

Note that the call-by-name derivation is longer because the expression (tail [1]) *is evaluated twice.*

The duplication of work is the reason to consider a further strategy, which is called *"call-by-need"* (or *lazy* in some contexts). The idea is to compute on *references to expressions* rather than the expressions themselves. Then call-by-need copies such references only but never complete expressions. For this purpose the language of expressions has to be extended by the introduction of such references.

Example 1.1.11 (Call-By-Need) *In order to avoid copying the sub expression* (tail [1]) *during the evaluation of* (double (tail [1])) *(as developed in Example 1.1.10 abvoce) the expression is reformulated like this, cf. the treatment in [Maraist et al., 1998]:*

```
let x=tail [1] in double x
```

The according call-by-need derivation could look like this:

```
let x=tail [1] in double x = let x=tail [1] in app x x
                           = let x=[]        in app x x
                           = let x=[]        in x
```

Note that the derivation has not more steps than the call-by-value evaluation from Example 1.1.10. Indeed, it is well known that call-by-need derivations need

1.1. DECLARATIVE PROGRAMMING LANGUAGES

less or equal many steps than call-by-value in general and that the set of values computable by call-by-name and call-by-need are equal (for purely functional programming languages).

When references are copied, as in the expression (`let x=tail [1] in app x x`) from the above example, we say that the sub expression `tail [1]` is *shared*.

For functional programming languages the semantics of call-by-value and call-by-name dier only with regard to (non-)terminating derivations. Furthermore, call-by-name and call-by-need dier with regard to e ciency, only. The dierences become more prominent, however, when functional languages are extended by logic features.

1.1.2 Functional Logic Languages

In contrast to logic programming languages like Prolog, this work is concerned with declarative programming languages which share all of the aforementioned features of current functional programming languages. Especially, this includes static typing, abstract data types, higher-order functions, and lazy evaluation as discussed in Section 1.1.1. There are several approaches to extend logic programming languages by special notational constructs for functions. The languages Mercury [Somogyi and Henderson, 1996] and HAL [García de la Banda et al., 2002], for instance, feature both a type system and notation for higher-order functions. Also the Ciao dialect of Prolog has been extended by a functional notation [Casas et al., 2006] and the language Oz [Smolka, 1995b] does also feature special treatment for functions. All of the languages mentioned above, however, feature call-by-value as the underlying semantics. The seamless integration of *lazy* functional programming languages with logic features, however, seems to be especially promising and is the leading principle of the languages Toy [López-Fraguas and Sánchez-Hernández, 1999] and Curry [Hanus (ed.), 2006]. This work is concerned with this latter branch of functional logic programming languages and our examples will be given in the syntax of Curry (which coincides with the syntax of Haskell for functional programs). For the general topic of the integration of functional and logic programming into a single paradigm the interested reader is referred to a survey by Hanus [2007b].

Functional logic languages in the sense described above extend functional programming languages by the possibility to define *non-deterministic operations* and to compute with partial information by employing *free variables*. Each of these topics will be introduced in a separate section below. With regards to semantics, we will discuss the notions of *run-time choice* vs. *call-time choice* in Section 1.1.2.3 which parallels the distinction between call-by-value, call-by-name and call-by-need in functional languages.

1.1.2.1 Non-Deterministic Operations

When, for a given expression, pattern matching (see Section 1.1.1.1) does identify more than one rule to be applicable, functional languages like Haskell choose the first rule appearing in the program. In functional *logic* programs, however, this situation induces a *non-deterministic choice* among all applicable rules.

Example 1.1.12 (Non-Determinism)

```
insert :: a    [a]     [a]
insert x xs     = x : xs
insert x (y:ys) = y : insert x ys
```

In Haskell the expression (`insert 1 [2,3]`) *evaluates to* [1,2,3] *as the second rule would be eectively ignored. Changing the order of the rules in the program,* (`insert 1 [2,3]`) *would evaluate to* [2,3,1]. *If the program is interpreted as a Curry program, however, the definition of* `insert` *implies that* x *is inserted as new head or somewhere in the tail of a non-empty list. Therefore, the expression* (`insert 1 [2,3]`) *non-deterministically evaluates to* [1,2,3], [2,1,3] *or* [2,3,1].

When non-determinism is involved, we will usually use the term *operation* rather than *function*. Whenever there are multiple matching rules we say that these rules *overlap*.

For future reference we note that the following operation is a kind of archetype of non-deterministic operations.

```
(?) :: a    a     a
x ? _ = x
_ ? y = y
```

The operator (`?`) induces a non-deterministic choice between its two arguments. Using the operation (`?`), often referred to as *choice*, we can easily formulate the simplest non-deterministic operation `coin`.

Example 1.1.13 (Operation `coin`)

```
coin :: Bool
coin = True ? False
```

For a call to `coin` *there are two derivations to* `True` *and to* `False`.

1.1.2.2 Free Variables and Narrowing

In addition to non-deterministic choice, functional logic languages also allow computation with partial information. Functions and operations can be called with unknown arguments that are instantiated in order to apply a rule. Whenever there are more than one applicable rules, an instantiation will be chosen non-deterministically. This mechanism is called *narrowing* [Slagle, 1974]. In Curry unknown arguments are introduce as (`let x free in e`) for some expression e. (Note that this notation is similar and related to the one discussed in the context of call-by-need in Section 1.1.10.)

Example 1.1.14 (Narrowing) *Most standard examples for the expressive power of narrowing are defined for* Peano *numbers:*

1.1. DECLARATIVE PROGRAMMING LANGUAGES

```
data Peano = 0 | S Peano

add :: Peano   Peano   Peano
add 0     m = m
add (S n) m = S (add n m)
```

A Peano number is either zero or the successor of another Peano number. The number two, for example, is therefore represented by (S (S 0)). *Calling* add *with a free variable as the second argument, e.g.,* (let x free in add (S 0) x), *we get the derivation:*[4]

```
let x free in add (S 0) x = let x free in S (add 0 x)
                          = let x free in S x
```

This can be read as "adding 1 to anything yields the successor of anything." If, however, we call add *with a free variable in the position of the first argument, e.g.,* (let x free in add x (S 0)), *the following derivation is possible.*

```
let x free in add x (S 0) = let x=0 in S 0
```

Here, x *has been instantiated to* 0. *As noted above, the choice of rule is non-deterministic and, therefore, we could also get the following derivation, among many others.*

```
  let x free in add x (S 0)
= let y free in let x=S y in S (add y (S 0))
= let y=0 in let x=S y in S (S 0)
```

Note, however, that the instantiation of free variables is solely induced by the program rules to be applied. Therefore, (let x free in S x) *is the only value that the expression* (let x free in add (S 0) x) *can be derived to and it is not possible that narrowing instantiates* x *in this situation.*

The narrowing mechanism integrates the functional concept of reduction with the nondeterministic search known from logic programming. Using narrowing, we can also solve equations as the following example illustrates.

Example 1.1.15 *Consider the following program.*

```
equal :: Peano   Peano   Bool
equal 0     0     = True
equal (S x) (S y) = equal x y

guard :: Bool   a   a
guard True x = x
```

In the context of this program together with the definitions of Example 1.1.14 above, the expression (let x free in guard (equal (add x x) (S (S 0))) x) *can be used to find a solution for the equation* $x + x = 2$.

---

[4]Note that the needed narrowing evaluation strategy [Antoy et al., 1994] is defined by employing substitutions rather than let bindings. The representation used here is rather informal and employed for introductory purposes only.

```
    let x free in guard (equal (add x x) (S (S 0))) x
  = let y free in let x=S y in guard (equal (S (add y x)) (S (S 0))) x
  = let y free in let x=S y in guard (equal (add y x) (S 0)) x
  = let y=0 in let x=S y in guard (equal x (S 0)) x
  = let y=0 in let x=S y in guard (equal y 0) x
  = let y=0 in let x=S y in guard True x
  = let y=0 in let x=S y in x
```

As expected, the result is (S 0) *as* x = 1 *is a solution for the represented equation. Note that this is the only possible derivation of a value and that the needed narrowing strategy [Antoy et al., 1994] tries only three additional possibilities, namely* x=0, x=S (S 0) *and* x=S (S (S z)) *for some free variable z, and that this su ces to ensure that no further solutions exist.*

1.1.2.3 Call-Time and Run-Time Choice

The interaction of laziness and logic programming features—especially non-determinism—is not trivial both semantically, as well as operationally, i.e., from the point of view of an implementation. Current lazy functional logic programming languages have agreed on a model coined *Call-Time Choice*[5] that supports the intuition that variables are placeholders for *values* rather than possibly non-deterministic computations. An important consequence of this computational model is that a call-by-need computation has the same results as a call-by-value computation in the context of the same program (if the latter computation terminates).

The semantic consequences of call-time choice are usually illustrated with a variation of the following tiny program:

Example 1.1.16 *Consider the following program together with the definitions for* not *and* coin *from Example 1.1.3 and 1.1.13.*

```
selfEq :: Bool     Bool
selfEq b = iff b b

iff :: Bool    Bool    Bool
iff True  b = b
iff False b = not b
```

The function selfEq *checks whether its argument is equivalent to itself using the Boolean equivalence test* iff. *There are two call-by-value derivations for the goal* (selfEq coin):

```
selfEq coin = selfEq True  = iff True  True  = True

selfEq coin = selfEq False = iff False False = not False = True
```

If we evaluate the same goal with call-by-name, we get

```
selfEq coin = iff coin coin
```

---
[5]For a detailed discussion of the notions call-tim e and run-tim e choice the interested reader is referred to [Hußm ann, 1993].

1.1. DECLARATIVE PROGRAMMING LANGUAGES 23

and this copying of the expression `coin` *yields four derivations where the additional two have a result that cannot be obtained with call-by-value.*

```
iff coin coin = iff True coin = coin = True
iff coin coin = iff True coin = coin = False

iff coin coin = iff False coin = not coin = not True = False
iff coin coin = iff False coin = not coin = not False = True
```

In a call-by-need derivation of the goal, i.e., in a lazy programming language, we have

```
let x=coin in selfEq x = let x=coin in iff x x
```

and `coin` *is evaluated only once. The result of* (`selfEq coin`) *is* `True`:

```
  let x=coin in iff x x
= let x=True in selfEq x x
= let x=True in x

  let x=coin in iff x x
= let x=False in selfEq x x
= let x=False in not x
= let x=False in True
```

In general the essence of call-time choice can be coined as "shared non-deterministic sub computations evaluate to the same value".

Current lazy functional logic programming languages conform to call-time choice semantics following the *principle of least astonishment* because — like in the context of functional programming — it is very natural to think of variables as place holders for values. Many people would intuitively say, for instance, that a definition like the one for `selfEq` above could not sensibly ever yield `False`. The point is further illustrated by the following example, in which a function `sort :: [Int]` `[Int]` should be tested with non-deterministic choices for arguments.

Example 1.1.17 (Non-Deterministic Tests) *Assume a function* `sort` *which for a given list of, e.g, numbers computes a sorted version of that list. Then for the following program*

```
sortTests :: ([Int],[Int])
sortTests = (l, sort l) where l free
```

users will most likely expect the second component of the pair to be a sorted reordering of the first. And they will still expect this behavior if they use a non-deterministic generator for non-negative numbers instead of a free variable[6]:

---

[6]We will show in Section 3.2 that logic variables can be simulated using such non-deterministic generators and this result relies on call-time choice semantics, cf. [Antoy and Hanus, 2006].

24   CHAPTER 1. INTRODUCTION AND MOTIVATION

```
sortTests :: ([Int],[Int])
sortTests = (l, sort l) where l = natList

natList :: [Int]
natList = []
natList = nat : natList

nat :: Int
nat = 1
nat = nat + 1
```

If run-time choice is assumed, however, the two appearances of the variable l *in* (l, sort l) *are completely independent such that* (l, sort l) where l=natList *is equivalent to* (natList, sort natalist). *This implies that, for example, the pair* ([3,1],[4,5,6]) *would be a possible value.*

The sort function can be defined in a functional logic language using the *test-of-generate* pattern [Hanus and Réty, 1998] where the definition of insert was given in Example 1.1.12.

Example 1.1.18 (Permutation Sort)

```
sort :: [Int]      [Int]
sort l | sorted p = p where p = permute l

sorted :: [Int]       Bool
sorted []          = True
sorted [_]         = True
sorted (m:n:ns) = m ≤ n && sorted (n:ns)

permute :: [a]       [a]
permute []      = []
permute (x:xs) = insert x (permute xs)
```

The definition of sort *is only reasonable with call-time choice, i.e., if both occurrences of* p *(in the guard and in the right-hand side of* sort*) denote the same value. Otherwise, an arbitrary permutation of the input would be returned if any permutation is sorted. Thanks to lazy evaluation, permutations need to be computed only as much as is necessary in order to decide whether they are sorted. For example, if the first two elements of a permutation are already out-of-order, then a presumably large number of possible completions can be discarded. Permutations of a list are computed recursively by inserting the head of a list at an arbitrary position in the permutation of the tail.*

Permutation sort demonstrates nicely the semantic eect of call-time choice and the operational eect of laziness which prunes away large parts of the search space by not evaluating unsorted permutations completely. Thus, it is a characteristic example for a search problem expressed in the more intuitive *generate-and-test* style but solved in the more e cient *test-of-generate* style. This pattern generalizes to other problems and is not restricted to sorting (which is, of course, usually not expressed as a problem employing non-deterministic search).

1.1. DECLARATIVE PROGRAMMING LANGUAGES

1.1.2.4 Controlling Search

One last topic concerning the seamless integration of functional and logic programming languages into a single paradigm is the *control of logic search*. Classic logic programming languages like Prolog have a fixed strategy when searching for solutions, i.e., *depth-first search*. Somewhat similar to the discussed distinction between call-by-value and call-by-name/call-by-need, this search strategy can be implemented efficiently but is not *complete*. This means that there are examples that have a solution for which depth-first search induces a non-terminating evaluation.

Example 1.1.19 (Depth-First Search) *Of course, a bit-wise representation of numbers is more efficient than using the Peano definition of zero and successor.*[7] *Therefore, a more realistic representation of numbers as algebraic data types is given by:*

```
data Nat = IHi | O Nat | I Nat
```

Natural numbers are represented in binary notation with the least significant bit first. *The* most significant bit *is always one and, therefore, denoted* IHi. *The values of type* Nat *can be related to natural numbers as follows, where* nat(n) *denotes the representation of the number* n *as value of type* Nat:

$$\begin{aligned} \text{IHi} &\mathrel{\hat=} 1 \\ \text{O (nat(n))} &\mathrel{\hat=} 2n \\ \text{I (nat(n))} &\mathrel{\hat=} 2n+1 \end{aligned}$$

A non-deterministic choice between all possible numbers could be defined as follows. (Compare this with the definition for nat *given in Example 1.1.17.)*

```
nat = IHi
nat = O nat
nat = I nat
```

The problem when employing depth-first search is now, that it will always be biased towards one of the rules nat=O nat *or* nat=I nat. *This means that, e.g., one of the simple equations like* $2 * x = 4 + x$ *or* $3 * x = 3 + x$ *cannot be solved by the system.* Breadth-first search, *in contrast, will find a solution for both equations as all rules are tried in turn.*

An important idea for advanced programming of logic search is that the programmer should be able to influence the search strategy from within his program, leads to the concept of *encapsulated search*. Encapsulated search is employed whenever different values of one expression have to be related in some way, e.g., to compute a list of all values or to find the minimal value and also to formulate a search strategy. A first approach to encapsulated search in functional logic programming was given in [Hanus and Steiner, 1998] where a

---

[7]See [Braßel et al., 2008] for an elaboration on the topic of bit-wise number representation in functional logic languages.

primitive operator `try` was proposed. This operator allows to easily program dierent search strategies. The first mature implementation of `try` for the functional logic language Curry was presented by Lux [1999] for the "Münster Curry Compiler" (MCC), while a dierent approach to encapsulated search was taken in the PAKCS compilation system [Hanus et al., 2010]. With both approaches however, the discussion of how to approach encapsulated search could not be considered as solved. Braßel et al. [2004b] show in many examples and considerations that the interactions between encapsulation, laziness and sharing is complicated and prone to problems. Braßel et al. [2004b] also present a wishlist for future implementations of encapsulation. The approach to encapsulated search presented in Section 6.6 fulfills all the points of that list. The problems when connecting encapsulated search with laziness is illustrated by the following example.

Example 1.1.20 (Encapsulated Search)
Reconsider the representation of numbers as algebraic data types introduced in Example 1.1.19. Next we define a test whether a given number is a prime number. As you know, a prime number is any number dierent from 1 which can be divided without rest only by 1 and itself. Assume a suitable definition of the rest of division `mod`, *which computes the remainder for a division as an optional value of type* `Maybe`.[8] *With this operation we can define this test quite concisely as follows.*

```
divisorOf :: Nat    Nat    Nat
divisorOf n m | mod n m =:= Nothing = m

prime :: Nat    Success
prime n = (n == 1) =:= False
       & length (allValues (divisorOf n nat)) =:= 2
```

Here, the operation `allValues` performs encapsulated search to yield a list containing all pairwise dierent values of its argument. To express the conditions, we use the strict equality operator (=:=)) which implements unification. The two conditions are expressed as two constraints connected by the operator (`&`). (`&`) is called "concurrent conjunction" and is a primitive, i.e., an externally defined operator in Curry. The adjective "concurrent" suggests that the result should not depend on the order in which the constraints are evaluated. But if `allValues` is based on encapsulated search as available in PAKCS, the result of, e.g., `prime (3?4)` does indeed depend on the order of evaluation. If the constraint (n==1) =:=False is solved first then the computation in PAKCS is successful and if the second constraint is preferred, the computation yields no solution. We will not explain how this behavior comes to pass and refer to the work of Braßel et al. [2004b] for a detailed discussion. Here, it is only important that this problem also stems from the connection of laziness with logic search and is caused by the sharing of `n` in both constraints.

---

[8]The type `Maybe` is defined by "`data Maybe a = Just a | Nothing`. See [Braßel et al., 2008] for a definition for `mod` on the presented data type.

In an alternative approach by Lux [1999] the result does not depend on the order in which the two constraints are evaluated. The computation of (prime (3?4)) fails for any order of evaluation, cf. the work by Braßel et al. [2004b] for details. Although the approach by Lux [1999] does not require any knowledge about the order of evaluation, detailed knowledge about the compiler and the executed optimizations are needed to successfully employ encapsulated search in this manner. For instance, a program can yield dierent values if one writes (λ x   x=:=(0 ? 1)) instead of (=:=(0 ? 1)) although by the very definition of the language Curry [Hanus (ed)., 2006] the latter expression is just an abbreviation of the former.

In [Antoy and Braßel, 2007] the source of the above problems has been examined in a framework of graph rewriting. The aim of [Antoy and Braßel, 2007] was to elaborate su cient conditions to prohibit the problematic situations described in [Braßel et al., 2004b]. At the same time, however, [Antoy and Braßel, 2007] give also examples that allowing the problematic situations might lead to interesting programs.

In [Braßel and Huch, 2007a] the first approach to fulfill the wishlist of [Braßel et al., 2004b] is presented. With regard to the examples presented in [Antoy and Braßel, 2007], however, the approach of [Braßel and Huch, 2007a] was still not the end of development.

Recently, in [Antoy and Hanus, 2009] a theoretic approach to compute with set functions was presented. The idea is to keep a representation of the whole computation space and to traverse this representation upon total completion of evaluation to collect the values, [Antoy and Hanus, 2009, Definition 5]. We will present an implementation of this idea in Section 6.6.2.

The approach presented in this work extends the approach of Braßel and Huch [2007a]. We will examine the contribution to encapsulated search in Section 6.6.

1.2 Implementing Functional Logic Languages

Corresponding to the nature of functional logic languages, there are three basic ways to obtain an implementation:

- implement an abstract machine in a suitable base language like C or Java
- transform Curry programs into logic programs
- transform Curry programs into (lazy) functional programs

Each way has some advantages and disadvantages: Designing an abstract machine has the advantage of giving the developer full access to all features, allowing him to gather information about sharing, or control the search mechanisms in order to implement, for instance, encapsulated search. However, both functional and logic programming come with a long history of optimization techniques, knowledge of how to avoid space leaks, how to design garbage collection and so on. When implementing a new machine from scratch, all of this work has to be reimplemented and chances are high that the machine will be behind state-of-the-art forever. In addition, libraries of the base language are comparatively hard to include in the implemented language. From the point of view of the abstract machine, these libraries are strictly external.

This is what makes approaches to transformation into related languages promising. All of the optimization techniques for the base language will be the more eective the lesser the level of interpretation is. There is no need to reimplement garbage collection or reconsider discussions about space leaks. The greater the similarities between base and implemented language, the easier is the integration of the base language's libraries. Furthermore, transformation to an existing language can involve less work than implementing an abstract machine from scratch. This is because many of the base language's features can be used without reconsidering implementation details of these features.

On the other hand, the developer of a transformation to a declarative host language has less control on program execution. When transforming to a logic language, for instance, the developer has to rely on the base language features to control logic search. Implementing an own approach to encapsulated search, like the one proposed for Curry in [Braßel et al., 2004b], are hard or even impossible to realize. When transforming to a functional language, features like sharing are beyond access or have to be reimplemented at high costs.[9] This makes implementing Curry's features like call-time choice tricky to transform. Moreover, the developer has to comply with standards of the target language. For instance, in transforming to Prolog he has to consider implementing lazy evaluation in a strict language. When transforming to Haskell he has to obey the type system, if he wants to take advantage of all of Haskell's optimizations.

There have been several implementations of abstract machines for Curry in imperative languages. An early Java implementation [Hanus and Sadre, 1997] has by now been set aside, an implementation in C [Lux and Kuchen, 1999] has reached the state of usability. A second attempt to implement Curry in Java with new concepts is still under development [Antoy et al., 2005] and continuously extended by new ideas [Antoy et al., 2006b]. All of these implementations more or less follow the idea of compiling into code for an abstract machine or implement a graph rewriting strategy, respectively.

Also transformations of Curry into a logic programming language have been devised: The most mature system PAKCS [Hanus et al., 2010] transforms Curry programs to SICStus Prolog[10], thereby using Prolog's features of constraint solving, free variables and logic search.

In this work, however, we will discuss how to transform functional logic programs to purely functional programs, reusing the sharing of the host language.

---

[9]An example of a technique to transform functional logic to functional programs together with a reimplementation of sharing is given in [Fischer et al., 2009]. The benchmarks presented in Chapter 6 demonstrate that the cost of explicit sharing is indeed so high that the proposed translation technique results in programs which are usually much slower than current systems [Braßel et al., 2010].

[10]www.sics.se/isl/sicstuswww/site/index.html

1.2.1 Transformation to Functional Languages

Conceptually, the simplest way to provide logic features in functional languages is to express non-determinism using lists [Wadler, 1985] but in principal any instance of the class `MonadPlus` can be used for this purpose, for examples see [Hinze, 2000, Kiselyov, 2005, Naylor et al., 2007]. All these approaches model non-deterministic computations like in Prolog in the sense that all computations involving non-deterministic choices are *strict*. However, the *functional logic* paradigm is mainly motivated by the insight that laziness and non-deterministic search can be combined profitably, cf. Section 1.1.2.3. Especially, this combination allows to program in the expressive and intuitive *generate-and-test* style while eectively computing in the more e cient style of *test-of-generate* [Hanus and Réty, 1998], cf. Example 1.1.18. Recent applications of this technique show that it is well suited for the demand-driven generation of test data [Runciman et al., 2008, Fischer and Kuchen, 2008]. Functional logic design patterns [Antoy and Hanus, 2002] illustrate further benefits of combining lazy functional and logic programming.

By defining a suitable class of monads, it has recently been shown that functional logic programs can be translated to pure functional programs [Fischer et al., 2009, Braßel et al., 2010]. The monadic approach does, however, introduce a considerable overhead by the necessity to reimplement sharing, as will be examined in detail in Chapter 6.

In principle, choosing a *lazy functional* target language has several advantages [Braßel and Huch, 2009, 2007b]. It is possible to translate deterministic functions *without* imposing much overhead. Additionally, Haskell allows to implement sharing of computed values even across non-deterministic branches where other implementations, including [Fischer et al., 2009], need to reevaluate shared expressions. Finally, in contrast to a logic target language, the explicit encoding of non-determinism allows more fine grained control of logic search, cf. Section 1.1.2.4.

Although Prolog is also a declarative language, there are many dierences between Prolog and Curry, more than there are between Curry and Haskell. Curry is not only syntactically very close to Haskell, many Curry modules in fact *are* Haskell programs. A great part of every-day Curry programming is functional programming, and what makes the basic concepts of Curry powerful is that each function can be used to perform logic search without changing its definition. Whether a deterministic function is used logically or functionally only depends on the way it is called: Calling a given function with free variables as arguments automatically induces a search if these variables are needed, whereas a call without free variables implies a deterministic evaluation like in Haskell, cf. Section 1.1.14. This fact implies a great deal of potential optimization when translating Curry to Haskell: whenever we can make sure by analyzing the source program that a given expression does not induce non-determinism or binding of free variables, we can simply use the original Curry code without any transformation at all.[11] Clearly, this way and because the translated programs

---

[11]Note, however, that we use the code of the intermediate language flat Curry rather than

do not feature side effects we will automatically profit from all of Haskell's optimization techniques. Accordingly, the amount of interpretation is, even in case of potentially non-deterministic programs, much lesser than in Prolog. This leads to other advantages like easy integration of Haskell-libraries, at least for deterministic parts of Curry programs.

One last point in favor of a Haskell transformation stems from different approaches to encapsulated search, as discussed in Section 1.1.2.4. In [Braßel et al., 2004b] it was shown that new basic concepts are needed to provide a declarative access to search operators. Unfortunately, these concepts are not realizable if the features normally provided by Prolog are used. As logic search has to be added to the Haskell transformation, the developer has full control on this part of the implementation. Thus, a transformation to Haskell can provide a better, i.e. more declarative, way of implementing encapsulated logic search.

The challenge of targeting Haskell, however, is to preserve the laziness and sharing of the source language which allows the efficient execution of programs written in the generate-and-test style. Therefore, previous approaches to non-determinism in Haskell [Wadler, 1985, Hinze, 2000, Kiselyov, 2005, Naylor et al., 2007] do not preserve laziness while other approaches [Fischer et al., 2009] need to reimplement sharing, which results in a considerable overhead also for deterministic programs.

All in all the translation scheme developed in this work comprises the following advantages:

- It is the first scheme translating lazy functional logic programs to *purely* functional programs. Consequently, the resulting code can be *fully optimized*, in contrast to our previous approach [Braßel and Huch, 2009] which relied on unsafe side effects for generating labels.

- The transformation is *simple* — one could even say "off-the-shelf" as the only prerequisite is the generation of unique identifiers. Introducing such identifiers to a given program is a well known technique and there exist good implementations for current compiling systems [Augustsson et al., 1994].

- The results for translating *functional* Curry programs closely correspond to programs originally written in Haskell. This ensures, in contrast to [Fischer et al., 2009, Braßel et al., 2010] that these programs can be optimized as well as programs originally written in Haskell.

- The sharing of the host language is reused, resulting in less overhead especially for deterministic programs, again in contrast to [Fischer et al., 2009, Braßel et al., 2010].

---

the original program.

1.3 Debugging Functional Logic Programs

It is the basic credo of declarative programming that abstracting from certain aspects of program execution greatly improves the quality of the written code: Typical sources of errors are principally omitted, like issues of memory management, type errors and multiple allocation of variables. A declarative program is much nearer to the *logic* of the implemented algorithm than to its execution. This makes code much more readable, comprehensive and maintainable.

There seems to be at first glance, however, a great drawback to these techniques: As there is such a far abstraction from the actual program execution, the executed program becomes a black box. Where an imperative programmer is able to step through his program's execution and recognize parts of his programs, the declarative programmer is usually not able to draw any such connections. This is of course an especially severe problem for *debugging*.

1.3.1 Related Work

There are many approaches in the literature to close this gap between the source code and its execution. Among the many techniques proposed so far we can only name a few and give a broad categorization:

Visualization of Computation A straightforward approach to search bugs is to represent the actual program execution in a human readable form and to provide tools to comfortably browse this representation. Such tools, beginning with step-by-step debuggers, have been developed for many languages, imperative and declarative alike. These tools normally depend on a specific backend of the supported language and seldom aim at portability. Some very elaborated examples for declarative languages include ViMer [Cameron et al., 2003] for the logic language Mercury [Somogyi and Henderson, 1996], Ozcar [Lorenz, 1999] for the Mozart system[12], a backend for the language Oz [Smolka, 1995a] and TeaBag [Antoy and Johnson, 2004] for the FLVM implementation [Antoy et al., 2005] of the functional logic language Curry [Hanus (ed)., 2006].

Value Oriented Debugging approaches based on analyzing what values have been computed by evaluating a given expression within the program are, for instance, declarative debugging, cf. the book by Shapiro [1983] for logic, the work by Nilsson and Fritzson [1994], Nilsson and Sparud [1997b] for functional, the one by Caballero and Rodríguez-Artalejo [2004] for functional logic programming; Silva [2006] gives a general survey of declarative debugging for functional logic languages. Additional value oriented approaches are, e.g., observations for lazy languages (cf. the work by Gill [2001] for functional, the ones by Braßel et al. [2004a], Huch and Sadeghi [2006] for functional logic languages), backward stepping and redex trailing (for functional languages only [Booth and Jones, 1997, Sparud and Runciman, 1997c]).

---
[12]http://www.mozart-oz.org

Performance Oriented Sometimes the bug is not in the computed values but in its failing e ciency. The general approach to analyze the frequency and duration of function calls is mostly known as "profiling". Profilers measuring actual run times are naturally dependent on a specific backend. Traditional profiling methods do not readily translate to lazy languages. A solution to this problem – attributing execution costs to user defined cost centers – was proposed in [Sansom and Peyton Jones, 1997] for the GHC[13] for the functional language Haskell [Peyton Jones, 2003] and ported for PAKCS [Hanus et al., 2010], an implementation of the functional logic language Curry, in [Braßel et al., 2005]. In addition to run-time profiling, both approaches feature a more abstract and therefore much more portable approach to profiling which is called "symbolic profiling". Such abstract measurements are not only more portable but also accessible to verification.

Special Purpose Tools Under this catch-all category we would like to mention some approaches which give backend depending information about special features of the program execution. Among many existing systems are stack inspection for the GHC [Ennals and Peyton Jones, 2003], a statistic overview of the search space available in the Oz debugger [Lorenz, 1999], the graphical representation of profiling data for the GHC [Peyton Jones, 2003] and GHood, an animated graphical viewer of observations [Gill, 2001].

The tools and categories above can only give a remote hint to the magnitude of tools giving information about the execution of declarative programs. As is often the case with such a multi-faceted research field: the same problems are solved many times and many basic approaches have to be reinvented time and again. How to cope with large applications? How to obtain information if no direct access to the back end is given? Is the represented data correct and is it complete or do we miss something? Wouldn't it be nice to have the same tool they got for that other backend for our language? The first approach that gave the basic idea that these problems might be solvable after all was the further development of redex trailing as proposed in [Chitil et al., 2001]. There the authors observed that the data collected for redex trailing was also su cient to provide declarative debugging as in the systems Freja [Nilsson and Sparud, 1997b] and observations like in Hood [Gill, 2001]. The approach of [Chitil et al., 2001] is also more portable than Freja and a more powerful implementation of Hood. Freja was implemented as a special Haskell compiler available only for the Solaris operation system, and the more powerful version of Hood had to be integrated in the Haskell interpreter Hugs[14] in order to achieve some additional features. The key idea to obtain this portability was to transform the given program and collect the information by side eects rather than relying on a specific backend.

---

[13]http://www.haskell.org/ghc/
[14]http://www.haskell.org/hugs/

1.3.2 The Approach Presented in this Work

In [Braßel et al., 2006, 2004c], we have extended the basic ideas of [Chitil et al., 2001] in several ways. First, our approach supports the additional features available in functional *logic* languages, i.e., free variables and non-deterministic functions. In addition, we have based our approach on a *core language* which features the main concepts of functional logic languages. This language, called "Flat Curry", was introduced in [Albert et al., 2005] and is described in detail in the next chapter.

Functional logic languages like Toy [López-Fraguas and Sánchez-Hernández, 1999] or Curry can be translated to this core language (and actually are in some implementations of Curry). On one hand this is one step away from the original source program but on the other hand this approach has some important advantages:

Portability At least conceptually, our approach is open to be ported to all declarative languages which can be translated to Flat Curry, including lazy functional languages. The program transformation, cf. [Braßel et al., 2006], maps a valid Flat Curry program to another valid Flat Curry program. The only features the backend has to support in order to execute the transformed program are some basic functionality to create side eects like `unsafePerformIO`.

Verifiability A considerable part of the formal foundation of functional logic languages has been developed with respect to Flat Curry, cf. [Albert et al., 2005]. Therefore, we were able to give proofs about correctness and completeness of the collected data in [Braßel et al., 2004c] which was not yet possible for the approach of [Chitil et al., 2001][15]

Unfortunately, debugging tools based on our former approach [Braßel et al., 2006] share a basic problem with the construction of redex trails [Chitil et al., 2001]: the debugging tools based on both approaches do not scale up well to large programs because of the size of the recorded data, which makes these approaches not feasible for realistic applications involving computations of more than a few thousands of reductions.

In Section 6.10 of this work, we introduce an alternative approach to debugging lazy functional programs which was originally published as [Braßel et al., 2007]. Instead of storing a complete redex trail, we memorize only the information necessary to guide a call-by-value interpreter to produce the same results. To avoid unnecessary reductions, similarly to the lazy semantics, the call-by-value interpreter is controlled by a list of step numbers which allows us to know which redexes should not be evaluated. In the extreme case where every redex is evaluated even by a lazy strategy, the list of step numbers reduces to a single number—the total number of reduction steps in the complete computation—which demonstrates the compactness of our representation. In addition

---

[15]According to personal communication with O. Chitil, formal reasoning for the approach of [Chitil et al., 2001] is forthcoming.

to the basic idea we will present a debugging tool based on that approach and discuss that the translation scheme developed in this works makes it possible to transfer the technique to also cover debugging of functional logic programs.

1.4 Content of this Work

In Chapter 2 we will present the formal framework for the representation of functional logic programs and their semantics. In Chapter 3 we will transfer a result about the relation between free variables and generator functions to this framework. Chapter 4 presents a simplification of how functional logic programs can be represented in the framework of natural semantics and discusses the connection to term graph rewriting. All of this work aims at connecting the contents of Chapter 5 to the previous work in the field of functional logic programming. In that chapter we are concerned with a detailed examination of a technique to transform lazy functional logic programs to purely functional programs. The purpose of the subsequent Chapter 6 is to demonstrate that the developed translation scheme is indeed relevant for practice. In that chapter we present benchmarks for programs translated by our scheme which show that it is a serious alternative for existing compilation systems. Additionally, we present the implementation of various features to extend our approach. Some of these features can be found in existing compilation systems for functional logic programs, some are unique to our approach.

The basic idea of the transformation studied in Chapter 3 has been published in [Braßel and Huch, 2007a]. The proofs of formal correctness, however, are new and much more elaborated than the ones presented in [Braßel and Huch, 2007a]. The transformation scheme examined in Chapter 5 has been published as [Braßel and Fischer, 2008], although no proof of soundness was given there. A former version of the approach employing side eects was formally treated in [Braßel and Huch, 2007a]. All proofs have been substantially revised and extended for this work. The contents of Section 6.10 were published as [Braßel et al., 2007, Braßel and Siegel, 2008, Braßel, 2008].

Although there might be few if any direct correspondence between this text and those published, many of our previous approaches have contributed to the material in the presented level of maturity, including:

- [Braßel and Christiansen, 2008, Braßel and Christiansen, 2008] to the contents of Chapter 3 and 4

- [Braßel and Hanus, 2005, Braßel and Huch, 2009, Braßel et al., 2010] to the contents of Chapter 5, and especially

    - [Braßel et al., 2004b, Antoy and Braßel, 2007] to the contents of Section 6.6
    - [Braßel et al., 2008] to the contents of Section 6.8

- [Braßel et al., 2004a,c, 2005, 2006, Braßel, 2007] to Section 6.10

Chapter 2

Functional Logic Programs

This chapter contains basic definitions to formalize our notion of functional logic programs and their semantics. We will first define the syntax of expressions and programs (Section 2.1). After that we introduce a natural semantics [Albert et al., 2005] which has become the base of many publications (Section 2.2). We will then introduce some additional steps to simplify this formalism (Section 2.3). Parts of this chapter have been published as [Braßel and Huch, 2007a].

2.1 Signatures, Expressions and Programs

A **constructor-based signature** is a disjoint union of two sets of symbols $C_\Sigma \cup F_\Sigma$ along with a mapping from each symbol to a natural number, called the symbol's **arity**. We will write $s \in {}^{(n)}$ to denote that contains the symbol s and that the arity of s is n. Elements of the sets C_Σ and F_Σ are called **constructor** and **function symbols**, respectively.[1] We will use the symbols $c, c_1, \ldots, c_n$ for constructor symbols, $f, g, h, f_1, \ldots, f_n$ for function symbols and $s, s_1, \ldots, s_n$ for arbitrary symbols in $C_\Sigma \cup F_\Sigma$.

Example 2.1.1 (Signature) *The signature for the collected programs of Examples 1.1.1-1.1.4 is:*

$$
\begin{aligned}
{}^{(0)} &= \{\text{Success,True,False,Nil}\} \\
\cup \ {}^{(1)} &= \{\text{Finite,Infinite,not,head,tail}\} \\
\cup \ {}^{(2)} &= \{\text{Cons,iff,xor,app}\} \\
\cup \ {}^{(3)} &= \{\text{Date}\}
\end{aligned}
$$

This signature is partitioned into the two sets:

$$
\begin{aligned}
C_\Sigma &= \{\text{Success,True,False,Nil,Finite,Infinite,Cons,Date}\} \\
F_\Sigma &= \{\text{not,head,iff,xor,app}\}
\end{aligned}
$$

---
[1] As discussed in Section 1.1.1.2 we will consider our programs to be first order.

As mentioned in Section 1.1.1.1, further type information apart from a symbol's arity will be ignored in this work.

In general we use the notation $\overline{o_n}$ to denote a **sequence of objects** $o_1, \ldots, o_n$. If the exact length and elements of the sequence are arbitrary we may write $\bar{o}$.

In the following, we consider a fixed set of **variables** Var. Variables are denoted by $x, y, z, x_1, \ldots, x_n$. For a given signature the set of **values** V is the set of terms constructed from C_Σ and Var, only, i.e., $V \ni v ::= x \mid c(\overline{v_n})$ where $x \in$ Var and $c \in C_\Sigma{}^{(n)}$. The set of **expressions** E is defined by $e \in E$ i e is inductively constructed from the following rules. Expressions are denoted by $e, e_1, \ldots, e_n$.

$$\begin{array}{rcll}
e & ::= & x & \text{(variable } x \in \text{Var)} \\
  & \mid & c(\overline{e_n}) & \text{(constructor call } c \in C_\Sigma \cap {}^{(n)}) \\
  & \mid & f(\overline{e_n}) & \text{(function call } f \in F_\Sigma \cap {}^{(n)}) \\
  & \mid & \textsf{case } e \textsf{ of } \{\overline{p_n \to e_n}\} & \text{(case expression, } n > 0) \\
  & \mid & e_1 \ ?\ e_2 & \text{(disjunction)} \\
  & \mid & \textsf{let } \overline{x_n = e_n} \textsf{ in } e & \text{(let binding } \overline{x_n} \in \text{Var}, n > 0) \\
p & ::= & c(\bar{x}) & \text{(pattern , } \bar{x} \text{ must be pairwise dierent)}
\end{array}$$

Accordingly, we have $V \subseteq E$. For **constants**, i.e., symbols with arity 0, we will often omit the argument brackets and write, e.g., `Nil` instead of `Nil()`. Note that in contrast to the work of Albert et al. [2005], we do not distinguish between *flexible* and *rigid* case expressions.

In Chapter 1.1 we have seen many examples of expressions including let-expressions in Sections 1.1.10 and 1.1.2.3 and expressions of the form (e_1 ? e_2) in Example 1.1.13. Note that the symbol "?" was treated as a defined operation in Example 1.1.13 but is considered a primitive to introduce a non-deterministic disjunction from now on. To keep expressions containing multiple disjunctions more readable, we omit brackets for ? expressions and assume that ? binds left associatively. Expressions of the form case e of $\{\overline{p_k \to e_k}\}$ are used to represent *pattern matching*, cf. Section 1.1.1.1.

Example 2.1.2 (Pattern Matching using Case) *The pattern matching for* not *(Example 1.1.3) is defined using* case*-expressions like this:*

    not x = case x of { True   False, False   True }

As case-*expressions are defined to match a shallow pattern, only, i.e., one constructor at a time, the function* equal *from Example 1.1.15 needs a nested* case *expression.*

    equal(a,b) = case a of { 0   case b of 0   True,
                             S(x)   case b of S(y)   equal(x,y) }

For overlapping rules, pattern matching may have to make use of ? *in addition to* case-*expressions. The operation* insert *(Example 1.1.12) is represented as follows.*

2.1. SIGNATURES, EXPRESSIONS AND PROGRAMS

```
insert(x,xs) = Cons(x,xs)
             ? (case xs of Cons(y,ys)    Cons(y,insert(x,ys)))
```

The general transformation of pattern matching to disjunctions and case-expressions can be studied in [Hanus and Prehofer, 1999]. As we think that case-expressions are much less readable than the programs introduced in Chapter 1, one of our aims in this chapter will be to regain some of the readability of the original programs in Section 4.

We say that a binding x = e in a let-expression and a branch x → e in a case-expression **introduces** the variable x. We say that an expression e has **unique variables** i every variable is introduced at most once in e. The astute reader may have noticed that we have not given a special syntax to introduce free variables like in Example 1.1.14. The convention is that **free variables** are introduced as circular let bindings of the form (let {x = x} in e).

A special class of terms with unique variables is called **linear**. In a linear term every variable occurs at most once. We will often need to give inductive definitions over the structure of expressions. One such definition is the set of **variables occurring in an expression** e, denoted by $vars(e)$, defined by:

$$
\begin{aligned}
vars(\mathrm{x}) &= \{\mathrm{x}\} \\
vars(\mathrm{s}(\overline{\mathrm{e}_n})) &= \bigcup_{1 \le i \le n} vars(\mathrm{e}_i) \\
vars(\mathsf{case}\ \mathrm{e}\ \mathsf{of}\ \{\overline{\mathrm{p}_k \to \mathrm{e}_k}\}) &= vars(\mathrm{e}) \cup \bigcup_{1 \le i \le k} vars(\mathrm{e}_i) \\
vars(\mathrm{e}_1\ ?\ \mathrm{e}_2) &= vars(\mathrm{e}_1) \cup vars(\mathrm{e}_2) \\
vars(\mathsf{let}\ \{\overline{\mathrm{x}_k = \mathrm{e}_k}\}\ \mathsf{in}\ \mathrm{e}) &= vars(\mathrm{e}) \cup \bigcup_{1 \le i \le k} vars(\mathrm{e}_i)
\end{aligned}
$$

A **substitution** $\sigma : \mathrm{Var} \to E$ is a mapping from variables to expressions such that only for a finite subset of Var we have $\sigma(\mathrm{x}) \ne \mathrm{x}$. We denote this finite subset of Var, the **domain** of σ, by $dom(\sigma)$ and, accordingly, by $rng(\sigma)$, the **range** of σ, the set $\{\sigma(\mathrm{x}) \mid \sigma(\mathrm{x}) \ne \mathrm{x}\}$. A concrete substitution will be given by explicating the behavior on the domain, e.g., we will write $\{\mathrm{x} \mapsto \mathtt{not\ True}, \mathrm{y} \mapsto \mathtt{False}\}$ to denote the substitution that maps the variable x to the expression `not True` and the variable y to `False`. For a set of variables $\mathrm{v} \subseteq \mathrm{Var}$, we denote by $\sigma \setminus \mathrm{v}$ the substitution that behaves like σ on $\mathrm{Var} \setminus \mathrm{v}$ and like the identity on v. The *homomorphic extension* of a substitution σ, denoted by $\underline{\sigma}$, is inductively defined as follows.

$$
\begin{aligned}
\underline{\sigma}(\mathrm{x}) &= \sigma(\mathrm{x}) \\
\underline{\sigma}(\mathrm{s}(\overline{\mathrm{e}_n})) &= \mathrm{s}(\overline{\underline{\sigma}(\mathrm{e}_n)}) \\
\underline{\sigma}(\mathsf{case}\ \mathrm{e}\ \mathsf{of}\ \{\overline{\mathrm{p}_k \to \mathrm{e}_k}\}) &= \mathsf{case}\ \underline{\sigma}(\mathrm{e})\ \mathsf{of}\ \{\overline{\mathrm{p}_k \to \underline{\sigma \setminus vars(\mathrm{p}_k)}(\mathrm{e}_k)}\} \\
\underline{\sigma}(\mathrm{e}_1\ ?\ \mathrm{e}_2) &= \underline{\sigma}(\mathrm{e}_1)\ ?\ \underline{\sigma}(\mathrm{e}_2) \\
\underline{\sigma}(\mathsf{let}\ \{\overline{\mathrm{x}_k = \mathrm{e}_k}\}\ \mathsf{in}\ \mathrm{e}) &= \mathsf{let}\ \{\overline{\mathrm{x}_k = \underline{\sigma \setminus \{\overline{\mathrm{x}_k}\}}(\mathrm{e}_k)}\}\ \mathsf{in}\ \underline{\sigma \setminus \{\overline{\mathrm{x}_k}\}}(\mathrm{e})
\end{aligned}
$$

In most cases we will call the extension of σ also a substitution for simplicity and we will reuse the symbol σ (instead of $\underline{\sigma}$). A substitution σ whose range is a subset of Var is called a **variable renaming**.[2] The *sub terms* of a given

---

[2] Often in the literature one finds the additional requirement that a variable renaming must be *injective*. In this work, we will explicitly say "injective variable renaming", whenever this additional property is needed.

expression e, defined in the usual inductive way, will be denoted by $sub(\mathsf{e})$.

A bit prematurely, Example 2.1.2 already introduced how our formalization of programs looks like. Accordingly, a **program** over signature consists of a sequence of function definitions (D) where each definition introduces a dierent function symbol ($\mathsf{f} \in F_\Sigma$) and consists of a pair of a left-hand side of the form $\mathsf{f}(\overline{\mathsf{x}})$ and an expression ($\mathsf{e} \in E$) on the right-hand side.

P	::=	$\overline{\mathsf{D}}$	(program)	each D defines dierent symbol f
D	::=	$\mathsf{f}(\overline{\mathsf{x}}) = \mathsf{e}$	(declaration)	$\mathsf{f}(\overline{\mathsf{x}})$ linear, e has unique variables, for all $\mathsf{x} \in vars(\mathsf{e})$ we have that x is either introduced in e or is an element of $\{\overline{\mathsf{x}_n}\}$ but not both.

Programs were already given in Example 2.1.2.

Somewhat informal, we call a variable **fresh** if it does not appear anywhere in the context it depends on, but in Section 2.2.3 we will give a more concrete notion of freshness.

When we refer to a rule within a program, we want to be independent of the names of variables occurring in that rule. Especially, as program rules are always identified by their left-hand side, we want the variables introduced in the right-hand side to be fresh. Therefore, when we write $\mathsf{l} = \mathsf{r} \in \mathsf{P}$ for a program P we mean that $\mathsf{l} = \mathsf{r}$ is a **variant of a program rule**, i.e., there is an injective variable renaming σ and a rule $\mathsf{l}' = \mathsf{r}'$ in the program P such that $\sigma(\mathsf{l}) = \mathsf{l}', \sigma(\mathsf{r}) = \mathsf{r}'$ such that $vars(\mathsf{r}) \setminus vars(\mathsf{l})$ are fresh and r has unique variables.

2.2 Natural Semantics of Case-Based Programs

By now there are many dierent approaches to capture the semantics of functional logic programs. Many approaches are based on a rewriting logic [González-Moreno et al., 1999a] or one of the various extension thereof. Another main stream in the study of functional logic programming are based on term graph rewriting [Antoy, 2005]. The semantics employed in this work [Albert et al., 2005] is an operational semantics for functional logic programs in a style which is often referred to as "natural". But there are many more approaches with less impact on the literature. The situation with this multitude of approaches is not fortunate. We hope that one of the contributions of this work will help the situation at least a little by bringing closer the approaches of [Antoy, 2005] and [Albert et al., 2005] with the results of chapter 4.

The natural semantics [Albert et al., 2005] is based on a special subset of expressions, called *flat expressions* (Section 2.2.1) and a central notion of this semantics is that of a *heap* and a *configuration* (Section 2.2.2). The idea is that a heap contains bindings for variables as is necessary to obtain call-by-need semantics, see Section 1.1.10. A configuration additionally contains the expression which is currently evaluated. The semantics itself is then defined as a set of rules to relate configurations (Section 2.2.3). There will be some notable dierences

2.2. NATURAL SEMANTICS OF CASE-BASED PROGRAMS

in our definition from the original approach which are examined in Section 2.2.4. Finally, section 2.2.5 will introduce an abstraction of the operational semantics which will allow to make express the results of this work more concisely.

2.2.1 Flat Expressions

An important subset of the expressions are the **flat expressions**. Flat expressions may *only contain variables as arguments of constructor and function applications*. The left-hand sides and the patterns of the above definition are examples of flat expressions. The presence of let bindings makes it possible to transform arbitrary case-based expressions to a flat expression. One possible transformation is the operation *flat*:

$$\begin{aligned}
\mathit{flat}(\mathtt{x}) &= \mathtt{x} \\
\mathit{flat}(\mathtt{s}(\overline{\mathtt{e}_n})) &= \mathsf{let}\ \overline{\{\mathtt{y}_m = \mathit{flat}(\mathtt{e}'_m)\}}\ \mathsf{in}\ \mathtt{s}(\overline{\mathtt{x}_n}) \\
&\quad (\overline{\mathtt{y}_m}, \overline{\mathtt{e}'_m}, \overline{\mathtt{x}_n}) = \mathit{varArgs}(\overline{\mathtt{e}_n}) \\
\mathit{flat}(\mathsf{case}\ \mathtt{e}\ \mathsf{of}\ \overline{\{\mathtt{p}_k \to \mathtt{e}_k\}}) &= \mathsf{case}\ \mathit{flat}(\mathtt{e})\ \mathsf{of}\ \overline{\{\mathtt{p}_k \to \mathit{flat}(\mathtt{e}_k)\}} \\
\mathit{flat}(\mathtt{e}_1\ \mathtt{?}\ \mathtt{e}_2) &= \mathit{flat}(\mathtt{e}_1)\ \mathtt{?}\ \mathit{flat}(\mathtt{e}_2) \\
\mathit{flat}(\mathsf{let}\ \overline{\{\mathtt{x}_k = \mathtt{e}_k\}}\ \mathsf{in}\ \mathtt{e}) &= \mathsf{let}\ \overline{\{\mathtt{x}_k = \mathit{flat}(\mathtt{e}_k)\}}\ \mathsf{in}\ \mathit{flat}(\mathtt{e}) \\
\mathit{varArgs}(\varepsilon) &= (\varepsilon, \varepsilon, \varepsilon) \\
\mathit{varArgs}(\mathtt{e} \cdot \overline{\mathtt{e}_n}) &= \begin{cases} (\mathtt{y} \cdot \overline{\mathtt{y}_m}, \mathtt{e} \cdot \overline{\mathtt{e}'_m}, \mathtt{y} \cdot \overline{\mathtt{x}_n}) & \text{, if } \mathtt{e} \notin \mathit{Var} \\ (\overline{\mathtt{y}_m}, \overline{\mathtt{e}_m}, \mathtt{e} \cdot \overline{\mathtt{x}_n}) & \text{, if } \mathtt{e} \in \mathit{Var} \end{cases}
\end{aligned}$$

where y fresh and $(\overline{\mathtt{y}_m}, \overline{\mathtt{e}'_m}, \overline{\mathtt{x}_n}) = \mathit{varArgs}(\overline{\mathtt{e}_n})$

In the above definition and in the following, we make the convention that, for $k = 0$, the "expression" let $\overline{\{\mathtt{x}_k = \mathtt{e}_k\}}$ in e is just a complicated way to write e. For example, we have $\mathit{flat}(\mathtt{True}) = \mathtt{True}$. The set of **flat expressions** for signature will be denoted by FE in the following and, naturally, we have $FE \subseteq E$.

Example 2.2.1 (Flattening) *For the expression* xor(True,False), *cf. Example 1.1.3, we have*

$$\mathit{flat}(\mathtt{xor}(\mathtt{True},\mathtt{False})) = \mathsf{let}\ \{\mathtt{x}_1 = \mathtt{True}, \mathtt{x}_2 = \mathtt{False}\}\ \mathsf{in}\ \mathtt{xor}(\mathtt{x}_1, \mathtt{x}_2)$$

Flattening may produce nested let*-bindings as for the following expression, cf. Example 1.1.10.*

$$\begin{aligned}&\mathit{flat}(\mathtt{double}(\mathtt{Cons}(\mathtt{1},\mathtt{Nil})))\\ =\ &\mathsf{let}\ \{\mathtt{x}_1 = \mathsf{let}\ \{\mathtt{x}_2 = \mathtt{1}, \mathtt{x}_3 = \mathtt{Nil}\}\ \mathsf{in}\ \mathtt{Cons}(\mathtt{x}_2, \mathtt{x}_3)\}\ \mathsf{in}\ \mathtt{double}(\mathtt{x}_1)\end{aligned}$$

Variable arguments are not touched by flattening, as illustrated by flattening (a variant of) the right-hand side of the recursive rule defining app *from Example 1.1.4.*

$$\mathit{flat}(\mathtt{Cons}(\mathtt{x}, \mathtt{app}(\mathtt{y}, \mathtt{z}))) = \mathsf{let}\ \{\mathtt{x}_1 = \mathtt{app}(\mathtt{y}, \mathtt{z})\}\ \mathsf{in}\ \mathtt{Cons}(\mathtt{x}, \mathtt{x}_1)$$

The purpose of flattening is to obtain call-by-need and call-time choice, as discussed informally in Sections 1.1.10 and 1.1.2.3 and formalized in the following section.

2.2.2 Heaps and Configurations

For the set of variables Var and the set of flat expressions FE, as defined in Section 2.2.1, a **heap** is a finite subset of $Var \times FE$ such that each element $x \in Var$ appears at most once in a pair (x, e) within the set. In other words a heap represents a partial function from Var to FE. Heaps will be denoted with upper case Greek letters (e.g. $\Gamma, \Delta, \ldots$) and we adopt the usual notation for functions to write $\Gamma(x) = e$ for $(x, e) \in \Gamma$. A **heap update** $\Gamma[x \mapsto e]$ is an abbreviation for $(\Gamma \setminus \{(x, \Gamma(x))\}) \cup \{(x, e)\}$. In analogy to construction and pattern matching of values in programs, we use the same notation to construct and deconstruct heaps. More clearly, if we say that a heap Γ' is equal to $\Gamma[x \mapsto e]$ we not only imply that Γ' is the result of an update of Γ by (x, e) but also that $\Gamma = (\Gamma' \setminus \{(x, e)\})$. For a concrete example of this notation consider the rule (VarExp) in Figure 2.1 as discussed below. We will also make use of the usual notations $dom(\Gamma)$ and $rng(\Gamma)$ to denote the **domain** and **range** of a heap, respectively. Note that an updated heap is again a heap and that for all heaps Γ the equation $\Gamma[x \mapsto e'][x \mapsto e] = \Gamma[x \mapsto e]$ holds.

A **configuration** $\Gamma : e$ is a pair of a heap and a flat expression. A **well-formed configuration** additionally satisfies the condition that no variable in $dom(\Gamma)$ is introduced in any of the expressions in $E := \{e\} \cup rng(\Gamma)$, all expressions in E have unique variables and there are no $(x_1, e_1), (x_2, e_2) \in \Gamma$, $x_1 \neq x_2$, $y \in Var$ such that y is introduced in more than one of the expression e, e_1 or e_2. In other words, each variable is introduced at most once in the configuration.

The definitions of occurring variables and substitution are generalized to heaps and configurations. The **variables occurring in a heap** Γ are defined as $vars(\Gamma) := dom(\Gamma) \cup \bigcup \{vars(e) \mid e \in rng(\Gamma)\}$. The **variables occurring in a configuration** $\Gamma : e$ are those occurring in Γ or in e. For an injective variable renaming σ we define $\sigma(\Gamma) := \{(\sigma(x), \sigma(e)) \mid (x, e) \in \Gamma\}$ and $\sigma(\Gamma : e) := \sigma(\Gamma) : \sigma(e)$. Note that by injectivity of σ, for any heap Γ we have that $\sigma(\Gamma)$ is again a heap and that for a well formed configuration $\Gamma : e$ the result $\sigma(\Gamma : e)$ is again well-formed.

2.2.3 Statements and their Derivation

Two configurations are related in a **statement** of the form $\Gamma : e \Downarrow \Delta : v$, called the **in-** and the **out-**configuration of that statement. Such statements are interpreted as: the expression e in the context of the heap Γ evaluates to the value v with the heap Δ, according to the rules of Figure 2.1.

Note that this semantics is referred to as $\Downarrow_0$. This is because the following sections introduce several steps of modification denoted by $\Downarrow_1 \Downarrow_2, \ldots$ When we give a definition for all the dierent versions we simply use $\Downarrow$, like, e.g., in the definition of a statement above.

2.2. NATURAL SEMANTICS OF CASE-BASED PROGRAMS

(Val) $\Delta : v \Downarrow_0 \Delta : v$ where $v = c(\overline{x_n})$ or $(\ v) = v$

(VarCons) $\Delta[x \mapsto c(\overline{x_n})] : x \Downarrow_0 \Delta[x \mapsto c(\overline{x_n})] : c(\overline{x_n})$

(VarExp) $\dfrac{\Delta : e \Downarrow_0 \Delta : v}{\Delta[x \mapsto e] : x \Downarrow_0 \Delta[x \mapsto v] : v}$

             where $e \neq x$ and $e \neq c(\overline{y_n})$

(Fun) $\dfrac{\Delta : \mathit{flat}(e) \Downarrow_0 \Delta : v}{\Delta : f(\overline{x_n}) \Downarrow_0 \Delta : v}$ where $f(\overline{x_n}) = e \in P$

(Let) $\dfrac{\Delta[\overline{x_k \mapsto e_k}] : e \Downarrow_0 \Delta : v}{\Delta : \text{let } \{\overline{x_k = e_k}\} \text{ in } e \Downarrow_0 \Delta : v}$

(Or) $\dfrac{\Delta : e_i \Downarrow_0 \Delta : v}{\Delta : e_1\ ?\ e_2 \Downarrow_0 \Delta : v}$ where $i \in \{1,2\}$

(Select) $\dfrac{\Delta : e \Downarrow_0 \Delta : c(\overline{x_n}) \quad \Delta : \sigma(e_i) \Downarrow_0 \Delta' : v}{\Delta : \text{case } e \text{ of } \{\overline{p_k \mapsto e_k}\} \Downarrow_0 \Delta' : v}$

             where $i \in \{1, \ldots, k\}$ and $c(\overline{x_n}) = \sigma(p_i)$

(Guess) $\dfrac{\Delta : e \Downarrow_0 \Delta' : x \quad \Delta'[\overline{x_n \mapsto x_n}][x \mapsto c(\overline{x_n})] : e_i \Downarrow_0 \Delta'' : v}{\Delta : \text{case } e \text{ of } \{\overline{p_k \mapsto e_k}\} \Downarrow_0 \Delta'' : v}$

             where $p_i = c(\overline{x_n})$ and $i \in \{1, \ldots, k\}$

Figure 2.1: Natural Semantics for Functional Logic Programs

We give a short explanation of the rules in Figure 2.1 followed by examples.

(VarCons) This rule is used to evaluate a variable x which is bound to a constructor-rooted term t in the heap. It returns t as a result of the evaluation.

(VarExp) In order to evaluate a variable x that is bound to an expression $e = \Delta(x)$ (which is not a value), this rule starts a sub computation for e. If a value v is eventually computed, the variable x is updated in the heap with the binding $[x \mapsto v]$.

(Val) A value, i.e., a constructor term or a free variable, is returned without modifying the heap.

(Fun) This rule performs a simple function unfolding employing a variant of a rule in the program P. (P is a global parameter of the calculus.) Note that we allow programs to contain more than only flat expressions. For convenience, the right-hand sides of the program rules are flattened by the application of this rule. Note that the variables in $f(\overline{x_n}) = e$ are fresh due to our definition of a "variant of a program rule" at the end of Section 2.1.

(Let) In order to reduce a let construct, this rule adds the bindings to the heap and proceeds with the evaluation of the main argument of let.

(Or) This rule non-deterministically evaluates a disjunction by either evaluating the first or the second argument.

(Select) and (Guess) These rules initiate the evaluation of a case expression by evaluating the case argument. If a constructor-rooted term is reached, the rule (Select) is applied to select the appropriate branch and continue with the evaluation of this branch. If a free variable is returned then rule (Guess) is used to non-deterministically choose one alternative and continue with the evaluation of the according branch. Moreover, the heap is updated with the binding of the free variable to the corresponding pattern.[3]

A **proof** or **proof tree** of a statement corresponds to a derivation sequence using the rules of Figure 2.1. We frequently refer to *the configurations* or *heaps* or *expressions occurring in a proof* and give inductive proofs on the *structure of a proof tree*.

Example 2.2.2 (Proof Trees) *We repeat the program from Example 1.1.9 in the formalism of this section.*

```
ones = Cons(1,ones)
head x = case x of { Cons(y,ys)     y }
```

The evaluation of the expression flat(head ones) employing the rules of Figure 2.1 looks like this where $= \emptyset\,[x \mapsto 1, y \mapsto \text{ones}]$ *and* $' = [\ x_1 \mapsto \text{Cons}(x, y)]$:

$$
\cfrac{
 \cfrac{
  \cfrac{
   \cfrac{
    \cfrac{
     \cfrac{\emptyset\,[x \mapsto 1]\,[y \mapsto \text{ones}] : \text{Cons}(x, y) \Downarrow_0 \;:\; \text{Cons}(x, y)}
           {\emptyset : \text{let } \{x = 1, y = \text{ones}\} \text{ in } \text{Cons}(x, y) \Downarrow_0 \;:\; \text{Cons}(x, y)}
    }
    {\emptyset : \text{ones} \Downarrow_0 \;:\; \text{Cons}(x, y)}
   }
   {\emptyset\,[x_1 \mapsto \text{ones}] : x_1 \Downarrow_0 [\ x_1 \mapsto \text{Cons}(x, y)] : \text{Cons}(x, y)} \quad ' : x \Downarrow_0 \; ' : 1
  }
  {\emptyset\,[x_1 \mapsto \text{ones}] : \text{case } x_1 \text{ of } \{\text{Cons}(y_1, y_2) \mapsto y_1\} \Downarrow_0 \; ' : 1}
 }
 {\emptyset\,[x_1 \mapsto \text{ones}] : \text{head}(x_1) \Downarrow_0 \; ' : 1}
}
{\emptyset : \text{let } \{x_1 = \text{ones}\} \text{ in } \text{head}(x_1) \Downarrow_0 \; ' : 1}
$$

---

[3] In the original setting [Albert et al., 2005] rule **(Guess)** is only applicable for special **case**-expressions, called *flexible*. We will not make this distinction here.

2.2. NATURAL SEMANTICS OF CASE-BASED PROGRAMS 43

Sometimes the following alternative layout for proof trees is more readable.

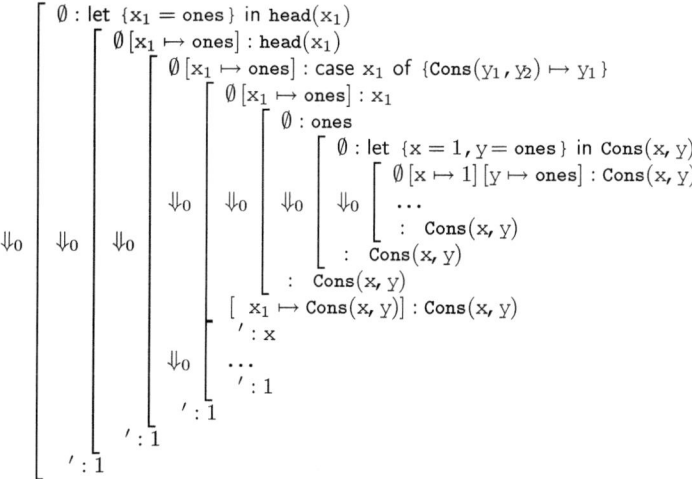

2.2.4 Correspondence to the Original Approach

The rules of Figure 2.1 feature some dierences to the original setting [Albert et al., 2005]. For example, we flatten the program rules in each function application (rule (**Fun**)) instead of requiring programs to feature flat expressions only. For most changes it should be obvious that both definitions are equivalent since they are a simple change of notation. There are two exceptions, however. The first change is that in rule (**VarExp**) we go from configuration $[\ x \mapsto e] : x$ to $: e$ instead of $[\ x \mapsto e] : e$. In other words we remove the binding $x \mapsto e$ from the heap. This change has semantic implications and will be discussed in Section 2.3.1 below. The second change is that we do not invent fresh variables nor perform a renaming in the rules (**Let**) and (**Guess**). Especially, this change requires the assumption that the rules are applied to statements about *well-formed* configurations initially. It is then easy to see that the rules will preserve the invariant that all configurations in a proof are well-formed (Proposition 2.2.3 below). This eectively means that no "name clashes" are possible. Before we can show this simple result we have to be a bit more precise about the freshness of the variables introduced in a derivation.

The **dependence sequence** of the configurations in a proof tree is inductively defined as

$$dep(\quad : e \Downarrow \quad ' : e') \;=\; \quad : e, \quad ' : e'$$

$$dep(\frac{T_1}{: e \Downarrow \quad ' : e'}) \;=\; \quad : e, dep(T_1),\; ' : e'$$

$$dep(\frac{T_1 \quad T_2}{: e \Downarrow \quad ' : e'}) \;=\; \quad : e, dep(T_1), dep(T_2),\; ' : e'$$

and we say that in a proof a configuration C' **depends on** another configuration C, denoted by C ≺ C', when C is before C' in the dependence sequence of the proof. With this notion we can be more precise about the freshness of variables. Fresh variables are (silently) introduced in the rule (Fun) by employing the definitions of the variant of a program rule and the *flat* operation. We now require that a variable in a configuration C = : *flat*(e) is fresh within a proof i it does not appear in any of the configurations C depends on (in this proof).

Proposition 2.2.3 *Let : e be a well-formed configuration. Then any proof tree of a statement : e $\Downarrow_0$ Δ : v contains only well-formed configurations.*

Proof. By induction on the structure of the proof tree.
Base cases:
(Val): the claim holds trivially.
(VarCons): If the claim holds for [x ↦ c($\overline{x_n}$)] : x then it also holds for [x ↦ c c($\overline{x_n}$) as neither c($\overline{x_n}$) nor the rule introduce new variables.
Inductive cases:
(VarExp): If the claim holds for [x ↦ e] : x then it also holds for : e where e ≠ x and e ≠ c($\overline{y_n}$) as e is not present in the heap and all the variables introduced in e cannot, by assumption, be introduced by any other expression in . Therefore, Δ : v is covered by induction hypothesis. In consequence, the claim also holds for Δ [x ↦ v] : v since v does not introduce new variables.
(Fun): If the claim holds for : f($\overline{x_n}$) then it also holds for : *flat*(e) where f($\overline{x_n}$) = e ∈ P as the definitions of a program variant and of the operation *flat* ensure that all variables in *flat*(e) are either in {$\overline{x_n}$} or fresh. Therefore, Δ : v is covered by induction hypothesis.
(Let): If the claim holds for : let {$\overline{x_k = e_k}$} in e then it also holds for [$\overline{x_k \mapsto e_k}$] : e as by assumption the variables introduced by let do not appear in . Therefore, Δ : v is covered by induction hypothesis.
(Or): If the claim holds for : e_1 ? e_2 then it also holds for : e_i where i ∈ {1,2} as e_i is a sub term of e_1 ? e_2. Therefore, Δ : v is covered by induction hypothesis.
(Select): If the claim holds for : case e of {$\overline{p_k \mapsto e_k}$} then it also holds for : e as e is a sub term. Therefore, Δ : c($\overline{x_n}$) is covered by induction hypothesis. In consequence, the claim also holds for Δ : $\sigma(e_i)$ since $\sigma(e_i)$ cannot introduce other variables than e_i. In addition the variables in Δ are either fresh or were already present in *vars*() or *vars*(e). If they are fresh they cannot be introduced in $\sigma(e_i)$ since : case e of {$\overline{p_k \mapsto e_k}$} ≺ Δ : $\sigma(e_i)$. If they are in *vars*()

2.2. NATURAL SEMANTICS OF CASE-BASED PROGRAMS   45

they cannot be introduced in $\sigma(e_i)$ by assumption that the initial configuration $\vcentcolon$ case e of $\{\overline{p_k \mapsto e_k}\}$ is well-formed. If they are in $vars(e)$ they can also not be introduced in $\sigma(e_i)$ as otherwise case e of $\{\overline{p_k \mapsto e_k}\}$ would not have unique variables. Consequently, the configuration $\Delta \vcentcolon \sigma(e_i)$ must be well-formed. The claim for $\vcentcolon$ v is again covered by induction hypothesis.

(Guess): If the claim holds for $\vcentcolon$ case e of $\{\overline{p_k \mapsto e_k}\}$ then it also holds for $\vcentcolon$ e as e is a sub term. Therefore, $\Delta \vcentcolon$ x is covered by induction hypothesis. In consequence, the claim also holds for $\Delta \left[\overline{x_n \mapsto x_n}\right][x \mapsto c(\overline{x_n})] \vcentcolon e_i$ since analogue to the discussion for rule (Select) above, no sub term of case e of $\{\overline{p_k \mapsto e_k}\}$, especially not e_i, can introduce variables present in Δ. Also e_i cannot introduce any of the variables $\overline{x_n}$, since that would imply that case e of $\{\overline{p_k \mapsto e_k}\}$ does not have unique variables. Finally, e_i can also not introduce the variable x since in order to be a result of the statement $\vcentcolon$ e $\Downarrow_0 \Delta \vcentcolon$ x, x must be present in Δ. The claim for $\vcentcolon$ v is again covered by induction hypothesis.   □

For future reference we note some simple observations about derivations with the rules of Figure 2.1. The reader should be able to verify that these observations can be proven very easily such that any formal treatment can be omitted. Indeed, we silently assume that the same observations hold for all variants of natural semantics introduced in this work.

The first observation is that for a rule like (VarExp) the update of the result heap will not overwrite a value: the variable taken from the heap will not be reintroduced because all introduced variables are fresh by definition. The second observation is that if a free variable x is the result of a derivation, it must also be in the domain of the result heap.

Observation 2.2.4

1) $\left[\, x \mapsto e\right] \vcentcolon x \Downarrow \Delta \left[x \mapsto v\right] \vcentcolon v$ *implies* $x \notin dom(\Delta)$

2) $\vcentcolon$ e $\Downarrow \Delta \vcentcolon$ x *implies* $x \in dom(\Delta)$ *and* $\Delta(x) = x$

3) $\left[\, x \mapsto e'\right] \vcentcolon e \Downarrow \Delta \vcentcolon x$ *where* x *is not reachable from* e *implies* $\Delta = \Delta'\left[x \mapsto e'\right]$

2.2.5 A More Abstract Notion of Semantics

The strength of natural semantics lies in the fact that it easily incorporates the evaluation strategy in the formal framework. Additionally, the concept is comparably close to that of possible implementations as aspects like sharing are taken into accord. When we develop the formal setting of Section 2.2.3 in the remainder of this work, we will strive to give results as strong as possible. Especially, we will always show how to construct a derivation with respect to some rules for $\Downarrow_i$ from a derivation with respect to $\Downarrow_j$ and the constructed derivations will be as close as possible. However, we also wish to give a more intuitive account of our results along the lines of "the values derivable from expression e are the same for $\Downarrow_j$ and $\Downarrow_i$, respectively," To formulate such a result we need a more abstract notion of semantics as introduced in the next definition.

Definition 2.2.5 (Abstract Semantics of an Expression) *Let P be a program over a constructor-based signature Σ and let e be a Σ-expression. Then the semantics of an expression $[\![e]\!]_i^P$ (with respect to P and $\Downarrow_i$) is defined by*

$$[\![e]\!]_i^P := \{\sigma(\overline{*(x_n)}) \mid \emptyset : \mathit{flat}(e) \Downarrow_i \sigma : c(\overline{x_n})\} \cup \{x \mid \emptyset : \mathit{flat}(e) \Downarrow_i \sigma : x\}$$

where $\sigma^*(\cdot)$ is defined by:

$$\sigma^*(x) = x \quad , \text{ if } x \notin \mathit{dom}(\sigma)$$

$$[x \mapsto y]^*(x) = \begin{cases} x & , \text{ if } x = y \\ \sigma^*(y) & , \text{ if } x \neq y \end{cases}$$

$$[x \mapsto c(\overline{x_n})]^*(x) = c(\overline{\sigma^*(x_n)})$$
$$[x \mapsto f(\overline{x_n})]^*(x) = x$$
$$[x \mapsto \text{let } \{\overline{x_k = e_k}\} \text{ in } e]^*(x) = [\overline{x_k \mapsto e_k}, x \mapsto e]^*(x)$$
$$[x \mapsto \text{case } e \text{ of } \{\overline{p_k \rightarrow e_k}\}]^*(x) = x$$

We may omit the program P if it is clear from the context. Note that, because of the choice of fresh variables in the calls to flat($\cdot$), the sets $[\![\cdot]\!]^P$ are infinite whenever any value contains a variable. The usual way to cope with this phenomenon is to consider equivalence classes with respect to renaming of variables. For this we define between two sets of constructor terms M, N the quasi order $\preceq$ as:

$$M \preceq N :\Leftrightarrow \forall v \in M : \exists \sigma, v' \in N : \sigma(v) = v'$$

where each σ is an injective variable renaming. It is easy to see that $\preceq$ is indeed a quasi order and it is well known that each quasi order induces an equivalence relation [Berghammer, 2008]:

$$M \equiv N :\Leftrightarrow M \preceq N \wedge N \preceq M$$

It is with respect to this equivalence relation that we consider equivalence classes of a given set of constructor terms M by the notation $\lfloor M \rfloor$.

Note that the given notion of semantics is indeed *an abstraction* from the original operational semantics in the sense that certain aspects, especially with regard to the function symbols employed, are disregarded. It is in this sense that we call $[\![e]\!]_i^P$ the "(abstract) semantics of" e (in the context of program P).

Example 2.2.6 (Abstract Semantics) *In correspondence with Example 2.2.2 the semantics of* (head(ones)) *is*

$$[\![\text{head(ones)}]\!]_0^P = \lfloor \{1\} \rfloor$$

For a more interesting example the reader might want to reconsider the definitions from Examples 1.1.4 and 1.1.10 to verify that the semantics of the expression double(Cons(1,Nil)) *is:*

$$[\![\text{double(Cons(1,Nil))}]\!]_0^P = \lfloor \{\text{Cons(1,x)}\} \rfloor$$

The next step will be a justification of our change to rule (VarExp) followed by a simplification of the rules of Figure 2.1.

2.3 Modifications of the Semantics

We will apply two modifications to the original semantics [Albert et al., 2005]. Firstly, we will discuss why we changed rule (VarExp) (Section 2.3.1), followed by a discussion of rule (VarCons) which can be eliminated from the calculus (Section 2.3.2).

2.3.1 Changing Rule (VarExp)

Unfortunately, the design of the original semantics [Albert et al., 2005] shows an anomaly for circular let bindings when the evaluation of the bindings induces non-deterministic branching. The root of the problem can be associated with the rule (VarExp). In contrast to the original work for functional languages by Launchbury [1993], Albert et al. [2005] do not remove a binding looked up in the heap. Whereas the corresponding original rule, (called "Variable" [Launchbury, 1993]) looks more like our rule (VarExp) of Figure 2.1, the version of Albert et al. is defined as follows.

$$(\text{OrigVarExp}) \quad \frac{[\ x \mapsto e] : e \Downarrow' \Delta : v}{[\ x \mapsto e] : x \Downarrow' \Delta [x \mapsto v] : v}$$
$$\text{where } e \neq x \text{ and } e \neq c(\overline{y_n})$$

The following excerpt of [Albert et al., 2005] demonstrates that the authors clearly think that this decision "does not affect the natural semantics since black holes have no value", but that it is only a step towards the work of Sestoft [1997].

> (VarExp) This rule achieves the effect of sharing. If the variable to be evaluated is bound to some expression in the heap, then the expression is evaluated and the heap is updated with the computed value; finally, we return this value as the result. In contrast to Launchbury (1993), we do not remove the binding for the variable from the heap; this becomes useful to generate fresh variable names easily. Sestoft (1997) solves this problem by introducing a variant of Launchbury's relation which is labeled with the names of the already used variables. The only disadvantage of our approach is that black holes (a detectably self-dependent infinite loop) are not detected at the semantical level. However, this does not affect the natural semantics since black holes have no value. [Albert et al., 2005, p.13]

In contrast to Launchbury's approach [Launchbury, 1993] a variable looked up in the heap is not deleted from the heap when evaluating its binding to head-normal form. In a deterministic setting, omitting this "black hole detection" does indeed not affect the semantics. The difference only consists of a finitely failing derivation on the one hand and the attempt to construct an infinite proof tree on the other hand. But in combination with non-determinism, multiple (possibly different) updates of a variable in the heap are possible. Therefore, it may happen that "black holes" have a value after all, as the following derivation shows:

$$\cfrac{\cfrac{\cfrac{\cfrac{\Delta : T \Downarrow' \Delta : T}{\Delta : T \;?\; ... \Downarrow' \Delta : T}}{\Delta : x \Downarrow' [x \mapsto T] : T} \quad [x \mapsto T] : F \Downarrow' [x \mapsto T] : F}{\Delta : \mathsf{case}\; x \;\mathsf{of}\; \{T \mapsto F\} \Downarrow' [x \mapsto T] : F}}{\cfrac{\Delta : T \;?\; \mathsf{case}\; x \;\mathsf{of}\; \{T \mapsto F\} \Downarrow' [x \mapsto T] : F}{\Delta : x \Downarrow' [x \mapsto T][x \mapsto F] : F}}}{\emptyset : \mathsf{let}\; \{x = T \;?\; \mathsf{case}\; x \;\mathsf{of}\; \{T \mapsto F\}\} \;\mathsf{in}\; x \Downarrow' [x \mapsto T][x \mapsto F] : F}$$

where $\Delta := \emptyset [x \mapsto T \;?\; \mathsf{case}\; x \;\mathsf{of}\; \{T \mapsto F\}]$

The variable x is looked up in the heap twice. Each time a different non-deterministic branch is chosen. Hence, x is bound to T as well as to F. In consequence, the given rule (OrigVarExp) violates the single assignment property which would otherwise hold for the calculus. In addition "black holes" now may have a value against the explicit statement quoted above.

In contrast, the rule (VarExp) from Figure 2.1 does not induce a similar behavior. With this rule the problematic derivation is no longer valid because there is no rule to cover the situation that x is looked up in the empty heap.

$$\cfrac{\cfrac{\cfrac{\cfrac{\emptyset : x \Downarrow_0 \langle\langle \text{result undefined} \rangle\rangle}{\emptyset : \mathsf{case}\; x \;\mathsf{of}\; \{T \mapsto F\} \Downarrow_0}}{\emptyset : T \;?\; \mathsf{case}\; x \;\mathsf{of}\; \{T \mapsto F\} \Downarrow_0}}{\emptyset [x \mapsto T \;?\; \mathsf{case}\; x \;\mathsf{of}\; \{T \mapsto F\}] : x \Downarrow_0}}{\emptyset : \mathsf{let}\; \{x = T \;?\; \mathsf{case}\; x \;\mathsf{of}\; \{T \mapsto F\}\} \;\mathsf{in}\; x \Downarrow_0}$$

We think that this speaks clearly for the version of the rule which we have chosen.

2.3.2 Elimination of (VarCons)

An observation about the rules of Figure 2.1 is that the rule (VarCons) is not really needed. If the rule (VarExp) could also be applied in the case that $e = c(\overline{x_n})$, (VarCons) would be a simple short-cut for applying rule (VarExp) directly followed by (Val). Therefore, a simplifying step introduces the following rule instead of the two rules (VarCons) and (VarExp).

$$(\mathsf{Var}) \quad \cfrac{\Delta : e \Downarrow_1 \Delta' : v}{[x \mapsto e]\Delta : x \Downarrow_1 \Delta'[x \mapsto v] : v} \quad \text{where } e \neq x$$

For ease of reference the whole semantics is shown in Figure 2.2. It is easy to see

2.3. MODIFICATIONS OF THE SEMANTICS

$$\text{(Val)} \quad \frac{}{: v \Downarrow_1 : v} \quad \text{where } v = c(\overline{x_n}) \text{ or } (\ v) = v$$

$$\text{(Var)} \quad \frac{: e \Downarrow_1 \Delta : v}{[\ x \mapsto e] : x \Downarrow_1 \Delta\ [x \mapsto v] : v} \quad \text{where } e \neq x$$

$$\text{(Fun)} \quad \frac{:\ \mathit{flat}(e) \Downarrow_1 \Delta : v}{:\ f(\overline{x_n}) \Downarrow_1 \Delta : v} \quad \text{where } f(\overline{x_n}) = e \in P$$

$$\text{(Let)} \quad \frac{[\ \overline{x_k \mapsto e_k}] : e \Downarrow_1 \Delta : v}{:\ \text{let } \{\overline{x_k = e_k}\} \text{ in } e \Downarrow_1 \Delta : v}$$

$$\text{(Or)} \quad \frac{:\ e_i \Downarrow_1 \Delta : v}{:\ e_1\ ?\ e_2 \Downarrow_1 \Delta : v} \quad \text{where } i \in \{1, 2\}$$

$$\text{(Select)} \quad \frac{:\ e \Downarrow_1 \Delta : c(\overline{x_n}) \quad \Delta : \sigma(e_i) \Downarrow_1\ :\ v}{:\ \text{case } e \text{ of } \{\overline{p_k \mapsto e_k}\} \Downarrow_1\ :\ v}$$
$$\text{where } i \in \{1, \ldots, k\} \text{ and } c(\overline{x_n}) = \sigma(p_i)$$

$$\text{(Guess)} \quad \frac{:\ e \Downarrow_1 \Delta : x \quad \Delta\ [\overline{x_n \mapsto x_n}]\ [x \mapsto c(\overline{x_n})] : e_i \Downarrow_1\ :\ v}{:\ \text{case } e \text{ of } \{\overline{p_k \mapsto e_k}\} \Downarrow_1\ :\ v}$$
$$\text{where } p_i = c(\overline{x_n}) \text{ and } i \in \{1, \ldots, k\}$$

Figure 2.2: Semantics without rule VarCons

that this change of the rules does not imply a change in the actual semantics, which is the content of the following theorem.

Lemma 2.3.1 $\quad :\ e \Downarrow_0 \Delta : v\ i \quad :\ e \Downarrow_1 \Delta : v$

Proof. "$\Rightarrow$": Replace any application $[\ x \mapsto c(\overline{x_n})] : x \Downarrow_0 [\ x \mapsto c(\overline{x_n})] : c(\overline{x_n})$ of rule (VarCons) by the derivation

$$\frac{:\ c(\overline{x_n}) \Downarrow_1\ :\ c(\overline{x_n})}{[\ x \mapsto c(\overline{x_n})] : x \Downarrow_1 [\ x \mapsto c(\overline{x_n})] : c(\overline{x_n})}$$

"$\Leftarrow$": For any application of rule (Var) of the form

$$\frac{:\ e \Downarrow_1 \Delta : v}{[\ x \mapsto e] : x \Downarrow_1 \Delta\ [x \mapsto v] : v}$$

there are two cases.

a) e is not of the form $c(\overline{x_n})$, then we can replace the application by an application of rule (VarExp) to get

$$\frac{:\ e \Downarrow_1 \Delta : v}{[\ x \mapsto e] : x \Downarrow_1 \Delta\ [x \mapsto v] : v}$$

b) e is of the form $c(\overline{x_n})$, then the derivation must be of the following form.

$$\frac{:\ c(\overline{x_n}) \Downarrow_1\ :\ c(\overline{x_n})}{[\ x \mapsto c(\overline{x_n})]\ :\ x \Downarrow_1\ [\ x \mapsto c(\overline{x_n})]\ :\ c(\overline{x_n})}$$

Therefore we have Δ = and v = e and we can replace the application by an application of rule (VarCons).

$$[\ x \mapsto e]\ :\ x \Downarrow_1 \Delta\ [x \mapsto v]\ :\ v$$

$\square$

Corollary 2.3.2 *For all expressions* e *holds* $[\![e]\!]_0^P = [\![e]\!]_1^P$.

Proof. Direct consequence of Definition 2.2.5 and Lemma 2.3.1. $\square$

The next chapter can also be seen as a simplification of the calculus in a certain sense. There we show that free variables can be replaced by generator functions, which is a transfer of results previously obtained by [Antoy and Hanus, 2006] and [Dios and López-Fraguas, 2006] to our setting. It is a simplification of the calculus since with that result it is possible to omit rule (Guess).

Chapter 3

Elimination of Free Variables

Antoy and Hanus [2006] presented a surprising result that under certain circumstances one can replace free variables by generator functions. Their results are proven for a term-rewriting based semantics which does not consider sharing. A similar result was presented in [Dios and López-Fraguas, 2006] in the context of the *Constructor-based ReWriting Logic (CRWL)*, a dierent semantic framework for functional logic languages [González-Moreno et al., 1999b], based on a rewriting logic which does also not explicitly consider sharing. It will turn out that the principle ideas of [Antoy and Hanus, 2006, Dios and López-Fraguas, 2006] will be very useful for our aim to translate functional logic programs into purely functional programs. For this reason, we extend these results to the more concrete and operational setting of the natural semantics introduced in the previous chapter. A first version of the contents of this chapter were published as Braßel and Huch [2007a], but all proofs have been substantially revised and extended.

The general contents of this chapter are:

a) The semantics defined in the previous chapter is extended to collect some crucial information about the occurrence of free variables in a derivation (Section 3.1).

b) The notion of a generator function is defined followed by a proof that the additional information from a) can be used to replace free variables by generator functions (Section 3.2).

c) A proof of the dual direction is given that for derivations in the context of programs employing generators we can construct an equivalent derivation with free variables (Section 3.2.3).

d) Finally, the results of this chapter are collected in a summarizing Theorem 3.3.

3.1 Treatment of Variable Chains

A heap contains a **variable chain** i there is an $x \in dom()$ such that (x) is a variable. The fact that logic variables are represented by trivial variable chains implies that also non-trivial chains cannot be avoided by simple syntactic restrictions, as illustrated by the following example.

Example 3.1.1 (Variable Chains) *The evaluation of the expression* let {x = x, y = id(x)} in head(y) *in the context of the empty heap will result in the configuration*

$$\emptyset \left[x_1 \mapsto x_1, x_2 \mapsto x_2, x \mapsto \text{Cons}(x_1, x_2), y \mapsto x \right] : x_1$$

Note especially that the resulting heap contains the variable chain (y, x). *Exactly the same result configuration is computed for the slightly dierent expression* let {x = x, y = x} in head(x).

Variable chains cause technical problems, especially when we consider the elimination of free variables in the next section. Even though we have not yet presented the idea of this elimination, the reader may be able to imagine the technical problems from looking at the above example. When constructing proof trees without free variables from trees with variables, we need to treat the derivations of the two expressions of Example 3.1.1 dierently. For the first expression we would like to see the variable y also updated to $\text{Cons}(x_1, x_2)$ and in the second derivation we would like to keep the variable chain as y has never been touched during the derivation. This is the reason that we have to add more information to derivations in order to distinguish the two cases. We call this new information **access tokens**. In this case, such a token is denoted by the symbol "∗" and the intended meaning is that such a token is added to those variables which have been accessed in the derivation. As we will use access tokens in another context later (cf. Section 3.2.1) we will assume any set T of tokens.

Definition 3.1.2 (Heap with Access Tokens) *Let* T *be a set, called the token set and* E′ ⊆ FE *a set of flat expressions. Then a* **heap with access tokens** *is a subset of* Var × FE ∪ Var × T × E′ *i the set* {(x, e) | (x, e) ∈ ∨ ∃t ∈ T : (x, t, e) ∈ ∧ e ∈ E′} *is a heap. In other words the elements of a heap with access tokens are either of the form* (x, e) ∈ *or* (x, t, e′) ∈ *where* t ∈ T *and* e′ ∈ E′. *For a heap update we write as usual* [x ↦ e] *to add the binding* (x, e) *and* $\left[x \xrightarrow{t} e' \right]$ *to add the binding* (x, t, e′). *During derivation we will never lookup tokens in the heap. The matching* [x ↦ e] *will therefore denote that* x *is mapped to* e *in the considered heap regardless of with or without token.*

In this section we will consider heaps with T = {∗} and E′ = Var. As there is no matching on heap tokens the rules of Figure 3.1 clearly constitute a conservative extension of $\Downarrow_1$.

3.1. TREATMENT OF VARIABLE CHAINS   53

Example 3.1.3 (Access Tokens) *Reconsider the expressions of Example 3.1.1. With the rules of Figure 3.1 the evaluation of the expression* let $\{x = x, y = id(x)\}$ in $head(y)$ *in the context of the empty heap results in the configuration*

$$\emptyset \left[x_1 \xrightarrow{*} x_1, x_2 \mapsto x_2, x \mapsto \mathtt{Cons}(x_1, x_2), y \xrightarrow{*} x \right] : x_1$$

The evaluation of let $\{x = x, y = x\}$ in $head(x)$, *in contrast results in*

$$\emptyset \left[x_1 \xrightarrow{*} x_1, x_2 \mapsto x_2, x \mapsto \mathtt{Cons}(x_1, x_2), y \mapsto x \right] : x_1$$

With this we can see that y *was accessed in the first but not in the second derivation.*

The following proposition states that the rules of Figure 3.1 correctly keep track of those variable chains which have been accessed during evaluation. And the next definition introduces what we mean by this "correctness" of book keeping.

Definition 3.1.4 *A heap with access tokens Γ features **correct variable updates** iff for all* $x \in dom(\Gamma)$ *with* $(x, *, y) \in \Gamma$ *it holds that* Γ(y) *is of the form* $c(\overline{x_n})$ *whenever* $y \in dom(\Gamma)$.

Let z *be a variable. A heap with access tokens Γ features **correct variable updates with exception of** z iff* $(z, *, z) \in \Gamma$ *and for all* x, y *with* $(x, *, y) \in \Gamma$ *there are two cases:*

a) y = z *and, accordingly, we have* $(y, *, y) \in \Gamma$ *or*

b) y ≠ z *and* Γ(y) *is of the form* $c(\overline{x_n})$ *whenever* $y \in dom(\Gamma)$.

Proposition 3.1.5 *Let* $D := \Gamma : e \Downarrow_2 \Delta : v$ *be a derivation using the rules in Figure 3.1. If Γ features correct variable updates then so does any heap occurring in an in-configuration of* D *and for all out-configurations* $\Delta : v$ *in* D *holds that* Δ *features correct variable updates whenever* $v = c(\overline{x_n})$ *and* Δ *features correct variable updates with exception of* v *whenever* $v \in Var$.

Proof. By induction on the structure of the derivation D.
Base Cases:
(ValV): For $\Gamma[x \mapsto x] : x \Downarrow_2 \Gamma\left[x \xrightarrow{*} x\right] : x$ the claim holds because for all $z \in dom(\Gamma)$ with $(z, *, y) \in \Gamma\left[x \xrightarrow{*} x\right]$ we have two cases:

1. if z = x then we directly have y = x and therefore $(y, *, y) \in \Gamma\left[x \xrightarrow{*} x\right]$ by definition of heap update and

2. if z ≠ x then we have

$$(z, *, y) \in \Gamma\left[x \xrightarrow{*} x\right]$$
$$\Rightarrow (z, *, y) \in \Gamma[x \mapsto x] \qquad \text{def heap update}, z \neq x$$
$$\Rightarrow (y, c(\overline{x_n})) \in \Gamma[x \mapsto x] \vee y \notin dom(\Gamma) \quad \text{by assumption}$$
$$\Rightarrow (y, c(\overline{x_n})) \in \Gamma\left[x \xrightarrow{*} x\right] \vee y \notin dom(\Gamma) \quad \text{def heap}, y \neq x \text{ (def (ValV))}$$

CHAPTER 3. ELIMINATION OF FREE VARIABLES

$$
\begin{array}{ll}
\text{(ValV)} & [\ x \mapsto x] : x \Downarrow_2 \ \left[x \xrightarrow{*} x\right] : x \\[1ex]
\text{(ValC)} & : c(\overline{x_n}) \Downarrow_2 \ : c(\overline{x_n}) \\[1ex]
\text{(VarV)} & \dfrac{: e \Downarrow_2 \Delta : y}{[\ x \mapsto e] : x \Downarrow_2 \Delta \left[x \xrightarrow{*} y\right] : y} \quad \text{where } e \neq x \\[2ex]
\text{(VarC)} & \dfrac{: e \Downarrow_2 \Delta : c(\overline{x_n})}{[\ x \mapsto e] : x \Downarrow_2 \Delta \left[x \mapsto c(\overline{x_n})\right] : c(\overline{x_n})} \quad \text{where } e \neq x \\[2ex]
\text{(Fun)} & \dfrac{: \mathit{flat}(e) \Downarrow_2 \Delta : v}{: f(\overline{x_n}) \Downarrow_2 \Delta : v} \quad \text{where } f(\overline{x_n}) = e \in P \\[2ex]
\text{(Let)} & \dfrac{[\ \overline{x_k \mapsto e_k}] : e \Downarrow_2 \Delta : v}{: \mathsf{let}\ \{\overline{x_k = e_k}\}\ \mathsf{in}\ e \Downarrow_2 \Delta : v} \\[2ex]
\text{(Or)} & \dfrac{: e_i \Downarrow_2 \Delta : v}{: e_1\ ?\ e_2 \Downarrow_2 \Delta : v} \quad \text{where } i \in \{1,2\} \\[2ex]
\text{(Select)} & \dfrac{: e \Downarrow_2 \Delta : c(\overline{x_n}) \quad \Delta : \sigma(e_i) \Downarrow_2 \ : v}{: \mathsf{case}\ e\ \mathsf{of}\ \{\overline{p_k \mapsto e_k}\} \Downarrow_2 \ : v} \\[1ex]
& \qquad \text{where } i \in \{1,\ldots,k\} \text{ and } c(\overline{x_n}) = \sigma(p_i) \\[2ex]
\text{(Guess)} & \dfrac{: e \Downarrow_2 \Delta : x \quad \Delta\ [\overline{x_n \mapsto x_n}]\ [x \mapsto c(\overline{x_n})] : e_i \Downarrow_2 \ : v}{: \mathsf{case}\ e\ \mathsf{of}\ \{\overline{p_k \mapsto e_k}\} \Downarrow_2 \ : v} \\[1ex]
& \qquad \text{where } p_i = c(\overline{x_n}) \text{ and } i \in \{1,\ldots,k\}
\end{array}
$$

Figure 3.1: Conservative extension to keep track of updated variables

(ValC): For $: c(\overline{x_n}) \Downarrow_2 \ : c(\overline{x_n})$ the claim holds trivially.

Inductive Cases:
(VarV): If $[\ x \mapsto e]$ features correct variable updates then so does because $e \neq x$. Therefore, the induction hypothesis implies that Δ features correct variable updates with the exception of y. Especially, we have $(y, *, y) \in \Delta$ and $x \notin \mathit{dom}(\Delta)$ (cf. Observation 2.2.4) and, therefore, $\Delta \left[x \xrightarrow{*} y\right]$ also features correct variable updates with the exception of y because for all $(z, *, y') \in \Delta \left[x \xrightarrow{*} y\right]$ we have two cases:

1. If $z = x$ we have $y' = y$ and, thus, $(y, *, y) \in \Delta \left[x \xrightarrow{*} y\right]$ as $(y, *, y) \in \Delta$ by assumption.

3.1. TREATMENT OF VARIABLE CHAINS 55

2. If $z \neq x$ we have

$$(z, *, y') \in \Delta \left[x \xrightarrow{*} y\right]$$
$$\Rightarrow (z, *, y') \in \Delta \qquad \text{def heap update}, z \neq x$$
$$\Rightarrow \Delta(y') = v \vee y \notin dom()$$
$$\qquad \text{where } v = c(\overline{x_n}) \text{ or } v = y' = y \text{ by assumption}$$
$$\Rightarrow \Delta \left[x \xrightarrow{*} y\right](y') = v \vee y \notin dom()$$
$$x \notin dom(\Delta) \text{(Observation 2.2.4)}, y \in dom() \text{ implies } y' \neq x$$

(VarC): If [$x \mapsto e$] features correct variable updates then so does because $e \neq x$. Therefore, Δ features correct variable updates by induction hypothesis and, thus, so does Δ [$x \mapsto c(\overline{x_n})$] because for all $(z, *, y') \in \Delta$ [$x \mapsto c(\overline{x_n})$] holds:

$$(z, *, y) \in \Delta \ [x \mapsto c(\overline{x_n})]$$
$$\Rightarrow (z, *, y) \in \Delta \qquad \text{def heap update}$$
$$\Rightarrow (y, c'(\overline{y_m})) \in \Delta \vee y \notin dom() \qquad \text{by assumption}$$
$$\Rightarrow (y, c'(\overline{y_m})) \in \Delta \ [x \mapsto c(\overline{x_n})] \vee y \notin dom()$$
$$x \notin dom(\Delta) \text{ (Observation 2.2.4)}, y \in dom() \text{ implies } y \neq x$$

(Fun), (Or): The claim holds trivially or stems directly from the induction hypothesis because these rules do not change any heap nor the resulting value.
(Let): If features correct variable updates then so does [$\overline{x_k \mapsto e_k}$] because

- it holds that $\overline{x_k} \notin dom()$ as the configuration is well formed (cf. Proposition 2.2.3) and, thus, there cannot be $(x, *, x_i) \in$ for $x_i \in \{\overline{x_k}\}$ and

- none of the new heap entries are adorned with $*$ and therefore do not constrain the claim for [$\overline{x_k \mapsto e_k}$].

Thus, that Δ features correct variable updates with the possible exception of v directly stems from the induction hypothesis.
(Select):
As features correct variable updates the induction hypothesis yields that so does Δ (with no exception – the result value is of the form $c(\overline{x_n})$). Therefore, the claim for : v is also covered by induction hypothesis.
(Guess): As features correct variable updates by assumption Δ features correct variable updates with exception of x by induction hypothesis. This implies that the modified heap Δ [$\overline{x_n \mapsto x_n}$] [$x \mapsto c(\overline{x_n})$] features correct variable updates (with no exception) because

- it holds that $\overline{x_n} \notin dom()$ as the configuration is well formed (cf. Proposition 2.2.3) and, thus, there cannot be $(x, *, x_i) \in$ for $x_i \in \{\overline{x_n}\}$ and

- otherwise $(x, *, x)$ is exchanged by $(x, c(\overline{x_n}))$ by definition of variable update.

Therefore, the claim for : v is covered by induction hypothesis. □

(Val)   : $c(\overline{x_n}) \Downarrow_3$: $c(\overline{x_n})$

(Var) $\dfrac{:\ e \Downarrow_3 \Delta\ :\ v}{[\ x \mapsto e]\ :\ x \Downarrow_3 \Delta\ [x \mapsto v]\ :\ v}$

(Fun) $\dfrac{:\ \mathit{flat}(e) \Downarrow_3 \Delta\ :\ v}{:\ f(\overline{x_n}) \Downarrow_3 \Delta\ :\ v}$ where $f(\overline{x_n}) = e \in P$

(Let) $\dfrac{[\ \overline{x_k \mapsto e_k}]\ :\ e \Downarrow_3 \Delta\ :\ v}{:\ \mathsf{let}\ \{\overline{x_k = e_k}\}\ \mathsf{in}\ e \Downarrow_3 \Delta\ :\ v}$

(Or) $\dfrac{:\ e_i \Downarrow_3 \Delta\ :\ v}{:\ e_1\ ?\ e_2 \Downarrow_3 \Delta\ :\ v}$ where $i \in \{1,2\}$

(Select) $\dfrac{:\ e \Downarrow_3 \Delta\ :\ c(\overline{x_n})\quad \Delta\ :\ \sigma(e_i) \Downarrow_3\ :\ v}{:\ \mathsf{case}\ e\ \mathsf{of}\ \{\overline{p_k \mapsto e_k}\} \Downarrow_3\ :\ v}$
where $i \in \{1, \ldots, k\}$ and $c(\overline{x_n}) = \sigma(p_i)$

Figure 3.2: Semantics without free variables

Note especially that the empty heap features correct variable updates. Therefore, it is no restriction that we only treat $\Downarrow_2$ derivations in the following.

As a last thought on the topic of variable chains: why do we not simply forbid variable chains on the syntactic level? The answer is twofold. Firstly, example 3.1.1 shows that variable chains may come up during evaluation anyway. It is the case, however, that such chains are always of a special form (namely either trivial (x, x) or of at most length 1, i.e., $(x, y), (y, v)$ where v is either y or a value $c(\overline{x_n})$. Secondly, therefore, in order to eliminate variables we would have to prove this fact about the form of variable chains. And that proof would not be any easier than the one of Proposition 3.1.5. (Indeed it would look very similar.) All in all we prefer to not restrict programs artificially and rather take the complication of changing the calculus. The first solution would aect the future use of the calculus, while the second is an intermediate step, only.

3.2 Elimination of Free Variables

We now introduce the idea of a generator. As hinted above, generators will allow us to replace free variables by non-deterministic derivations. This will allow us to exchange the derivation rules used so far by the new rules shown in Figure 3.2.

Replacing free variables by generators is a program transformation of a given program over signature which adheres to the following basic idea.

3.2. ELIMINATION OF FREE VARIABLES

$$(\text{Val}) \quad : \; c(\overline{x_n}) \Downarrow_4 \; : \; c(\overline{x_n}) \mid ()$$

$$(\text{Var}) \quad \frac{: \; e \Downarrow_4 \Delta \; : \; v \mid (y)}{[\, x \mapsto e\,] : x \Downarrow_4 \Delta \; \left[\, x \xrightarrow{\text{ad}(x,e,(y))} v \,\right] : v \mid \text{ad}(x, e, (y))}$$

$$(\text{Fun}) \quad \frac{: \; \mathit{flat}(e) \Downarrow_4 \Delta \; : \; v \mid (x)}{: \; f(\overline{x_n}) \Downarrow_4 \Delta \; : \; v \mid (x)} \quad \text{where } f(\overline{x_n}) = e \in P$$

$$(\text{Let}) \quad \frac{[\, \overline{x_k \mapsto e_k}\,] : e \Downarrow_4 \Delta \; : \; v \mid (x)}{: \; \text{let } \{\overline{x_k = e_k}\} \text{ in } e \Downarrow_4 \Delta \; : \; v \mid (x)}$$

$$(\text{Or}) \quad \frac{: \; e_i \Downarrow_4 \Delta \; : \; v \mid (x)}{: \; e_1 \; ? \; e_2 \Downarrow_4 \Delta \; : \; v \mid (x)} \quad \text{where } i \in \{1, 2\}$$

$$(\text{Select}) \quad \frac{: \; e \Downarrow_4 \Delta \; : \; c(\overline{x_n}) \mid (x) \quad \text{ud}_{(x)}(\Delta) : \sigma(e_i) \Downarrow_4 \; : \; v \mid (y)}{: \; \text{case } e \text{ of } \{\overline{p_k \mapsto e_k}\} \Downarrow_4 \; : \; v \mid (y)}$$
$$\text{where } i \in \{1, \ldots, k\} \text{ and } c(\overline{x_n}) = \sigma(p_i)$$

Figure 3.3: Conservative extension: keep track of updated generator values

1. Add to each program the definition of the special function **generate**:
$$\begin{aligned}\textbf{generate} \; &= \; (\text{let } \{\overline{x_{n_1} = \textbf{generate}}\} \text{ in } c_1(\overline{x_{n_1}})) \\ &? \; \ldots \\ &? \; (\text{let } \{\overline{x_{n_k} = \textbf{generate}}\} \text{ in } c_k(\overline{x_{n_k}}))\end{aligned}$$
where $\overline{c_k}$ are all constructors in C_Σ and c_i has arity n_i for all $1 \leq i \leq k$.

2. Replace in each configuration and each expression in the program bindings of the form $x = x$ or $x \mapsto x$ by $x = \textbf{generate}$ or $x \mapsto \textbf{generate}$, respectively.

Note that the generator normally is type oriented, i.e., it generates only values of the correct type. This greatly prunes the search space and can be implemented by approaches analogous to those used for type classes [Wadler and Blott, 1989].

We now turn to the proof that all free variables in a derivation and program can be replaced by such generators. Naturally, we have to show two directions, namely that from any derivation with free variables we can construct one without (Section 3.2.2) and vice versa (Section 3.2.3). Finally, in Section 3.3 we will put together the obtained results in the form of a Theorem.

In order to obtain the strongest possible result, we will map derivations in $\Downarrow_2$ (Figure 3.1) not to the rules without free variables (Figure 3.2) but to a conservative extension of those rules as shown in Figure 3.3 (Section 3.2.1).

3.2.1 Keeping Track of Generator Updates

As seen in the previous section we need to conservatively extend the calculus with free variables to obtain information about variable updates. Analogously,

58   CHAPTER 3. ELIMINATION OF FREE VARIABLES

we also need a conservative extension of the calculus without free variables (Figure 3.2) to obtain information about the evaluated generators. We will again use access tokens for this extension (Definition 3.1.2). This time we will use so called *adornments* as tokens. Such an adornment is either empty () or a variable x. The notation (x) should denote an adornment which might be either () or x, i.e., a matching on any information possible. As can be seen in Figure 3.3 adornments are always added to value updates. With regard to the definition of heaps with access tokens 3.1.2 we have therefore T = {()} ∪ Var and that E′ is the set of flat constructor terms (values). Whenever the binding of a variable x is marked with the token y it means that x was updated with a value which stems from an erlier evaluation of a generator originally found in the heap as the binding of y.

The rules of Figure 3.3 do not only add adornments to the heap but also to each out-configuration. This adornment witnesses whether the current result value stems from evaluating a generator. In Figure 3.3 we make use of two auxiliary functions ad and ud, (adorn and unadorn, respectively). The function ad defines whether the current adornment has to be changed to x or whether to keep the old adornment. The function ud eliminates a given adornment from the given heap.

Definition 3.2.1 (Functions ad and ud) *Selecting an adornment depending on expression* e:

$$\text{ad}(x, e, (y)) = \begin{cases} x & , \text{if } e = \text{generate} \\ (y) & , \text{otherwise} \end{cases}$$

Eliminating an adornment from a heap:

$$\begin{array}{rcl}
\text{ud}_{()}(\Delta) & = & \Delta \\
\text{ud}_x(\Delta) & = & \Delta \qquad \text{if there is no } e \text{ with } (x, x, e) \in \Delta \\
\text{ud}_x(\Delta \left[x \xrightarrow{x} e \right]) & = & \Delta \left[x \mapsto e \right]
\end{array}$$

The following derivation serves several purposes. It illustrates the evaluation of a generator and the calculation with adornments. In addition it will be useful for future reference in proofs. As seen below, the evaluation of the special function generate is a linear proof tree which non-deterministically chooses one of the constructors of the program as a value.

Proposition 3.2.2

$$[\ x \mapsto \text{generate}] : x \Downarrow_4 [\ \overline{x_n \mapsto \text{generate}}] \left[x \xrightarrow{x} c(\overline{x_n}) \right] : c(\overline{x_n}) \mid x$$

3.2. ELIMINATION OF FREE VARIABLES

Proof.

$$\dfrac{\dfrac{\dfrac{\Delta := [\ \overline{x_n} \mapsto \textsf{generate}] : c(\overline{x_n}) \Downarrow_4 \Delta : c(\overline{x_n}) \mid ()}{: e_i = \textsf{let } \{\overline{x_n} = \textsf{generate}\} \textsf{ in } c(\overline{x_n}) \Downarrow_4 \Delta : c(\overline{x_n}) \mid ()}}{\times_{j=1}^{i-1} \left(\begin{array}{c} : e_{j+1} \ ? \ \ldots \ ? \ e_k \Downarrow_4 \Delta : c(\overline{x_n}) \mid () \\ : e_j \ ? \ e_{j+1} \ ? \ \ldots \ ? \ e_k \Downarrow_4 \Delta : c(\overline{x_n}) \mid () \end{array} \right)}{: \textsf{generate} \Downarrow_4 \Delta : c(\overline{x_n}) \mid ()}}{[\ x \mapsto \textsf{generate}] : x \Downarrow_4 [\ \overline{x_n} \mapsto \textsf{generate}] \left[x \xrightarrow{x} c(\overline{x_n}) \right] : c(\overline{x_n}) \mid x}$$

$\square$

3.2.2 Replacing Free Variables by Generators

We eliminate free variables in configurations, heaps, expressions, and programs by replacing them with a call to the special function generate. This replacement is realized by a family of mappings gen($\cdot$). On some occasions we also need to replace the current free variable with a value of the form $c(\overline{x_n})$. This value will then be an additional parameter of gen($\cdot$), written $\textsf{gen}^{c(\overline{x_n})}(\cdot)$. Likewise, when we transform the binding of a variable x we need to know that variable. This will also be an additional parameter and in this case we write $\textsf{gen}_x(\cdot)$.

Definition 3.2.3 (Free Variable Elimination gen())

$$\textsf{gen}(: e) = \textsf{gen}() : \textsf{gen}(e)$$
$$\textsf{gen}^{c(\overline{x_n})}(\Delta : c'(\overline{y_m})) = \textsf{gen}(\Delta : c'(\overline{y_m})) \mid ()$$
$$\textsf{gen}^{c(\overline{x_n})}(\Delta : x) = \textsf{gen}^{c(\overline{x_n})}(\Delta\ [\overline{x_n} \mapsto \overline{x_n}]) : c(\overline{x_n}) \mid x$$

$$\textsf{gen}() = \{(x, \textsf{gen}_x(e)) \mid (x, e) \in\ \}$$
$$\cup\ \{(x, y, (\ y)) \mid (x, *, y) \in\ , y \in dom()\ \}$$
$$\cup\ \{(x, y) \mid (x, *, y) \in\ , y \notin dom()\ \}$$

$$\textsf{gen}^{c(\overline{x_n})}(\Gamma) = \begin{cases} \textsf{gen}(\Gamma'\ [x \mapsto c(\overline{x_n})])\left[x \xrightarrow{x} c(\overline{x_n})\right] & \textit{if } \Gamma = \Gamma'\left[x \xrightarrow{*} x\right] \\ \textsf{gen}(\Gamma) & \textit{otherwise} \end{cases}$$

$$\textsf{gen}_x(x) = \textsf{generate}$$
$$\textsf{gen}_x(e) = \textsf{gen}(e), \textit{ if } e \neq x$$
$$\textsf{gen}(x) = x$$
$$\textsf{gen}(s(\overline{e_n})) = s(\overline{\textsf{gen}(e_n)})$$
$$\textsf{gen}(e_1\ ?\ e_2) = \textsf{gen}(e_1)\ ?\ \textsf{gen}(e_2)$$
$$\textsf{gen}((f)\textsf{case } e \textsf{ of } \{\overline{p_k \to e_k}\}) = \textsf{case } \underline{\textsf{gen}(e)} \textsf{ of } \{\overline{p_k \to \textsf{gen}(e_k)}\}$$
$$\textsf{gen}(\textsf{let } \{\overline{x_k = e_k}\} \textsf{ in } e) = \textsf{let } \{\overline{x_k = \textsf{gen}_{x_k}(e_k)}\} \textsf{ in } \textsf{gen}(e)$$

$$\textsf{gen}(P) = \overline{l_n = \textsf{gen}(r_n)} \textit{ where } P = \overline{l_n = r_n}$$

Apart from the introduction of generator operations, the main aspect to note about Definition 3.2.3 is that variable chains with an access token (x, *, y) are

60   CHAPTER 3. ELIMINATION OF FREE VARIABLES

replaced by the binding of the chained variable, i.e., (x, x, (y)) whenever y ∈ dom(). We will soon see that this detail plays a crucial role when constructing derivations with generators from ones without. Before we will indulge in the details of the corresponding proof, we need to consider a rather technical detail concerning the relation between the transformations of expressions gen(·) and flat(·).

Proposition 3.2.4 *For any expression* e *holds that*

$$flat(gen(e)) = gen(flat(e))$$

Proof. By a simple induction on the structure of e where the only non-trivial case is $e = s(\overline{e_n})$:

$$
\begin{aligned}
&flat(gen(s(\overline{e_n}))) \\
&= flat(s(\overline{gen(e_n)})) & &\text{def } gen() \\
&= \text{let } \overline{\{y_m = flat(e'_m)\}} \text{ in } s(\overline{x_n}) \\
&\quad \text{where } (\overline{y_m}, \overline{e'_m}, \overline{x_n}) = varArgs(\overline{gen(e_n)}) & &\text{def } flat() \\
&= \text{let } \overline{\{y_m = flat(gen(e''_m))\}} \text{ in } s(\overline{x_n}) \\
&\quad \text{where } (\overline{y_m}, \overline{gen(e''_m)}, \overline{x_n}) = varArgs(\overline{gen(e_n)}) & &\text{def } varArgs() \\
&= \text{let } \overline{\{y_m = flat(gen(e''_m))\}} \text{ in } s(\overline{x_n}) \\
&\quad \text{where } (\overline{y_m}, \overline{e''_m}, \overline{x_n}) = varArgs(\overline{e_n}) & &\text{def } varArgs(), gen(x){=}x \\
&= \text{let } \overline{\{y_m = gen(flat(e''_m))\}} \text{ in } s(\overline{x_n}) \\
&\quad \text{where } (\overline{y_m}, \overline{e''_m}, \overline{x_n}) = varArgs(\overline{e_n}) & &\text{ind. hyp.} \\
&= \text{let } \overline{\{y_m = gen_{y_m}(flat(e''_m))\}} \text{ in } s(\overline{x_n}) \\
&\quad \text{where } (\overline{y_m}, \overline{e''_m}, \overline{x_n}) = varArgs(\overline{e_n}) & &\overline{flat(e''_m) \neq y_m} \text{ by defs} \\
&= \text{let } \overline{\{y_m = gen_{y_m}(flat(e''_m))\}} \text{ in } s(\overline{gen(x_n)}) \\
&\quad \text{where } (\overline{y_m}, \overline{e''_m}, \overline{x_n}) = varArgs(\overline{e_n}) & &\text{def } gen() \\
&= gen(\text{let } \overline{\{y_m = flat(e''_m)\}} \text{ in } s(\overline{x_n}) \\
&\quad \text{where } (\overline{y_m}, \overline{e''_m}, \overline{x_n}) = varArgs(\overline{e_n}) & &\text{def } gen() \\
&= gen(flat(s(\overline{e_n}))) & &\text{def } flat()
\end{aligned}
$$

□

The next proposition illustrates how gen(·) behaves on heaps and configurations.

Proposition 3.2.5 (Generator Evaluation) *For any heap which features correct variable updates (Definition 3.1.4) and any variable x with (x) = x, any n-ary constructor c, and any fresh variables $\overline{x_n}$ we have*

$$gen([\ x \mapsto x]:x) \Downarrow_4 gen^{c(\overline{x_n})}(\left[x \xrightarrow{*} x\right]:x)$$

3.2. ELIMINATION OF FREE VARIABLES

Proof. We have by Definition 3.2.3

$$\begin{aligned}
&\text{gen}([\ x \mapsto x] : x) \\
&= \text{gen}([\ x \mapsto x]) : \text{gen}(x) \\
&= \text{gen}()[\ x \mapsto \text{generate}] : x
\end{aligned}$$

and

$$\begin{aligned}
&\text{gen}^{c(\overline{x_n})}(\ \left[x \xrightarrow{*} x\right] : x) \\
&= \text{gen}^{c(\overline{x_n})}(\ \left[x \xrightarrow{*} x\right][\overline{x_n \mapsto x_n}]) : c(\overline{x_n}) \mid x & \text{def 3.2.3} \\
&= \text{gen}^{c(\overline{x_n})}(([\ \overline{x_n \mapsto x_n}]\left[x \xrightarrow{*} x\right]) : c(\overline{x_n}) \mid x & \text{def heap update} \\
&= \text{gen}([\ \overline{x_n \mapsto x_n}][x \mapsto c(\overline{x_n})])\left[x \xrightarrow{x} c(\overline{x_n})\right] : c(\overline{x_n}) \mid x & \text{def 3.2.3} \\
&= \text{gen}([\ \overline{x_n \mapsto x_n}])\left[x \xrightarrow{x} c(\overline{x_n})\right] : c(\overline{x_n}) \mid x & \text{def heap update} \\
&= \text{gen}()\ \left[\overline{x_n \mapsto \text{generate}}, x \xrightarrow{x} c(\overline{x_n})\right] : c(\overline{x_n}) \mid x & \text{def 3.2.3}
\end{aligned}$$

The step stemming on Definition 3.1.4 is noteworthy. Since by assumption $[\ x \mapsto x]$ features correct variable updates there cannot exist $(y, *, x) \in$. Therefore it holds that $\text{gen}([\ x \mapsto c(\overline{x_n})]) = \text{gen}()[\ x \mapsto c(\overline{x_n})]$.

Because of the equalities derived above the claim is a direct consequence of Proposition 3.2.2. □

Next we show that any derivation with free variables can be reconstructed as a derivation with generators.

Lemma 3.2.6 *Let* P *be a program over signature . For all well formed configurations* : e, Δ : v *where features correct variable updates and all constructor symbols* $c' \in$ $^{(m)} \cap C_\Sigma$ *and all variables* $\overline{y_m}$ *we have that* : $e \Downarrow_2 \Delta$: v *implies* $\text{gen}(\ :\ e) \Downarrow_4 \text{gen}^{c'(\overline{y_m})}(\Delta : v)$ *in* $\text{gen}(P)$.

The central idea of the following proof is that whenever the intermediate result of a sub computation in $\Downarrow_2$ is a free variable, the corresponding application of (Val) : $x \Downarrow_2$: x is replaced by the generator evaluation constructed for the proof of Proposition 3.2.2. The diferences between the resulting heaps is eectively eliminated when the rule (Guess) is applied for $\Downarrow_2$. The remaining proof is concerned with the technical details of showing that the mappings of Definition 3.2.3 correctly replace free variables by calls to the generator function to the chosen constructor, respectively.

Proof. (Of Lemma 3.2.6) By induction on the structure of the proof tree.
Base cases:
(ValV): We have $[\ x \mapsto x] : x \Downarrow_2 \left[x \xrightarrow{*} x\right]$: x implies $\text{gen}([\ x \mapsto x] : x) \Downarrow_4$ $\text{gen}^{c'(\overline{y_m})}(\ \left[x \xrightarrow{*} x\right] : x)$ by Proposition 3.2.5.

(ValC): We have : $c(\overline{x_n}) \Downarrow_2$: $c(\overline{x_n})$ implies $\text{gen}(\ :\ c(\overline{x_n})) \Downarrow_4 \text{gen}^{c'(\overline{y_m})}(\ :$ $c(\overline{x_n})$) because $\text{gen}^{c'(\overline{y_m})}(\ :\ c(\overline{x_n})) = \text{gen}(\ :\ c(\overline{x_n})) \mid () = \text{gen}()\ :\ c(\overline{x_n}) \mid ()$.
Inductive cases:

(VarV): The induction hypothesis in this case is that : e $\Downarrow_2$ Δ : y implies gen(: e) $\Downarrow_4$ gen$^{c'(\overline{y_m})}$(Δ : y) where e $\neq$ x. With this assumption we have to show that $[\ x \mapsto e] : x \Downarrow_2 \Delta \left[x \xrightarrow{*} y\right]$: y implies gen($[\ x \mapsto e] : x$) $\Downarrow_4$ gen$^{c'(\overline{y_m})}$($\Delta \left[x \xrightarrow{*} y\right]$: y). This claim holds because we have

$$\frac{\text{gen}(\ :\ e) \Downarrow_4 \text{gen}^{c'(\overline{y_m})}(\Delta\ :\ y)}{= \text{gen}()\ :\ \text{gen}(e) \Downarrow_4 \text{gen}(\Delta\ [\overline{y_m \mapsto y_m}]\ [y \mapsto c'(\overline{y_m})])\left[y \xrightarrow{y} c'(\overline{y_m})\right]}$$

$$\frac{\text{gen}()[\ x \mapsto \text{gen}_x(e)] : x \Downarrow_4 \text{gen}(\Delta\ [\overline{y_m \mapsto y_m}]\ [y \mapsto c'(\overline{y_m})])[x \mapsto c'(\overline{y_m})]}{= \text{gen}([\ x \mapsto e] : x) \Downarrow_4 \text{gen}^{c'(\overline{y_m})}(\Delta\ \left[x \xrightarrow{*} y\right]\ :\ y)}$$

as by Proposition 3.1.5 we have (y, *, y) $\in \Delta$ and in this case gen$_x$(e) = gen(e).
(VarC): The induction hypothesis in this case is that : e $\Downarrow_2$ Δ : c($\overline{x_n}$) implies gen(: e) $\Downarrow_4$ gen$^{c'(\overline{y_m})}$(Δ : c($\overline{x_n}$)) where e $\neq$ x. With this assumption we have to show that $[\ x \mapsto e] : x \Downarrow_2 \Delta\ [x \mapsto c(\overline{x_n})]$: c($\overline{x_n}$) implies gen($[\ x \mapsto e] : x$) $\Downarrow_4$ gen$^{c'(\overline{y_m})}$($\Delta\ [x \mapsto c(\overline{x_n})]$: c($\overline{x_n}$)). This claim holds because we have

$$\frac{\text{gen}(\ :\ e) \Downarrow_4 \text{gen}^{c'(\overline{y_m})}(\Delta\ :\ c(\overline{x_n}))}{= \text{gen}()\ :\ \text{gen}(e) \Downarrow_4 \text{gen}(\Delta\ )\ :\ c(\overline{x_n})\ |\ ()}$$

$$\frac{\text{gen}()[\ x \mapsto \text{gen}_x(e)] : x \Downarrow_4 \text{gen}(\Delta\ )\ [x \mapsto c(\overline{x_n})] : c(\overline{x_n})\ |\ ()}{= \text{gen}([\ x \mapsto e] : x) \Downarrow_4 \text{gen}^{c'(\overline{y_m})}(\Delta\ [x \mapsto c(\overline{x_n})] : c(\overline{x_n}))}$$

where gen($\Delta\ [x \mapsto c(\overline{x_n})]$) = gen($\Delta\ )\ [x \mapsto c(\overline{x_n})]$ as features correct variable updates, in consequence, Δ does by Proposition 3.1.5.
(Fun): The induction hypothesis in this case is that : $flat$(e) $\Downarrow_2$ Δ : v implies gen(: $flat$(e)) $\Downarrow_4$ gen$^{c'(\overline{y_m})}$(Δ : v) where f($\overline{x_n}$) = e $\in$ P . With this assumption we have to show that : f($\overline{x_n}$) $\Downarrow_2$ Δ : v implies gen(: f($\overline{x_n}$)) $\Downarrow_4$ gen$^{c'(\overline{y_m})}$(Δ : v). This claim holds because we have

$$\frac{\text{gen}(\ :\ flat(e)) \Downarrow_4 \text{gen}^{c'(\overline{y_m})}(\Delta\ :\ v)}{= \text{gen}()\ :\ flat(\text{gen}(e)) \Downarrow_4 \text{gen}^{c'(\overline{y_m})}(\Delta\ :\ v)}$$

$$\frac{\text{gen}()\ :\ f(\overline{x_n}) \Downarrow_4 \text{gen}^{c'(\overline{y_m})}(\Delta\ :\ v)}{= \text{gen}(\ :\ f(\overline{x_n})) \Downarrow_4 \text{gen}^{c'(\overline{y_m})}(\Delta\ :\ v)}$$

because f($\overline{x_n}$) = gen(e) $\in$ gen(P) and gen($flat$(e)) = $flat$(gen(e)) by Proposition 3.2.4.
(Let): The induction hypothesis in this case is that $[\ \overline{x_k \mapsto e_k}]$: e $\Downarrow_2$ Δ : v implies gen($[\ \overline{x_k \mapsto e_k}]$: e) $\Downarrow_4$ gen$^{c'(\overline{y_m})}$(Δ : v). With this assumption we have to show that : let $\{\overline{x_k = e_k}\}$ in e $\Downarrow_2$ Δ : v implies gen(: let $\{\overline{x_k = e_k}\}$ in e) $\Downarrow_4$ gen$^{c'(\overline{y_m})}$(Δ : v). This claim holds because we have

$$\frac{\text{gen}([\ \overline{x_k \mapsto e_k}] : e) \Downarrow_4 \text{gen}^{c'(\overline{y_m})}(\Delta\ :\ v)}{= \text{gen}()\left[\overline{x_k \mapsto \text{gen}_{x_k}(e_k)}\right] : \text{gen}(e) \Downarrow_4 \text{gen}^{c'(\overline{y_m})}(\Delta\ :\ v)}$$

$$\frac{\text{gen}()\ :\ \text{let}\ \{\overline{x_k = \text{gen}_{x_k}(e_k)}\}\ \text{in gen}(e) \Downarrow_4 \text{gen}^{c'(\overline{y_m})}(\Delta\ :\ v)}{= \text{gen}(\ :\ \text{let}\ \{\overline{x_k = e_k}\}\ \text{in e}) \Downarrow_4 \text{gen}^{c'(\overline{y_m})}(\Delta\ :\ v)}$$

3.2. ELIMINATION OF FREE VARIABLES

where the bindings of $\overline{x_k}$ can be drawn out of the scope of gen(), as the in-configuration is well formed and features correct variable updates by assumption.

(Or): The induction hypothesis in this case is that : $e_i \Downarrow_2 \Delta$: v implies gen(: e_i) $\Downarrow_4$ gen$^{c'(\overline{y_m})}(\Delta$: v) where i∈ {1,2}. With this assumption we have to show that : e_1 ? $e_2 \Downarrow_2 \Delta$: v implies gen(: e_1 ? e_2) $\Downarrow_4$ gen$^{c'(\overline{y_m})}(\Delta$: v). This claim holds because we have

$$\begin{array}{rl} & \text{gen}(: \ e_i) \Downarrow_4 \text{gen}^{c'(\overline{y_m})}(\Delta : v) \\ = & \text{gen}() : \ \text{gen}(e_i) \Downarrow_4 \text{gen}^{c'(\overline{y_m})}(\Delta : v) \\ \hline & \text{gen}() : \ \text{gen}(e_1) \ ? \ \text{gen}(e_2) \Downarrow_4 \text{gen}^{c'(\overline{y_m})}(\Delta : v) \\ = & \text{gen}(: \ e_1 \ ? \ e_2) \Downarrow_4 \text{gen}^{c'(\overline{y_m})}(\Delta : v) \end{array}$$

(Select): The induction hypothesis in this case is that : $e \Downarrow_2 \Delta$: $c(\overline{x_n})$ implies gen(: e) $\Downarrow_4$ gen$^{c'(\overline{y_m})}(\Delta$: $c(\overline{x_n})$) and Δ : $\sigma(e_i) \Downarrow_2$: v implies gen(Δ : $\sigma(e_i)$) $\Downarrow_4$ gen$^{c'(\overline{y_m})}($: v) where i∈ {1,...,k} and $c(\overline{x_n}) = \sigma(p_i)$. With this assumption we have to show that : case e of $\{\overline{p_k \mapsto e_k}\} \Downarrow_2$: v implies gen(: case e of $\{\overline{p_k \mapsto e_k}\}) \Downarrow_4$ gen$^{c'(\overline{y_m})}($: v). This claim holds because we have

$$\left[\begin{array}{l} \quad \text{gen}(: \text{ case } e \text{ of } \{\overline{p_k \mapsto e_k}\}) \\ = \text{gen}() : \text{ case gen}(e) \text{ of } \{\overline{p_k \mapsto \text{gen}(e_k)}\} \\ \left[\begin{array}{l} \text{gen}(: e) = \text{gen}( ) : \text{ gen}(e) \\ \ldots \\ \text{gen}^{c'(\overline{y_m})}(\Delta : c(\overline{x_n})) = \text{gen}(\Delta) : c(\overline{x_n}) \mid () \\ \quad \text{gen}(\Delta : \sigma(e_i)) \\ = \text{ud}_{()}(\text{gen}(\Delta)) : \sigma(\text{gen}(e_i)) \\ \ldots \\ \text{gen}^{c'(\overline{y_m})}(: v) \end{array}\right. \\ \text{gen}^{c'(\overline{y_m})}(: v) \end{array}\right.$$

because gen$(\sigma(e_i)) = \sigma(\text{gen}(e_i))$ as σ is a renaming of fresh variables.

(Guess): The induction hypothesis in this case is that : $e \Downarrow_2 \Delta$: x implies gen(: e) $\Downarrow_4$ gen$^{c'(\overline{y_m})}(\Delta$: x) and $\Delta \ [\overline{x_n \mapsto x_n}] [x \mapsto c(\overline{x_n})]$: $e_i \Downarrow_2$: v implies gen($\Delta \ [\overline{x_n \mapsto x_n}] [x \mapsto c(\overline{x_n})]$: e_i) $\Downarrow_4$ gen$^{c'(\overline{y_m})}($: v) where $p_i = c(\overline{x_n})$ and i∈ {1,...,k}. With this assumption we have to show that : case e of $\{\overline{p_k \mapsto e_k}\} \Downarrow_2$: v implies gen(: case e of $\{\overline{p_k \mapsto e_k}\}) \Downarrow_4$ gen$^{c'(\overline{y_m})}($:

v). This claim holds because we have

$$\begin{bmatrix} \text{gen}(\ :\ \text{case e of } \{\overline{p_k \mapsto e_k}\}) \\ =\ \text{gen}()\ :\ \text{case gen}(e) \text{ of } \{\overline{p_k \mapsto \text{gen}(e_k)}\} \\ \begin{bmatrix} \text{gen}(\ :\ e) = \text{gen}()\ :\ \text{gen}(e) \\ \ldots \\ \text{gen}^{c'(\overline{y_m})}(\Delta\ :\ x) = \text{gen}(\Delta\ [\overline{y_m \mapsto y_m}]\ [x \mapsto c'(\overline{y_m})])\ \left[x \xrightarrow{x} c'(\overline{y_m})\right]\ :\ c'(\overline{y_m})\ |\ x \\ \text{gen}(\Delta\ [\overline{y_m \mapsto y_m}]\ [x \mapsto c'(\overline{y_m})]\ :\ e_i) \\ =\ \text{ud}_x(\text{gen}(\Delta\ [\overline{y_m \mapsto y_m}]\ [x \mapsto c'(\overline{y_m})])\ \left[x \xrightarrow{x} c'(\overline{y_m})\right])\ :\ \text{gen}(e_i) \\ \ldots \\ \text{gen}^{c'(\overline{y_m})}(\ :\ v) \\ \text{gen}^{c'(\overline{y_m})}(\ :\ v) \end{bmatrix} \end{bmatrix}$$

as by Proposition 3.1.5 we have $(x, *, x) \in \Delta$. $\square$

3.2.3 Reintroduction of Free Variables

In this section we show how to construct derivations employing free variables from those using generators. A first observation is that the rules of Figure 3.3 preserve a certain invariant concerning the adornments added during evaluation. This invariant will later prove crucial for our purpose.

Definition 3.2.7 *A heap is called **unadorned** i there exists no variable x such that $(x, x, e) \in$ (for any e).*

*A heap is called **adorned** with variable x i there exists a value $c(\overline{x_n})$ such that $\{(x, x, c(\overline{x_n})), \overline{(x_n, \text{generate})}\} \subseteq$ and $\setminus \{(x, x, c(\overline{x_n}))\}$ is unadorned.*

Proposition 3.2.8 *Let be an unadorned heap and D be a derivation of the form $: e \Downarrow_4 C$. Then any heap of an in-configuration of D is unadorned and for any out-configuration $\Delta : v \mid (x)$ holds that*

a) Δ is unadorned if $(x) = ()$ and

b) Δ is adorned with x if $(x) = x$.

Proof. By induction on the structure of D.
Base Case:
(Val): the claim holds trivially.
Inductive Cases:
(Var): If $[\ x \mapsto e]$ is unadorned then so is , obviously. Therefore, the claim holds for $\Delta : v \mid (y)$ by induction hypothesis. We distinguish the following cases,

1. If $e = \text{generate}$ we know by Proposition 3.2.5 that

$$\Delta : v \mid (y) = [\ \overline{x_n \mapsto \text{generate}}] : c(\overline{x_n}) \mid ()$$

Therefore Δ is unadorned by induction hypothesis. As $\text{ad}(x, e, (y)) = x$ in this case we have that $\Delta \left[x \xrightarrow{\text{ad}(x,e,(y))} v\right]$ is indeed adorned with x, the adornment of the result configuration, as required.

3.2. ELIMINATION OF FREE VARIABLES

2. If $e \neq$ generate then, as $x \notin dom(\Delta)$ (cf. Observation 2.2.4), we have $ad(x, e, (y)) = (y) \neq x$ and the claim holds for $\Delta \left[x \xrightarrow{ad(x,e,(y))} v \right] : v \mid$ $ad(x, e, (y))$ because it holds for $\Delta : v \mid (y)$.

(Fun), (Or): The claim holds trivially for these rules since neither any heap nor the adornment is changed.
(Let): If is unadorned then so is $[\;\overline{x_k \mapsto e_k}]$, obviously. Therefore the claim for $\Delta : v \mid (x)$ directly stems from the induction hypothesis.
(Select): By induction hypothesis the claim holds for $\Delta : c(\overline{x_n}) \mid (x)$. For $ud_{(x)}(\Delta)$ we distinguish the following cases.

1. If $(x) = ()$ then $ud_{(x)}(\Delta) = \Delta$ and therefore $ud_{(x)}(\Delta)$ is unadorned by induction hypothesis.

2. If $(x) = x$ then we have by induction hypothesis $(x, x, e') \in \Delta$ for some e' and $ud_{(x)}(\Delta) = (\Delta \setminus \{(x, x, e')\}) \cup \{(x, e')\}$. Therefore, $ud_{(x)}(\Delta)$ is unadorned by Definition 3.2.7.

As $ud_{(x)}(\Delta)$ is unadorned in both cases the claim for $\;\;: v \mid (y)$ follows by induction hypothesis. □

We can now turn to define the transformation which introduces free variables instead of generator functions. This definition corresponds closely to the one of Definition 3.2.3.

Definition 3.2.9 (Free Variable (Re-)Introduction free($\cdot$)**)** *We introduce free variables in configurations, heaps, expressions, and programs by replacing calls to the special function* generate. *Note that the form of the first equation is justified by Proposition 3.2.8 plus Definition 3.2.7.*

$$\text{free}(\Delta \left[\overline{x_n \mapsto \text{generate}}, x \xrightarrow{x} c(\overline{x_n})\right] : e \mid x) = \text{free}(\Delta \left[x \xrightarrow{x} c(\overline{x_n})\right]) : x$$
$$\text{free}(\Delta : e \mid ()) = \text{free}(\Delta) : \text{free}(e)$$
$$\text{free}(\;\; : \;\; e) = \text{free}(\;\;) : \text{free}(e)$$
$$\text{free}(\;\;) = \{(x, \text{free}_x(e)) \mid (x, (), e) \in \;\;\} \cup \{(x, y) \mid \exists e : (x, y, e) \in \;\;\}$$
$$\text{free}_x(\text{generate}) = x$$
$$\text{free}_x(e) = \text{free}(e), \; \textit{if } e \neq \text{generate}$$
$$\text{free}(x) = x$$
$$\text{free}(s(\overline{e_n})) = s(\overline{\text{free}(e_n)})$$
$$\text{free}(e_1 \; ? \; e_2) = \text{free}(e_1) \; ? \; \text{free}(e_2)$$
$$\text{free}((f)\text{case } e \text{ of } \{\overline{p_k \to e_k}\}) = \text{case free}(e) \text{ of } \{\overline{p_k \to \text{free}(e_k)}\}$$
$$\text{free}(\text{let } \{\overline{x_k = e_k}\} \text{ in } e) = \text{let } \{\overline{x_k = \text{free}_{x_k}(e_k)}\} \text{ in free}(e)$$
$$\text{free}(P) = \overline{l_n = \text{free}(r_n)} \textit{ where } P = \overline{l_n = r_n}$$

Next we show a simple proposition which parallels Proposition 3.2.4.

Proposition 3.2.10

1. $flat(\text{free}(e)) = \text{free}(flat(e))$

2. $\text{free}(\text{gen}(e)) = e$

Proof. The proof for 1 is fully analogue to the proof of Proposition 3.2.4 and the proof of 2 is by a simple induction. □

We are now ready to prove our result about how to construct derivations with free variables from those featuring generators. The restriction that e might not be a direct call to a generator is merely technical and not severe. One can simply evaluate, e.g., let $\{x = \text{generate}\}$ in x instead.

Lemma 3.2.11 *Let* P *be a program without free variables possibly employing generators,   an unadorned heap and e an expression such that* $e \neq \textbf{generate}$*. Then we have*

$$\begin{array}{rl} & : \ e \Downarrow_4 \Delta \ : v \ | \ (x) \\ implies & \text{free}(\ : \ e) \Downarrow_1 \text{free}(\Delta \ : v \ | \ (x)) \end{array}$$

Proof. (Of Lemma 3.2.11) By induction on the structure of the proof tree.
Base cases:
(Val): We have

$$\begin{array}{rl} & : \ c(\overline{x_n}) \Downarrow_4 \ : \ c(\overline{x_n}) \ | \ () \\ implies & \text{free}(\ : \ c(\overline{x_n})) \Downarrow_1 \text{free}(\ : \ c(\overline{x_n}) \ | \ ()) \end{array}$$

as the latter is equal to $\text{free}() : \ c(\overline{x_n}) \Downarrow_4 \text{free}() : \ c(\overline{x_n})$
Inductive cases:
(Var): The induction hypothesis in this case is that

$$\begin{array}{rl} & : \ e \Downarrow_4 \Delta \ : v \ | \ (y) \\ implies & \text{free}(\ : \ e) \Downarrow_1 \text{free}(\Delta \ : v \ | \ (y)) \end{array}$$

. With this assumption we have to show that

$$\begin{array}{rl} & [\ x \mapsto e] : x \Downarrow_4 \Delta \left[x \xrightarrow{ad(x,e,(y))} v \right] : v \ | \, \text{ad}(x, e, (y)) \\ implies & \text{free}([\ x \mapsto e] : x) \Downarrow_1 \text{free}(\Delta \left[x \xrightarrow{ad(x,e,(y))} v \right] : v \ | \, \text{ad}(x, e, (y))) \end{array}$$

. This claim holds because we have

$$\begin{array}{rl} & \text{free}(\ : \ e) \Downarrow_1 \text{free}(\Delta \ : v \ | \ (y)) \\ = & \text{free}() : \ \text{free}(e) \Downarrow_1 \text{free}(\Delta) : v \\ \hline & \text{free}() [\ x \mapsto \text{free}_x(e)] : x \Downarrow_1 \text{free}(\Delta) [x \mapsto v] : v \\ = & \text{free}([\ x \mapsto e] : x) \Downarrow_1 \text{free}(\Delta \left[x \xrightarrow{ad(x,e,(y))} v \right] : v \ | \, \text{ad}(x, e, (y))) \end{array}$$

3.2. ELIMINATION OF FREE VARIABLES

whenever $e \neq \text{generate}$ and $(y) = ()$ because $\text{free}_x(e) = \text{free}(e)$ and $\text{ad}(x, e, (y)) = ()$ in this case.

For $e \neq \text{generate}$ but $(y) = y$ we first note that by Proposition 3.2.8 the heap Δ must be of the form $\Delta' \left[y \xrightarrow{y} c(\overline{x_n}) \right] [\overline{x_n \mapsto \text{generate}}]$ and therefore we have $\text{free}(\Delta : v \mid y) = \text{free}(\Delta' \left[y \xrightarrow{y} c(\overline{x_n}) \right]) : y$ and we can construct

$$\frac{\frac{\text{free}(\ : \ e) \Downarrow_4 \text{free}(\Delta : v \mid y)}{= \ \text{free}() : \ \text{free}(e) \Downarrow_4 \text{free}(\Delta' \left[y \xrightarrow{y} c(\overline{x_n}) \right]) : y}}{\text{free}() [\ x \mapsto \text{free}_x(e)] : x \Downarrow_4 \text{free}(\Delta' \left[y \xrightarrow{y} c(\overline{x_n}) \right]) [x \mapsto y] : y}$$
$$= \ \text{free}([\ x \mapsto e] : x) \Downarrow_4 \text{free}(\Delta \left[x \xrightarrow{y} v \right] : v \mid y)$$

Finally, if $e = \text{generate}$ Proposition 3.2.2 states that we have

$$[\ x \mapsto \text{generate}] : x \Downarrow_4 [\ \overline{x_n \mapsto \text{generate}}] \left[x \xrightarrow{x} c(\overline{x_n}) \right] : c(\overline{x_n}) \mid x$$

and therefore we can construct

$$\text{free}([\ x \mapsto \text{generate}] : x) \Downarrow_1 \text{free}([\ \overline{x_n \mapsto \text{generate}}] \left[x \xrightarrow{x} c(\overline{x_n}) \right] : c(\overline{x_n}) \mid x)$$
$$= \ \text{free}() [\ x \mapsto \text{free}_x(\text{generate})] : x \Downarrow_1 \text{free}(\ \left[x \xrightarrow{x} c(\overline{x_n}) \right]) : x$$
$$= \ \text{free}() [\ x \mapsto x] : x \Downarrow_1 \text{free}() [\ x \mapsto x] : x$$

which is an axiomatic application of rule (Val).

(Fun): The induction hypothesis in this case is that

$$: \ \text{flat}(e) \Downarrow_4 \Delta : v \mid (x)$$
$$\text{implies} \quad \text{free}(\ : \ \text{flat}(e)) \Downarrow_1 \text{free}(\Delta : v \mid (x))$$

where $\mathtt{f}(\overline{x_n}) = e \in P$. With this assumption we have to show that

$$: \ \mathtt{f}(\overline{x_n}) \Downarrow_4 \Delta : v \mid (x)$$
$$\text{implies} \quad \text{free}(\ : \ \mathtt{f}(\overline{x_n})) \Downarrow_1 \text{free}(\Delta : v \mid (x))$$

. This claim holds because we have

$$\frac{\frac{\text{free}(\ : \ \text{flat}(e)) \Downarrow_1 \text{free}(\Delta : v \mid (x))}{= \ \text{free}() : \ \text{flat}(\text{free}(e)) \Downarrow_1 \text{free}(\Delta : v \mid (x))}}{\text{free}() : \ \mathtt{f}(\overline{x_n}) \Downarrow_1 \text{free}(\Delta : v \mid (x))}$$
$$= \ \text{free}(\ : \ \mathtt{f}(\overline{x_n})) \Downarrow_1 \text{free}(\Delta : v \mid (x))$$

as by Proposition 3.2.10.1 we have $\text{flat}(\text{free}(e)) = \text{free}(\text{flat}(e))$ and by definition of $\text{free}(P)$ we have $\mathtt{f}(\overline{x_n}) = \text{free}(e) \in \text{free}(P)$.

(Let): The induction hypothesis in this case is that

$$[\ \overline{x_k \mapsto e_k}] : e \Downarrow_4 \Delta : v \mid (x)$$
$$\text{implies} \quad \text{free}([\ \overline{x_k \mapsto e_k}] : e) \Downarrow_1 \text{free}(\Delta : v \mid (x))$$

. With this assumption we have to show that
$$\text{implies} \quad \begin{array}{l} \Gamma : \text{let } \{\overline{x_k = e_k}\} \text{ in } e \Downarrow_4 \Delta : v \mid (x) \\ \text{free}(\Gamma : \text{let } \{\overline{x_k = e_k}\} \text{ in } e) \Downarrow_1 \text{free}(\Delta : v \mid (x)) \end{array}$$

. This claim holds because we have

$$\begin{array}{rl} & \text{free}(\Gamma[\,\overline{x_k \mapsto e_k}] : e) \Downarrow_1 \text{free}(\Delta : v \mid (x)) \\ = & \text{free}(\Gamma) \left[\overline{x_k \mapsto \text{free}_{x_k}(e_k)} \right] : \text{free}(e) \Downarrow_1 \text{free}(\Delta : v \mid (x)) \\ \hline & \text{free}(\Gamma) : \text{let } \{\overline{x_k = \text{free}_{x_k}(e_k)}\} \text{ in free}(e) \Downarrow_1 \text{free}(\Delta : v \mid (x)) \\ = & \text{free}(\Gamma : \text{let } \{\overline{x_k = e_k}\} \text{ in } e) \Downarrow_1 \text{free}(\Delta : v \mid (x)) \end{array}$$

(Or): The induction hypothesis in this case is that
$$\text{implies} \quad \begin{array}{l} \Gamma : e_i \Downarrow_4 \Delta : v \mid (x) \\ \text{free}(\Gamma : e_i) \Downarrow_1 \text{free}(\Delta : v \mid (x)) \end{array}$$

where $i \in \{1,2\}$. With this assumption we have to show that
$$\text{implies} \quad \begin{array}{l} \Gamma : e_1 \text{ ? } e_2 \Downarrow_4 \Delta : v \mid (x) \\ \text{free}(\Gamma : e_1 \text{ ? } e_2) \Downarrow_1 \text{free}(\Delta : v \mid (x)) \end{array}$$

. This claim holds because we have

$$\begin{array}{rl} & \text{free}(\Gamma : e_i) \Downarrow_1 \text{free}(\Delta : v \mid (x)) \\ = & \text{free}(\Gamma) : \text{free}(e_i) \Downarrow_1 \text{free}(\Delta : v \mid (x)) \\ \hline & \text{free}(\Gamma) : \text{free}(e_1) \text{ ? free}(e_2) \Downarrow_1 \text{free}(\Delta : v \mid (x)) \\ = & \text{free}(\Gamma : e_1 \text{ ? } e_2) \Downarrow_1 \text{free}(\Delta : v \mid (x)) \end{array}$$

(Select): The induction hypothesis in this case is that
$$\text{implies} \quad \begin{array}{l} \Gamma : e \Downarrow_4 \Delta : c(\overline{x_n}) \mid (x) \\ \text{free}(\Gamma : e) \Downarrow_1 \text{free}(\Delta : c(\overline{x_n}) \mid (x)) \end{array}$$

and
$$\text{implies} \quad \begin{array}{l} \text{ud}_{(x)}(\Delta) : \sigma(e_i) \Downarrow_4 \Theta : v \mid (y) \\ \text{free}(\text{ud}_{(x)}(\Delta) : \sigma(e_i)) \Downarrow_1 \text{free}(\Theta : v \mid (y)) \end{array}$$

where $i \in \{1, \ldots, k\}$ and $c(\overline{x_n}) = \sigma(p_i)$. With this assumption we have to show that
$$\text{implies} \quad \begin{array}{l} \Gamma : \text{case } e \text{ of } \{\overline{p_k \mapsto e_k}\} \Downarrow_4 \Theta : v \mid (y) \\ \text{free}(\Gamma : \text{case } e \text{ of } \{\overline{p_k \mapsto e_k}\}) \Downarrow_1 \text{free}(\Theta : v \mid (y)) \end{array}$$

. This claim holds because we have

$$\left[\begin{array}{l} \text{free}(\Gamma : \text{case } e \text{ of } \{\overline{p_k \mapsto e_k}\}) \\ = \text{free}(\Gamma) : \text{case free}(e) \text{ of } \{\overline{p_k \mapsto \text{free}(e_k)}\} \\ \left[\begin{array}{l} \text{free}(\Gamma : e) = \text{free}(\Gamma) : \text{free}(e) \\ \ldots \\ \text{free}(\Delta : c(\overline{x_n}) \mid (x)) = \text{free}(\Delta) : c(\overline{x_n}) \\ \text{free}(\text{ud}_{(x)}(\Delta) : \sigma(e_i)) = \text{free}(\text{ud}_{(x)}(\Delta)) : \sigma(\text{free}(e_i)) \\ \ldots \\ \text{free}(\Theta : v \mid (y)) \end{array} \right. \\ \text{free}(\Theta : v \mid (y)) \end{array} \right.$$

in the case that $(x) = ()$ and, therefore, $\mathsf{ud}_{(x)}(\Delta) = \Delta$ and $\sigma(\mathsf{free}(\mathsf{e})) = \mathsf{free}(\sigma(\mathsf{e}))$ as σ is a variable renaming.

And in the case that $(x) = x$ it holds that by Proposition 3.2.8 the heap Δ must be of the form $\Delta' \left[x \xrightarrow{x} c(\overline{x_n}) \right] [\overline{x_n \mapsto \mathsf{generate}}]$ and therefore we have:

$$\mathsf{free}(\Delta : c(\overline{x_n}) \mid x) = \mathsf{free}(\Delta' \left[x \xrightarrow{x} c(\overline{x_n}) \right]) : x = \mathsf{free}(\Delta')[x \mapsto x] : x$$

Furthermore we have in this case

$$\begin{aligned}
\mathsf{free}(\mathsf{ud}_x(\Delta)) &= \mathsf{free}(\mathsf{ud}_x(\Delta' \left[x \xrightarrow{x} c(\overline{x_n}) \right] [\overline{x_n \mapsto \mathsf{generate}}])) \\
&= \mathsf{free}(\mathsf{ud}_x(\Delta' \left[x \xrightarrow{x} c(\overline{x_n}) \right]) [\overline{x_n \mapsto \mathsf{generate}}]) \\
&= \mathsf{free}(\mathsf{ud}_x(\Delta' \left[x \xrightarrow{x} c(\overline{x_n}) \right])) [\overline{x_n \mapsto x_n}] \\
&= \mathsf{free}(\Delta')[x \mapsto c(\overline{x_n}), \overline{x_n \mapsto x_n}]
\end{aligned}$$

and all in all we can construct the following application of rule (Guess).

$$\begin{bmatrix}
\mathsf{free}(: \ \mathsf{case} \ \mathsf{e} \ \mathsf{of} \ \{\overline{\mathsf{p}_k \mapsto \mathsf{e}_k}\}) \\
= \mathsf{free}() : \ \mathsf{case} \ \mathsf{free}(\mathsf{e}) \ \mathsf{of} \ \{\overline{\mathsf{p}_k \mapsto \mathsf{free}(\mathsf{e}_k)}\} \\
\begin{bmatrix} \mathsf{free}(: \ \mathsf{e}) = \mathsf{free}() : \ \mathsf{free}(\mathsf{e}) \\
\ldots \\
\mathsf{free}(\Delta : c(\overline{x_n}) \mid (x)) = \mathsf{free}(\Delta')[x \mapsto x] : x \\
\mathsf{free}(\mathsf{ud}_{(x)}(\Delta) : \sigma(\mathsf{e}_i)) = \mathsf{free}(\Delta')[x \mapsto c(\overline{x_n}), \overline{x_n \mapsto x_n}] : \sigma(\mathsf{free}(\mathsf{e}_i)) \\
\ldots \\
\mathsf{free}(: \ \mathsf{v} \mid (y)) \end{bmatrix} \\
\mathsf{free}(: \ \mathsf{v} \mid (y))
\end{bmatrix}$$

$\square$

3.3 Summary

In the previous sections we have constructed closely corresponding derivations for programs and expressions with free variables to the corresponding ones employing generators. The aim of this section is to summarize these results in the terms of the more abstract notion of semantics introduced in Section 2.2.5. For this we will first extract the values of derivations with generators. Then we show that neither of the mappings $\mathsf{gen}(\cdot)$ nor $\mathsf{free}(\cdot)$ have an influence of the value extraction from result configurations. Finally, we will show that the set of computable values is indeed the same for both kinds of derivations.

Definition 3.3.1 (Extracting Values from Generator Derivations)
Let P *be a program without free variables possibly employing generators and* e *an expression such that* $\mathsf{e} \neq \mathsf{generate}$. *Then*

$$\llbracket \mathsf{e} \rrbracket_4^P := \{c(\overline{{}^*(x_n)}) \mid \emptyset : \mathit{flat}(\mathsf{e}) \Downarrow_i \ : \ c(\overline{x_n}) \mid ()\}$$
$$\cup \ \{x \mid \emptyset : \mathit{flat}(\mathsf{e}) \Downarrow_i \ : \ c(\overline{x_n}) \mid x\}$$

where $*(\cdot)$ *was introduced in Definition 2.2.5.*

70   CHAPTER 3. ELIMINATION OF FREE VARIABLES

The dierence between $[\![e]\!]_4^P$ and $[\![e]\!]_4^P$ is in the treatment of generators evaluated at top level. For the semantics of $e = \text{let } \{x = \text{generate}\}$ in x holds:

$$[\![e]\!]_4^P = |\{c(\bar{y}) \mid c \in C_\Sigma\}|$$
$$[\![e]\!]_4^P = |\{x\}|$$

An important point about the reconstruction of heaps when mapping between derivations with or without free variables is that the final values with regard to $[\![e]\!]_1^P, [\![e]\!]_4^P$, or $[\![e]\!]_4^P$ are not changed. This is the content of the next proposition.

Proposition 3.3.2 (Value Extraction with free($\cdot$),gen())

1. Let   be a heap with access tokens (Definition 3.1.2) where $T = \{*\}$ and $E' = Var$ which features correct variable updates. Then we have for all x that $\,^*(x) = \text{gen}()\,^*(x)$.

2. Let   be a heap with access tokens where $T = Var$ and E' flat constructor terms which is unadorned. Then we have for all x that $\,^*(x) = \text{free}()\,^*(x)$.

Proof. The *size* of an expression e, denoted by $|e|$, is inductively defined by:

$$|x| = 1$$
$$|s(\overline{e_n})| = 1 + \sum_1^n |e_n|$$
$$|\text{case } e \text{ of } \{\overline{p_k \to e_k}\}| = 1 + |e| + \sum_1^k |e_k|$$
$$|\text{let } \{\overline{x_k = e_k}\} \text{ in } e| = 1 + |e| + \sum_1^k |e_k|$$
$$|e_1 \,?\, e_2| = 1 + |e_1| + |e_2|$$

The size $|\,\,|$ of a give heap $= \overline{\{(x_n, e_n)\}}$ is defined by $|\,\,| = \sum_1^n |e_n|$. (Note that heaps are by definition finite sets.)

1. Proof by Noetherian induction on the size of .
Base case, $|\,\,| = 0$ which implies $= \emptyset$: we have for any variable x that $\,^*(x) = \text{gen}()\,^*(x) = x$.
Inductive case: Let the claim hold for all heaps with a smaller size than . Then we have by the according Definitions 2.2.5 and 3.2.3:
If $x \notin dom()$ then $\,^*(x) = \text{gen}()\,^*(x) = x$.
If $= \,'\left[x \xrightarrow{*} y\right]$ then $x \neq y$ by assumption that   features correct updates. Therefore, we have $\,^*(x) = \,'^*(y)$ and $\text{gen}()\,^*(x) = \text{gen}(\,')^*(y)$ and the claim follows by induction hypothesis.
If $= \,'[x \mapsto x]$ then $\,^*(x) = x$ and $\text{gen}()\,^*(x) = \text{gen}(\,')[x \mapsto \text{generate}]^*(x) = x$.
If $= \,'[x \mapsto y]$ where $x \neq y$ then $\,^*(x) = \,'^*(y)$ and $\text{gen}()\,^*(x) = \text{gen}(\,')^*(y)$ and the claim follows by induction hypothesis.
If $= \,'[x \mapsto c(\overline{x_n})]$ then $\,^*(x) = c(\overline{\,'^*(x_n)})$ and $\text{gen}()\,^*(x) = c(\overline{\text{gen}(\,')^*(x_n)})$ and the claim follows by induction hypothesis.
If $= \,'[x \mapsto e]$ where e is a function call, a ?-expression or a case expression

3.3. SUMMARY

then $\sigma^*(x) = x$ and $\text{gen}(\sigma)\ \sigma^*(x) = \text{gen}(\sigma')[x \mapsto \text{gen}_x(e)]^*(x) = x$ as $\text{gen}_x(e)$ is also a function call, ?-expression or case expression, respectively.
If $\sigma = \sigma'[x \mapsto \text{let } \{\overline{x_k = e_k}\} \text{ in } e]$ then $\sigma^*(x) = \sigma'[\overline{x_k \mapsto e_k}, x \mapsto e]^*(x)$ and $\text{gen}(\sigma)\ \sigma^*(x) = \text{gen}(\sigma'[\overline{x_k \mapsto e_k}, x \mapsto e])^*(x)$ and the claim follows by induction hypothesis.

2. Again proof by Noetherian induction on the size of σ.
Base case, $|\sigma| = 0$: we have for any variable x that $\sigma^*(x) = \text{free}(\sigma)\ \sigma^*(x) = x$.
Inductive case: Let the claim hold for all heaps with a smaller size than σ. It cannot be the case that $\sigma = \sigma'\left[x \xrightarrow{y} e\right]$ since σ is by assumption unadorned. Therefore, the following case distinction in accordance with Definitions 2.2.5 and 3.2.9 is full:
If $x \notin dom(\sigma)$ then $\sigma^*(x) = \text{free}(\sigma)\ \sigma^*(x) = x$.
If $\sigma = \sigma'[x \mapsto x]$ then $\sigma^*(x) = x$ and $\text{free}(\sigma)\ \sigma^*(x) = \text{free}(\sigma')[x \mapsto x]^*(x) = x$.
If $\sigma = \sigma'[x \mapsto y]$ where $x \neq y$ then $\sigma^*(x) = \sigma'^*(y)$ and $\text{free}(\sigma)\ \sigma^*(x) = \text{free}(\sigma')^*(y)$ and the claim follows by induction hypothesis.
If $\sigma = \sigma'[x \mapsto c(\overline{x_n})]$ then $\sigma^*(x) = c(\sigma'^*(x_n))$ and $\text{free}(\sigma)\ \sigma^*(x) = c(\overline{\text{free}(\sigma')^*(x_n)})$ and the claim follows by induction hypothesis.
If $\sigma = \sigma'[x \mapsto e]$ where e is a function call, a ?−expressions or a case expression then $\sigma^*(x) = x$ and $\text{free}(\sigma)\ \sigma^*(x) = \text{free}(\sigma')[x \mapsto \text{free}_x(e)]^*(x) = x$ as $\text{free}_x(e)$ is either also a function call, ?-expression or case expression, respectively, or equal to x if e = generate.
If $\sigma = \sigma'[x \mapsto \text{let } \{\overline{x_k = e_k}\} \text{ in } e]$ then $\sigma^*(x) = \sigma'[\overline{x_k \mapsto e_k}, x \mapsto e]^*(x)$ and $\text{free}(\sigma)\ \sigma^*(x) = \text{free}(\sigma'[\overline{x_k \mapsto e_k}, x \mapsto e])^*(x)$ and the claim follows by induction hypothesis. □

We are now ready to the result of this chapter, namely that the set of values computable with regard to a program P is equal to that computable for the version with generators $\text{gen}(P)$.

Theorem 1 (Elimination of Free Variables) *Let* P *be a program over signature Σ and* e *be a Σ-expression. Then we have*

$$[\![e]\!]_0^P = [\![\text{gen}(e)]\!]_4^{\text{gen}(P)}$$

Proof. By Lemma 3.2.6 we have that $\emptyset : flat(e) \Downarrow_2 \sigma : c(\overline{x_n})$ in P implies

$$\begin{aligned}
& \text{gen}(\emptyset : flat(e)) \Downarrow_4 \text{gen}^{c'(\overline{y_m})}(\sigma : c(\overline{x_n})) \\
= \ & \emptyset : \text{gen}(flat(e)) \Downarrow_4 \text{gen}(\sigma) : c(\overline{x_n}) \mid () \qquad \text{Def 3.2.3} \\
= \ & \emptyset : flat(\text{gen}(e)) \Downarrow_4 \text{gen}(\sigma) : c(\overline{x_n}) \mid () \qquad \text{Prop 3.2.4}
\end{aligned}$$

in $\text{gen}(P)$ since $\emptyset$ features correct variable updates. And by Proposition 3.3.2 we have $c(\overline{\sigma^*(x_n)}) = c(\overline{\text{gen}(\sigma)^*(x_n)})$. Thus, we may conclude

$$\begin{aligned}
& \{c(\overline{\sigma^*(x_n)}) \mid \emptyset : flat(e) \Downarrow_1 \sigma : c(\overline{x_n}) \text{ in P}\} \\
\subseteq \ & \{c(\overline{\sigma'^*(x_n)}) \mid \emptyset : flat(\text{gen}(e)) \Downarrow_1 \sigma' : c(\overline{x_n}) \mid () \text{ in gen(P)}\}
\end{aligned} \qquad (1)$$

72 CHAPTER 3. ELIMINATION OF FREE VARIABLES

Likewise by Lemma 3.2.6 we have that $\emptyset : \mathit{flat}(e) \Downarrow_2 \; : \; x$ in P implies

$$
\begin{aligned}
& \mathsf{gen}(\emptyset : \mathit{flat}(e)) \Downarrow_4 \mathsf{gen}^{c'(\overline{y_m})}(: \; x) \\
= \; & \emptyset : \mathsf{gen}(\mathit{flat}(e)) \Downarrow_4 \mathsf{gen}^{c'(\overline{y_m})}([\;\overline{x_n \mapsto x_n}\;]) : c'(\overline{y_m}) \mid x \quad \text{Def 3.2.3} \\
= \; & \emptyset : \mathit{flat}(\mathsf{gen}(e)) \Downarrow_4 \mathsf{gen}^{c'(\overline{y_m})}([\;\overline{x_n \mapsto x_n}\;]) : c'(\overline{y_m}) \mid x \quad \text{Prop 3.2.4}
\end{aligned}
$$

in $\mathsf{gen}(P)$ and we may conclude also

$$
\begin{aligned}
& \{x \mid \emptyset : \mathit{flat}(e) \Downarrow_1 \; : \; x \text{ in P }\} \\
\subseteq \; & \{x \mid \emptyset : \mathit{flat}(\mathsf{gen}(e)) \Downarrow_1 \; ' : c'(\overline{x_n}) \mid x \text{ in } \mathsf{gen}(P)\}
\end{aligned} \quad (2)
$$

Lemma 3.2.11 entails that $\emptyset : \mathit{flat}(\mathsf{gen}(e)) \Downarrow_4 \; : \; c'(\overline{x_n}) \mid ()$ in $\mathsf{gen}(P)$ implies

$$
\begin{aligned}
& \mathsf{free}(\emptyset : \mathit{flat}(\mathsf{gen}(e))) \Downarrow_1 \mathsf{free}(: \; c'(\overline{x_n}) \mid ()) \\
= \; & \emptyset : \mathsf{free}(\mathit{flat}(\mathsf{gen}(e))) \Downarrow_1 \mathsf{free}() : \; c'(\overline{x_n}) \quad \text{Def 3.2.9} \\
= \; & \emptyset : \mathit{flat}(\mathsf{free}(\mathsf{gen}(e))) \Downarrow_1 \mathsf{free}() : \; c'(\overline{x_n}) \quad \text{Prop 3.2.10.1} \\
= \; & \emptyset : \mathit{flat}(e) \Downarrow_1 \mathsf{free}() : \; c'(\overline{x_n}) \quad \text{Prop 3.2.10.2}
\end{aligned}
$$

in $\mathsf{free}(\mathsf{gen}(P)) = P$ (Proposition 3.2.10.2) since $\emptyset$ is unadorned and for all - expressions e holds that $\mathsf{gen}(e) \neq \mathit{generate}$. And by Proposition 3.3.2 we have $c'(\overline{\;^*(x_n)}) = c'(\mathsf{free}()\;\overline{\;^*(x_n)})$. Thus, we may conclude

$$
\begin{aligned}
& \{c'(\overline{\;^*(x_n)}) \mid \emptyset : \mathit{flat}(\mathsf{gen}(e)) \Downarrow_4 \; : \; c'(\overline{x_n}) \mid () \text{ in } \mathsf{gen}(P)\} \\
\subseteq \; & \{c'(\overline{\;'^*(x_n)}) \mid \emptyset : \mathit{flat}(e) \Downarrow_1 \; ' : c'(\overline{x_n}) \text{ in P}\}
\end{aligned} \quad (3)
$$

Lemma 3.2.11 also entails that $\emptyset : \mathit{flat}(\mathsf{gen}(e)) \Downarrow_4 \; : \; c'(\overline{x_n}) \mid x$ in $\mathsf{gen}(P)$ implies

$$
\begin{aligned}
& \mathsf{free}(\emptyset : \mathit{flat}(\mathsf{gen}(e))) \Downarrow_1 \mathsf{free}(: \; c'(\overline{x_n}) \mid x) \\
= \; & \emptyset : \mathsf{free}(\mathit{flat}(\mathsf{gen}(e))) \Downarrow_1 \mathsf{free}() : \; x \quad \text{Def 3.2.9} \\
= \; & \emptyset : \mathit{flat}(\mathsf{free}(\mathsf{gen}(e))) \Downarrow_1 \mathsf{free}() : \; x \quad \text{Prop 3.2.10.1} \\
= \; & \emptyset : \mathit{flat}(e) \Downarrow_1 \mathsf{free}() : \; x \quad \text{Prop 3.2.10.2}
\end{aligned}
$$

in P and we conclude

$$
\begin{aligned}
& \{x \mid \emptyset : \mathit{flat}(\mathsf{gen}(e)) \Downarrow_4 \; : \; c'(\overline{x_n}) \mid x \text{ in } \mathsf{gen}(P)\} \\
\subseteq \; & \{x \mid \emptyset : \mathit{flat}(e) \Downarrow_1 \; ' : x \text{ in P}\}
\end{aligned} \quad (4)
$$

3.3. SUMMARY

Finally we can put all observations (1) − (4) together to get the validity of the following equations.

$$\llbracket e \rrbracket_0^P$$
$$= \llbracket e \rrbracket_1^P \qquad\qquad\qquad\qquad\qquad\qquad\qquad \text{Cor 2.3.2}$$
$$= \{c(\overline{{}^*(x_n)}) \mid \emptyset : \mathit{flat}(e) \Downarrow_1 \; : \; c(\overline{x_n})\} \cup$$
$$\quad \{x \mid \emptyset : \mathit{flat}(e) \Downarrow_1 \; : \; x\} \qquad\qquad \text{Def 2.2.5}$$
$$= \{c(\overline{{}^*(x_n)}) \mid \emptyset : \mathit{flat}(e) \Downarrow_2 \;_1 : c(\overline{x_n})\} \cup$$
$$\quad \{x \mid \emptyset : \mathit{flat}(e) \Downarrow_2 \;_1 : x\}$$
the step from $\Downarrow_1$ to $\Downarrow_2$ is a conservative extension, $_1^*(\cdot)$ ignores tokens
$$\subseteq \{c(\overline{{}_2^*(x_n)}) \mid \emptyset : \mathit{flat}(\mathsf{gen}(e)) \Downarrow_4 \;_2 : c(\overline{x_n})\} \cup$$
$$\quad \{x \mid \emptyset : \mathit{flat}(\mathsf{gen}(e)) \Downarrow_4 \;_2 : x\} \qquad \text{in } \mathsf{gen}(P) \; (1), (2)$$
$$= \llbracket e \rrbracket_4^{\mathsf{gen}(P)} \qquad\qquad\qquad\qquad\qquad \text{Def 3.3.1}$$
$$\subseteq \{c(\overline{{}_3^*(x_n)}) \mid \emptyset : \mathit{flat}(e) \Downarrow_1 \;_3 : c(\overline{x_n})\} \cup$$
$$\quad \{x \mid \emptyset : \mathit{flat}(e) \Downarrow_1 \;_3 : x\} \qquad\qquad \text{in } P \; (3), (4)$$
$$= \llbracket e \rrbracket_1^P \qquad\qquad\qquad\qquad\qquad\qquad \text{Def 2.2.5}$$
$$= \llbracket e \rrbracket_0^P \qquad\qquad\qquad\qquad\qquad\qquad \text{Cor 2.3.2}$$

□

Note that we also have $\llbracket e \rrbracket_4^P = \llbracket \mathsf{free}(e) \rrbracket_0^{\mathsf{free}(P)}$ for a program with generators P and an according expression $e \neq \mathsf{generate}$ as a simple implication of Theorem 1 and Proposition 3.2.10.2.

Theorem 1 is stated in terms of the semantics $\Downarrow_4$ (cf. Figure 3.3). Nevertheless, in the following we will work with the semantics $\Downarrow_3$ as introduced in Figure 3.2. This means especially, that we loose the information about generators evaluated at top level and will compute any constructor for, e.g., the expression let $\{x = \mathsf{generate}\}$ in x. This additional non-determinism with respect to the calculation with free variables can be seen as the major drawback for any approach employing generators solely. Especially, it is not obvious how to extend such a setting by standard logic features like unification. We will come back to this problem in Sections 6.7 and 6.8 and present a new solution.

Chapter 4
Uniform Programs

In this chapter we will transform the derivation rules considered so far in such a way that expressions can be restricted to a simpler syntactic structure. In the course of this chapter we will eliminate case-expressions and we will also omit let-expressions during evaluation, although they can still be used in programs. As a consequence, in the end we will be left with a calculus featuring only four rules. There are several advantages of the proposed transformations.

- programs and derivations become more readable
- formal considerations become less technical, cf. Section 4.3
- the resulting calculus is more concise and also closer to implementations
- a short excursus will show that the resulting calculus is closer to term-graph rewriting than the former

To obtain these advantages, we will first consider a standard transformation employed in many current compiling systems (Section 4.1). In Section 4.2 we will then introduce the new form of expressions and programs called *uniform*. After that (Section 4.3) we introduce the corresponding *flat* version of uniform expressions which is used in the according calculus. Before we prove the soundness of the proposed transformation (Section 4.5) a short excursus to term-graph rewriting will further motivate the results (Section 4.4).

4.1 Case Lifting

Most if not all compilers for the functional logic language Curry employ a transformation called *case lifting*. The idea is that a nested case expressions can be lifted by introducing a new function whose definition consists of the inner case expression (which is then no longer nested).

Example 4.1.1 (Case Lifting) *Reconsider the definition of* `equal` *from Example 1.1.15. The flat version looks like this:*

```
equal x y = case x of 0       case y of 0        True
                      S x'    case y of S y'     True
```
Case lifting of the definition would produce:
```
equal x y = case x of 0       equal_1 y
                      S x'    equal_2 y

equal_1 y = case y of 0       True
equal_2 y = case y of S y'    True
```

We need some helpful observations to prepare the proof of correctness of this transformation. Lemma 4.1.2 and Lemma 4.1.3 are concerned with invariants with respect to heaps in derivations. After that Proposition 4.1.4 claims that case-expressions with non-variable arguments can be replaced by expressions of the form (case x of $\{\overline{p_k \to e_k}\}$). We can then formalize the transformation in Definitions 4.1.5-4.1.8 followed by the correctness proof (Lemma 4.1.10).

The first useful observation is that no variables can get lost during evaluation.

Lemma 4.1.2 : $e \Downarrow_3 \Delta : v$ *implies* $dom() \subseteq dom(\Delta)$.

The proof is a simple induction where the interesting cases are rules (Var) and (Let) as only these rules introduce or update variables in the heap.

Proof. (Of Lemma 4.1.2) By induction on the structure of the proof tree.
Base cases:
(Val): We have : $c(\overline{x_n}) \Downarrow_3 : c(\overline{x_n})$ implies $dom() \subseteq dom()$.
Inductive cases:
(Var): The induction hypothesis in this case is that : $e \Downarrow_3 \Delta : v$ implies $dom() \subseteq dom(\Delta)$. With this assumption we have to show that $[\ x \mapsto e]$: $x \Downarrow_3 \Delta [x \mapsto v]$: v implies $dom([\ x \mapsto e]) \subseteq dom(\Delta [x \mapsto v])$. This claim holds because we have
$$\begin{aligned} & dom([\ x \mapsto e]) \\ =\ & dom() \cup \{x\} \\ \subseteq\ & dom(\Delta) \cup \{x\} \\ =\ & dom(\Delta [x \mapsto v]) \end{aligned}$$

(Fun): The induction hypothesis in this case is that : $flat(e) \Downarrow_3 \Delta : v$ implies $dom() \subseteq dom(\Delta)$ where $f(\overline{x_n}) = e \in P$. With this assumption we have to show that : $f(\overline{x_n}) \Downarrow_3 \Delta : v$ implies $dom() \subseteq dom(\Delta)$ which is a direct consequence of the induction hypothesis.
(Let): The induction hypothesis in this case is that $[\ \overline{x_k \mapsto e_k}] : e \Downarrow_3 \Delta : v$ implies $dom([\ \overline{x_k \mapsto e_k}]) \subseteq dom(\Delta)$. With this assumption we have to show that : let $\{\overline{x_k = e_k}\}$ in $e \Downarrow_3 \Delta : v$ implies $dom() \subseteq dom(\Delta)$. This claim holds because we have
$$\begin{aligned} & dom() \\ \subseteq\ & dom() \cup \{\overline{x_k}\} \\ =\ & dom([\ \overline{x_k \mapsto e_k}]) \\ \subseteq\ & dom(\Delta) \end{aligned}$$

4.1. CASE LIFTING

(Or): The induction hypothesis in this case is that : $e_i \Downarrow_3 \Delta'$: v implies $dom(\Delta) \subseteq dom(\Delta')$ where $i \in \{1,2\}$. With this assumption we have to show that : $e_1 ? e_2 \Downarrow_3 \Delta'$: v implies $dom(\Delta) \subseteq dom(\Delta')$ which is a direct consequence of the induction hypothesis.
(Select): The induction hypothesis in this case is that : $e \Downarrow_3 \Delta'$: $c(\overline{x_n})$ implies $dom(\Delta) \subseteq dom(\Delta')$ and $\Delta' : \sigma(e_i) \Downarrow_3 \Theta$: v implies $dom(\Delta') \subseteq dom(\Theta)$ where $i \in \{1,\ldots,k\}$ and $c(\overline{x_n}) = \sigma(p_i)$. With this assumption we have to show that Δ : case e of $\{\overline{p_k \mapsto e_k}\} \Downarrow_3 \Theta$: v implies $dom(\Delta) \subseteq dom(\Theta)$ which holds by inductive assumption and by transitivity of $\subseteq$. □

The second observation is that given a successful derivation we can add any fresh bindings to the initial heap without effecting the result value. Moreover, the added bindings will be found in the resulting heap without any change.

Lemma 4.1.3 : Δ $e \Downarrow_3 \Delta'$: v and $dom(\Delta) \cap dom(\Theta') = \emptyset$ imply ($\Delta \cup \Theta'$) : $e \Downarrow_3$ ($\Delta' \cup \Theta'$) : v.

The proof is a simple induction where the only notable insight used in rules (Var) and (Guess) is that for any two heaps Γ, Γ' such that $x \notin dom(\Gamma')$ it holds that $[x \mapsto e] \cup \Gamma'$ is equal to ($\Gamma \cup \Gamma'$)$[x \mapsto e]$.

Proof. (Of Lemma 4.1.3) By induction on the structure of the proof tree.
Base cases:
(Val): We have Δ : $c(\overline{x_n}) \Downarrow_3 \Delta$: $c(\overline{x_n})$ and $dom(\Delta) \cap dom(\Theta') = \emptyset$ imply ($\Delta \cup \Theta'$) : $c(\overline{x_n}) \Downarrow_3$ ($\Delta \cup \Theta'$) : $c(\overline{x_n})$.
Inductive cases:
(Var): The induction hypothesis in this case is that : $e \Downarrow_3 \Delta'$: v and $dom(\Delta) \cap dom(\Theta') = \emptyset$ imply ($\Delta \cup \Theta'$) : $e \Downarrow_3$ ($\Delta' \cup \Theta'$) : v. With this assumption we have to show that $[x \mapsto e] : x \Downarrow_3 \Delta [x \mapsto v]$: v and $dom(\Delta [x \mapsto v]) \cap dom(\Theta') = \emptyset$ imply ($[x \mapsto e] \cup \Theta'$) : $x \Downarrow_3$ ($\Delta [x \mapsto v] \cup \Theta'$) : v. This claim holds because we have ($[x \mapsto e] \cup \Theta'$) = ($\Delta \cup \Theta'$)$[x \mapsto e]$ and ($\Delta [x \mapsto v] \cup \Theta'$) = ($\Delta \cup \Theta'$)$[x \mapsto v]$.
(Fun): The induction hypothesis in this case is that : $flat(e) \Downarrow_3 \Delta'$: v and $dom(\Delta) \cap dom(\Theta') = \emptyset$ imply ($\Delta \cup \Theta'$) : $flat(e) \Downarrow_3$ ($\Delta' \cup \Theta'$) : v where $f(\overline{x_n}) = e \in P$. With this assumption we have to show that : $f(\overline{x_n}) \Downarrow_3 \Delta'$: v and $dom(\Delta) \cap dom(\Theta') = \emptyset$ imply ($\Delta \cup \Theta'$) : $f(\overline{x_n}) \Downarrow_3$ ($\Delta' \cup \Theta'$) : v which is a direct consequence of the induction hypothesis.
(Let): The induction hypothesis in this case is that $[\overline{x_k \mapsto e_k}] : e \Downarrow_3 \Delta'$: v and $dom(\Delta) \cap dom(\Theta') = \emptyset$ imply ($[\overline{x_k \mapsto e_k}] \cup \Theta'$) : $e \Downarrow_3$ ($\Delta' \cup \Theta'$) : v. With this assumption we have to show that Δ : let $\{\overline{x_k = e_k}\}$ in $e \Downarrow_3 \Delta'$: v and $dom(\Delta) \cap dom(\Theta') = \emptyset$ imply ($\Delta \cup \Theta'$) : let $\{\overline{x_k = e_k}\}$ in $e \Downarrow_3$ ($\Delta' \cup \Theta'$) : v. This claim holds because we have ($[\overline{x_k \mapsto e_k}] \cup \Theta'$) = ($\Delta \cup \Theta'$)$[\overline{x_k \mapsto e_k}]$ and since $\{\overline{x_k}\} \subseteq dom(\Delta)$ by Lemma 4.1.2.
(Or): The induction hypothesis in this case is that : $e_i \Downarrow_3 \Delta'$: v and $dom(\Delta) \cap dom(\Theta') = \emptyset$ imply ($\Delta \cup \Theta'$) : $e_i \Downarrow_3$ ($\Delta' \cup \Theta'$) : v where $i \in \{1,2\}$. With this assumption we have to show that : $e_1 ? e_2 \Downarrow_3 \Delta'$: v and $dom(\Delta) \cap dom(\Theta') = \emptyset$

imply $(\Delta \cup \Delta') : e_1 ? e_2 \Downarrow_3 (\Delta \cup \Delta') : v$ which is a direct consequence of the induction hypothesis.

(Select): The induction hypothesis in this case is that $\Delta : e \Downarrow_3 \Delta : c(\overline{x_n})$ and $dom(\Delta) \cap dom(\Delta') = \emptyset$ imply $(\Delta \cup \Delta') : e \Downarrow_3 (\Delta \cup \Delta') : c(\overline{x_n})$ and $\Delta : \sigma(e_i) \Downarrow_3 \Delta' : v$ and $dom(\Delta) \cap dom(\Delta') = \emptyset$ imply $(\Delta \cup \Delta') : \sigma(e_i) \Downarrow_3 (\Delta \cup \Delta') : v$ where $i \in \{1, \ldots, k\}$ and $c(\overline{x_n}) = \sigma(p_i)$. With this assumption we have to show that $\Delta :$ case e of $\{\overline{p_k \mapsto e_k}\} \Downarrow_3 \Delta' : v$ and $dom(\Delta) \cap dom(\Delta') = \emptyset$ imply $(\Delta \cup \Delta') :$ case e of $\{\overline{p_k \mapsto e_k}\} \Downarrow_3 (\Delta \cup \Delta') : v$ which holds by inductive assumption and by transitivity of $\subseteq$ along with the fact that for any sets M, N, O holds that M $\subseteq$ N and N $\cap$ O = $\emptyset$ implies M $\cap$ O = $\emptyset$. □

A very simple "transformation" allows us to eliminate non-variable expressions at the matching position of a case.

Proposition 4.1.4 (Case with Variable Arguments)
Programs can be equivalently reformulated such that all case expressions are of the form case x of $\{\overline{p_k \to e_k}\}$ *where* $x \notin \bigcup vars(e_k)$.

Proof. We can replace every expression of the form case e of $\{\overline{p_k \to e_k}\}$ by an expression let $\{x = e\}$ in case x of $\{\overline{p_k \to e_k}\}$. This is because we can replace every derivation of the form

$$\frac{\Delta : e \Downarrow_3 \Delta : c(\overline{x_n}) \quad \Delta : \sigma(e_i) \Downarrow_3 \Delta' : v}{\Delta : \text{case } e \text{ of } \{\overline{p_k \mapsto e_k}\} \Downarrow_3 \Delta' : v}$$

by a derivation

$$\frac{\Delta : e \Downarrow \Delta : c(\overline{x_n})}{[x \mapsto e] : x \Downarrow \Delta [x \mapsto c(\overline{x_n})] : c(\overline{x_n}) \quad \Delta [x \mapsto c(\overline{x_n})] : \sigma(e_i) \Downarrow [x \mapsto c(\overline{x_n})] : v}$$
$$\frac{[x \mapsto e] : \text{case } x \text{ of } \{\overline{p_k \to e_k}\} \Downarrow [x \mapsto c(\overline{x_n})] : v}{\Delta : \text{let } \{x = e\} \text{ in case } x \text{ of } \{\overline{p_k \to e_k}\} \Downarrow [x \mapsto c(\overline{x_n})] : v}$$

since by Lemma 4.1.3 $\Delta : \sigma(e_i) \Downarrow_3 \Delta' : v$ implies for the fresh variable $x \notin dom(\Delta)$ that $\Delta [x \mapsto c(\overline{x_n})] : \sigma(e_i) \Downarrow [x \mapsto c(\overline{x_n})] : v$. □

In the following we will assume that the considered programs feature only case expressions with variable arguments. With this we can move towards lifting case expressions. The following three definitions capture the according transformation. The first definition labels case expression such that they can be identified during evaluation. To be most precise, we should change the derivation rules in order to work on labelled case expressions. We hope, however, that it is obvious that such a change would just be a conservative extension of the rules. Thus, we silently take for granted that labelling case expressions does not change the semantics of programs and expressions.

Definition 4.1.5 (Labeling) *Let Σ be a signature and L an infinite but enumerable set of symbols such that* $L \cap \Sigma = \emptyset$. *Then we call L a set of labels*

4.1. CASE LIFTING

for and the labeling $cl(\cdot)$ is defined on expressions, heaps, configurations, statements, and programs by

$$
\begin{aligned}
cl(x) &= x \\
cl(s(\overline{e_n})) &= s(\overline{cl(e_n)}) \\
cl(\text{case } x \text{ of } \{\overline{p_k \to e_k}\}) &= (\text{f})\text{case}^l\ x \text{ of } \{\overline{p_k \to cl(e_k)}\} \text{ where } l\ \textit{fresh} \\
cl(\text{let } \{\overline{x_k = e_k}\} \text{ in } e) &= \text{let } \{\overline{x_k = cl(e_k)}\} \text{ in } cl(e) \\
cl(e_1\ ?\ e_2) &= cl(e_1)\ ?\ cl(e_2) \\[4pt]
cl(\ ) &= \{(\textsf{x}, cl(e))\ |\ (\textsf{x}, e) \in\ \} \\[4pt]
cl(\ :e) &= cl(\ ) : cl(e) \\[4pt]
cl(\overline{l = e}) &= \overline{l = cl(e)}
\end{aligned}
$$

We denote the set of labels occurring in a labeled program P by $\overline{l}(P)$.

The main challenge of case lifting is that the freshly introduced functions need to capture the full scope of the case branches. The possible problem is illustrated by the following example.

Example 4.1.6 *Consider the definition of the function* `zipWith`:

```
zipWith f []      _       = []
zipWith f _       []      = []
zipWith f (x:xs) (y:ys)   = f x y : zipWith f xs ys
```

With case expressions the function is expressed like this:

```
zipWith f xs ys = case xs of
                    []
                    (x:xs')   case ys of
                                []
                                (y:ys')   f x y : zipWith f xs' ys'
```

Lifting the nested case results in the following definition.

```
zipWith f xs ys = case xs of
                    []
                    (x:xs')   zipWith_1 f x xs' ys

zipWith_1 f x xs' z = case z of
                        []
                        (y:ys')   f x y : zipWith f xs' ys'
```

Note, that for the transformation all variables occurring free in the nested case expression have to be collected. We do so in order of textual appearance. Note also that while collecting we have to eliminate the double occurrence of the variable `f` *because a definition with a left-hand side* `zipWith_1 ys f x f xs'` *would be invalid by the definition of programs. The final thing to note is that the variable at the argument position of the case (here* `ys`*) is added as the last argument*

of the newly introduced function. The function's definition introduces a fresh
variable at this position. This detail is due to the fact that the variable might
also appear in the case branches.

Definition 4.1.7 (Sequence of Unbound Variables)
Let e be an expression. The sequence of unbound variables occurring in e apart
from $\overline{x_n}$, denoted by $uv_{\overline{x_n}}(e)$ is defined as follows.

$$uv_{\overline{x_n}}(x) = \begin{cases} \varepsilon & , \text{if } x \in \{\overline{x_n}\} \\ x & , \text{otherwise} \end{cases}$$

$$uv_{\overline{x_n}}(s(\overline{e_n})) = nub(\overline{uv_{\overline{x_n}}(e_1),\ldots,uv_{\overline{x_n}}(e_n)})$$

$$uv_{\overline{x_n}}((f)case^l\ x\ of\ \{\overline{p_k \to e_k}\}) = nub(uv_{\overline{x_n}}(x), \overline{uv_{V_k}(e_k)})$$
$$\text{where } V_i = \overline{x_n}, uv\ (p_i)$$

$$uv_{\overline{x_n}}(let\ \{\overline{y_k = e_k}\}\ in\ e) = nub(\overline{uv_{\overline{x_n},\overline{y_k}}(e_k)}, uv_{\overline{x_n},\overline{y_k}}(e))$$

$$uv_{\overline{x_n}}(e_1\ ?\ e_2) = nub(uv_{\overline{x_n}}(e_1), uv_{\overline{x_n}}(e_2))$$

where $nub(\cdot)$ removes all duplicates from a given sequence, keeping the first.

Using Definition 4.1.7 we can now formalize the transformation for case
lifting. We will define how to lift just a single case expression. When we have
shown that this single lifting results in an equivalent program a simple induction
shows that all nested cases can be eliminated in this way.

Definition 4.1.8 (Lifting) Let   be a signature, L a set of labels for   and
$l \in L$. Then

$$lift_l(x) = x$$
$$lift_l(s(\overline{e_n})) = s(\overline{lift_l(e_n)})$$
$$lift_l((f)case^l\ x\ of\ \{\overline{p_k \to e_k}\}) = l(\overline{uv_{uv\ (p_k)}(e_k)}, x)$$
$$lift_l((f)case^{l'}\ x\ of\ \{\overline{p_k \to e_k}\}) = (f)case^{l'}\ x\ of\ \{\overline{p_k \to lift_l(e_k)}\}, \text{ if } l' \neq l$$
$$lift_l(let\ \{\overline{y_k = e_k}\}\ in\ e) = let\ \{\overline{y_k = lift_l(e_k)}\}\ in\ lift_l(e)$$
$$lift_l(e_1\ ?\ e_2) = lift_l(e_1)\ ?\ lift_l(e_2)$$

$$lift_l(\ ) = \{(x, lift_l(e)) \mid (x, e) \in\ \}$$

$$lift_l(\ :\ e) = lift_l(\ ) :\ lift_l(e)$$

Let $P = \overline{l_n = r_n}$ be a labeled program and $l \in \bar{l}(P)$. Then the lifted program
$lift_l(P)$ is defined by $\overline{l_n = lift_l(r_n)}$ together with the rule

$$l(\overline{uv_{uv\ (p_k)}(e_k)}, y) = case\ y\ of\ \{\overline{p_k \to e_k}\}$$

where y fresh whenever the expression $(f)case^l\ x\ of\ \{\overline{p_k \to e_k}\}$ occurs in some
rule of P.

We have to make sure that programs transformed in this way are again
syntactically correct programs.

4.1. CASE LIFTING

Proposition 4.1.9 *Let Σ be a signature, L a set of labels for Σ and $1 \in$ L. Furthermore let P be a program over Σ containing the expression $e = $ (f)case^l x of $\{\overline{p_k \to e_k}\}$ in some rule. Then $lift_l(P)$ is a program over signature $\Sigma \cup \{1\}$ such that $1 \in F_\Sigma$ and $1 \in \Sigma^{(n+1)}$ where $\overline{x_n} = uv_{uv\ (p_k)}(e_k)$.*

Proof. As e appears in a syntactically correct program, the expression itself is well-formed, and, especially has unique variables. Therefore, we only have to ensure that

a) the left-hand side of the new function $1(\overline{x_n}, x)$ is linear and

b) all $x \in vars(e)$ are either introduced in e or in $\overline{x_n}$, x but not both.

a) holds by definition of $uv_{\overline{x_n}}(\cdot)$ which is defined by $nub(\cdot)$ whenever variables may occur multiple times and x is fresh.
b) can be shown by a simple induction on the structure of the $\overline{e_k}$ noting that all variables introduced in one of the $\overline{e_k}$, say e_i, is excluded from $uv_{uv\ (p_i)}(e_i)$ while all variables introduced in e_i will appear in $uv_{uv\ (p_i)}(e_i)$. □

When interpreting programs as equations it should be intuitively clear that the transformation of lifting cases is correct. Accordingly, the proof of correctness is quite simple.

Lemma 4.1.10 $\Delta : e \Downarrow_3 \Delta' : v$ *in* $lift_l(:\Delta : e) \Downarrow_3 lift_l(\Delta' : v)$ *in* $lift_l(P)$.

Proof.
($\Rightarrow$): Consider an expression of the form

$$flat(\text{case x of } \{\overline{p_k \to e_k}\}) = \text{case x of } \{\overline{p_k \to flat(e_k)}\}$$

that appears in a derivation $\Delta : e \Downarrow_3 \Delta' : v$ (remember that all expressions are flattened before evaluation). Then we can replace all applications of rule (Select) of the form

$$\frac{D_1 \quad D_2}{\Delta : \text{case}^l \text{ x of } \{\overline{p_k \to flat(e_k)}\} \Downarrow_3 \Delta' : v}$$

by the following combination of applications.

$$= \frac{\dfrac{D_1 \quad D_2}{\Delta : \text{case x of } \{\overline{p_k \to flat(e_k)}\} \Downarrow_3 \Delta' : v}}{\dfrac{\Delta : flat(\text{case x of } \{\overline{p_k \to e_k}\}) \Downarrow_3 \Delta' : v}{\Delta : 1(uv_{uv\ (p_k)}(e_k), x) \Downarrow_3 \Delta' : v}}$$

The application of rule (Fun) is valid because by definition the rule

$$1(uv_{uv\ (p_k)}(e_k), x) = \text{case x of } \{\overline{p_k \to e_k}\}$$

is a variant of a rule in $lift_l(P)$.
($\Leftarrow$): In the other direction we can simply drop the application of rule (Fun)

whenever a call to l is unfolded to construct a valid tree directly corresponding to the one above. □

The final result of this section is a simple Corollary of Lemma 4.1.10.

Corollary 4.1.11 *For every program* P *there is an equivalent program such that each rule is of the form* $f(\overline{x_n}, x) = $ case x of $\{\overline{p_k \to e_k}\}$ *such that no* e_i *in* $\{\overline{e_k}\}$ *contains a case expression.*

Proof. First by Proposition 4.1.4 there exists an equivalent program P' such that all case expressions in P' have variable arguments.

Now we make sure that does contain a symbol $c \in C_\Sigma \cap$ $^{(0)}$ (or otherwise introduce a new one to get a new signature). Then we consider if there is a symbol $f \in F_\Sigma \cap$ $^{(n)}$ such that f is defined in P' by the rule $f(\overline{x_n}) = r$ where r is not a case-expression. If such an f exists we can construct a new signature ' by replacing f by an n + 1-ary symbol f and a new program P'' by replacing the rule defining f by

$$f(\overline{x_n}, x) = \text{case x of } \{c \to r\}$$

and replacing all calls $f(\overline{e_n})$ in the program by $f(\overline{e_n}, c)$. The resulting program is equivalent which can be seen by contrasting the derivations

$$\frac{\dfrac{D}{: \ flat(r) \Downarrow_3 \Delta \ : v}}{: \ f(\overline{x_n}) \Downarrow_3 \Delta \ : v}$$

for program P' with the derivation

$$\frac{\dfrac{\cdots}{: \ x \Downarrow_3 \ : c} \quad \dfrac{D}{: \ flat(r) \Downarrow_3 \Delta \ : v}}{\dfrac{: \ \text{case x of } \{c \to flat(r)\} \Downarrow_3 \Delta \ : v}{= \ : \ flat(\text{case x of } \{c \to r\}) \Downarrow_3 \Delta \ : v}}{: \ f(\overline{x_n}, x) \Downarrow_3 \Delta \ : v}$$

in program P''.

Finally a simple induction on the number of nested case expressions in P'' shows the existence of a program P''' of the required form. □

With this result we can replace case-based programs with a more readable version which is closer to original programs.

4.2 Introduction of Uniform Programs

We are now ready to introduce the notion of uniform programs and expressions as shown in Figure 4.1.

4.2. INTRODUCTION OF UNIFORM PROGRAMS

$$
\begin{array}{rcll}
e & ::= & x & \text{(variable } x \in \text{Var)} \\
  & | & c(\overline{e_n}) & \text{(constructor call } c \in C_\Sigma \cap {}^{(n)}) \\
  & | & f(\overline{e_n}) & \text{(function call } c \in F_\Sigma \cap {}^{(n)}) \\
  & | & e_1 \; ? \; e_2 & \text{(disjunction)} \\
  & | & \text{let } \overline{x_n = e_n} \text{ in } e & \text{(let binding } \overline{x_n} \in \text{Var}, n > 0) \\
P & ::= & \overline{D} & \text{(program)} \\
D & ::= & f(\overline{x_n}, c(\overline{y_m})) = e & \text{(declaration, } f \in F_\Sigma \cap {}^{(n+1)} \\
  &   &   & \text{the } \overline{x_n}, \overline{y_m} \text{ are pairwise different,} \\
  &   &   & (vars(e) \setminus uv\,(e)) \cap vars(f(\overline{x},p)) = \emptyset, \\
  &   &   & uv\,(e) \subseteq \{\overline{x_n}, \overline{y_m}\}
\end{array}
$$

Figure 4.1: Uniform expressions and programs

Example 4.2.1 *Reconsider the function* `insert` *from example 1.1.12. It can be redefined with a uniform declaration as:*

```
insert(x,xs,()) = Cons(x,xs) ? insert2(x,xs)

insert2(x,Cons(y,ys)) = Cons(y,insert(x,ys,()))
```

In the following we will simply omit a dummy argument () for the sake of readability and write:

```
insert(x,xs) = Cons(x,xs) ? insert2(x,xs)

insert2(x,Cons(y,ys)) = Cons(y,insert(x,ys))
```

Complex pattern matching also requires the introduction of fresh operations. For example `sorted` *from Example 1.1.18 can be redefined as:*

```
sorted(Nil)        = True
sorted(Cons(m,xs)) = sorted2 m xs

sorted2(m,Nil)        = True
sorted2(m,Cons(n,ns)) = and(leq(m,n),sorted2(n,ns))
```

To achieve matching on the last argument sometimes we need to swap arguments. For example `append` *(Example 1.1.4) is redefined as:*

```
app(xs,ys) = app2(ys,xs)

app2(ys,Nil)        = ys
app2(ys,Cons(x,xs)) = Cons(x,app2(ys,xs))
```

From now on, it will be convenient to treat a program P as a mapping p from function symbols to a sequence of rules. For example we will write p(app) to denote the sequence of length 1 app(xs,ys)=app2(ys,xs) in the context of the program from Example 4.2.1 above.

$$
\begin{array}{ll}
\text{(Val)} & : \mathsf{c}(\overline{x_n}) \Downarrow_5 \; : \; \mathsf{c}(\overline{x_n}) \\[1em]
\text{(Var)} & \dfrac{: \; e \Downarrow_5 \Delta \; : \; v}{[\; x \mapsto e] : x \Downarrow_5 \Delta \; [x \mapsto v] \; : \; v} \\[1em]
\text{(Let)} & \dfrac{[\; \overline{x_k \mapsto e_k}] : e \Downarrow_5 \Delta \; : \; v}{: \; \text{let } \{\overline{x_k = e_k}\} \text{ in } e \Downarrow_5 \Delta \; : \; v} \\[1em]
\text{(Or)} & \dfrac{: \; e_i \Downarrow_5 \Delta \; : \; v}{: \; e_1 \; ? \; e_2 \Downarrow_5 \Delta \; : \; v} \quad \text{where } i \in \{1,2\} \\[1em]
\text{(Match)} & \dfrac{: \; x \Downarrow_5 \Delta \; : \; \mathsf{c}(\overline{y_m}) \quad \Delta \; : \; \mathit{flat}(e) \Downarrow_5 \; : \; v}{: \; \mathtt{f}(\overline{x_n}, x) \Downarrow_5 \; : \; v} \\
& \text{where } \mathtt{f}(\overline{x_n}, \mathsf{c}(\overline{y_m})) = e \in \mathtt{P}
\end{array}
$$

Figure 4.2: Natural Semantics for Uniform Programs

The rules to evaluate uniform expressions in the scope of uniform programs are given in Figure 4.2. With the result of Section 4.1 it is easy to see that for each program in the original sense there is an equivalent uniform program.

Proposition 4.2.2 *For each program in the sense of Section 2.1 there is an equivalent uniform program.*

Proof. By Corollary 4.1.11 we can construct an equivalent program P where each rule is of the form $\mathtt{f}(\overline{x_n}, x) = \text{case } x \text{ of } \{\overline{p_k \to e_k}\}$. For this program we construct a uniform program P' by defining

$$
\begin{aligned}
\mathtt{f}(\overline{x_n}, p_1) &= e_1 \\
&\vdots \\
\mathtt{f}(\overline{x_n}, p_k) &= e_k
\end{aligned}
$$

For these programs contrast the evaluations

$$
= \dfrac{\dfrac{\stackrel{D_1}{: \; x \Downarrow_3 \Delta \; : \; p_i} \quad \stackrel{D_2}{\Delta \; : \; \mathit{flat}(e_i) \Downarrow_3 \; : \; v}}{\dfrac{: \; \text{case } x \text{ of } \{\overline{p_k \to \mathit{flat}(e_k)}\} \Downarrow_3 \; : \; v}{\dfrac{: \; \mathit{flat}(\text{case } x \text{ of } \{\overline{p_k \to e_k}\}) \Downarrow_3 \; : \; v}{: \; \mathtt{f}(\overline{x_n}, x) \Downarrow_3 \; : \; v}}}
$$

and

$$
\dfrac{\stackrel{D_1}{: \; x \Downarrow_5 \Delta \; : \; p_i} \quad \stackrel{D_2}{\Delta \; : \; \mathit{flat}(e_i) \Downarrow_5 \; : \; v}}{: \; \mathtt{f}(\overline{x_n}, x) \Downarrow_5 \; : \; v}
$$

where $\mathtt{f}(\overline{x_n}, p_i) = e_i \in \mathtt{P}'$ by construction. □

4.3. FLAT UNIFORM PROGRAMS

$$\begin{array}{rcll} e & ::= & x & \text{(variable } x \in \text{Var)} \\ & | & s(\overline{x_n}) & (s \in {}^{(n)}) \\ & | & x \mathbin{?} y & \text{(disjunction)} \end{array}$$

Figure 4.3: Flat uniform expressions

4.3 Flat Uniform Programs

Now that we have simplified the structure of programs we can take one further step to simplify expressions with regard to let-bindings. One of the technical difficulties of the framework of natural semantics is the admission of let bindings in the course of evaluation. This unnecessarily distinguishes between heap bindings to be (possibly) made in the future and current heap bindings. With this distinctions constructing a mapping between different evaluations can be cumbersome.

Example 4.3.1 *For example evaluating the four expressions*

```
let z=let x=1,y=2 in (x,y) in (z,z)
let x=1,z=let y=2 in (x,y) in (z,z)
let y=2,z=let x=1 in (x,y) in (z,z)
let x=1,y=2,z=(x,y) in (z,z)
```

results in four different heaps although the intended semantics for all three is the same.

Especially, the above distinction is not relevant with regard to the implementation of functional logic languages. And, as we will see in the next section, omitting let-expressions during evaluation will take the framework a considerable step closer towards other approaches to the operational semantics of functional logic programs. As we will show the superfluous technical burden of let-expressions can be lifted and flat expressions can be restricted to the simple form shown in Figure 4.3. We will refer to the thus defined set of expressions as *FUE* .

The next step towards our goal is to redefine the flattening of expressions such that ?-expressions are also applied to variable arguments, only.

$$\begin{aligned} \mathit{flat}'(x) &= x \\ \mathit{flat}'(s(\overline{e_n})) &= \text{let } \overline{\{y_m = \mathit{flat}'(e'_m)\}} \text{ in } s(\overline{x_n}) \\ &\quad \text{where } (\overline{y_m}, \overline{e'_m}, \overline{x_n}) = \mathit{varArgs}(\overline{e_n}) \\ \mathit{flat}'(e_1 \mathbin{?} e_2) &= \text{let } \overline{\{y_m = e'_m\}} \text{ in } x_1 \mathbin{?} x_2 \\ &\quad \text{where } (\overline{y_m}, \overline{e'_m}, x_1, x_2) = \mathit{varArgs}(e_1, e_2) \\ \mathit{flat}'(\text{let } \overline{\{x_k = e_k\}} \text{ in } e) &= \text{let } \overline{\{x_k = \mathit{flat}'(e_k)\}} \text{ in } \mathit{flat}'(e) \end{aligned}$$

In order to restrict evaluations of uniform programs to flat uniform expressions, we need to redefine the way the calculus accesses the program rules. The idea is that whenever a rule for function symbol f matching a given constructor c is looked up in the program, the right-hand side of that rule is *fully normalized*. This means that all let bindings of that right-hand side are introduced to the heap *at once*. One advantage is that this is similar to what real implementations do, at least closer than the representation by let-expressions. Another advantage is that this way the number of possible heaps is reduced as discussed with Example 4.3.1.

The next proposition introduces the transformation of a flat expression such that all bindings can be introduced to the heap at once.

Proposition 4.3.2 *Let* e *be an expression. Then the repeated application of the following reduction rules to* $\mathit{flat}'(e)$ *has a result denoted by* $\mathit{norm}(e)$.

$$\text{let } \{\overline{x_i = e_i}\} \text{ in let } \{\overline{y_j = e'_j}\} \text{ in } e$$
$$\rightarrow \text{let } \{\overline{x_i = e_i}, \overline{y_j = e'_j}\} \text{ in } e$$

$$\text{let } \{\overline{x_i = e_i}, x = \text{let } \{\overline{y_j = e'_j}\} \text{ in } e, \overline{z_k = e''_k}\} \text{ in } e'$$
$$\rightarrow \text{let } \{\overline{x_i = e_i}, \overline{y_j = e'_j}, x = e, \overline{z_k = e''_k}\} \text{ in } e'$$

A simple induction on the number of let-expressions in the given expressions shows that

a) a repeated application of the rules must finally lead to an expression for which no rule is applicable and

b) that this result is of the form let $\{\overline{z_k = e_k}\}$ in e where e is an expression in the sense above.

With this restricted form of programs it is straight forward to come up with a version of natural semantics which does not have the above problems of distinguishing future from current bindings, cf. Figure 4.4.

4.4 Excursus Term-Graph Rewriting

Before we prove the semantic equivalence of derivations in $\Downarrow_5$ and $\Downarrow_6$, respectively, we will provide some more motivation for this cause. The main advantage of the new concept is that heap entries solely consist of either function or constructor calls. With this derivations can easily be seen as a series of term-graph reductions where the variables identify nodes and these nodes are labeled with constructor and function symbols, respectively.

As a simple example we depict the derivation of (selfEq coin) in the context of the program from Example 1.1.16.

Example 4.4.1 (Term-Graph Rewriting) *The term* (selfEq coin) *can be represented by a graph like this:*

4.4. EXCURSUS TERM-GRAPH REWRITING

$$\text{(Val)} \quad : \mathsf{c}(\overline{x_n}) \Downarrow_6 \; : \mathsf{c}(\overline{x_n})$$

$$\text{(Var)} \quad \dfrac{: e \Downarrow_6 \Delta \; : v}{[\, x \mapsto e] : x \Downarrow_6 \Delta \; [x \mapsto v] : v}$$

$$\text{(Or)} \quad \dfrac{: x_i \Downarrow_6 \Delta \; : v}{: x_1 \, ? \, x_2 \Downarrow_6 \Delta \; : v} \qquad \text{where } i \in \{1,2\}$$

$$\text{(Match)} \quad \dfrac{: x \Downarrow_6 \Delta : \mathsf{c}(\overline{y_m}) \quad \Delta \; [\overline{z_k \mapsto e_k}] : e \Downarrow_6 \; : v}{: \mathtt{f}(\overline{x_n}, x) \Downarrow_6 \; : v}$$
$$\text{where } \mathtt{f}(\overline{x_n}, \mathsf{c}(\overline{y_m})) = e' \in \mathrm{P} \text{ and let } \{\overline{z_k = e_k}\} \text{ in } e = norm(e')$$

Figure 4.4: Evaluating flat uniform programs

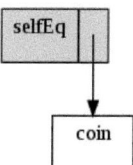

The filling of the node labeled with `selfEq` *denotes that we reduce this node in the next step to:*

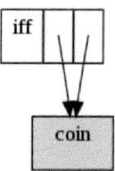

As discussed with Examples 1.1.16 the sharing of the sub term `coin` *is the reason why graphs are employed rather than trees. The next step has to unfold* `coin`.

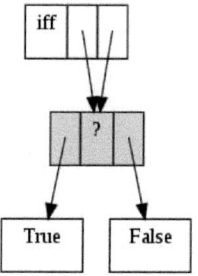

88   CHAPTER 4. UNIFORM PROGRAMS

The reduction of an ?-node is a non-deterministic choice discarding one of the arguments. And the remaining steps are further function unfoldings.

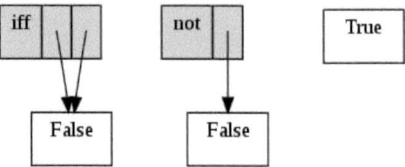

We will su ce ourselves with this informational introduction to term-graph rewriting and refer the interested reader to Echahed [2008]. The interesting fact with regard to this work is that term-graph rewriting has proven to be a convenient tool when investigating properties of functional logic programming, see, for example the works by Antoy et al. [2006b,a], Antoy and Braßel [2007], Antoy and Hanus [2009]. As we will show in the next example the calculus of Figure 4.4 can be seen as operating on term-graphs.

Example 4.4.2 (Encoding the Strategy in a Term-Graph)
In Example 4.4.1 we have seen how term-graph rewriting can be illustrated in general. We will now extend the picture by information about the control and the sequence of variables which are to be evaluated (and updated).[1]

In accordance to the previous example the control is represented by a gray filling. The derivation sequence therefore begins as before:

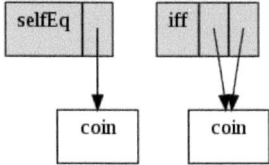

But now a matching on the first argument of iff *is needed and the according variable is put on the control. We depict the descend to this argument by a) moving the control to the node labeled with* coin *and b) marking the position which was demanded.*

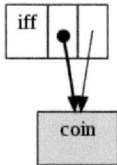

---
[1]For simplicity we will allow function unfolding without matching, e.g., to go directly from coin to True ? False without matching a constant constructor like ().

4.4. EXCURSUS TERM-GRAPH REWRITING

We can now proceed with an unfolding of `coin` *to get:*

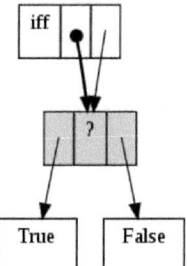

According to the rules before a non-deterministic step can occur, we need to compute the head normal form of one of the arguments. Like in Example 4.4.1 we decide on the second argument.

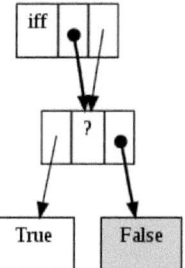

Now we have found a constructor term on the control. We follow back the bold arrow and perform the non-deterministic step on the ? we find at its end.

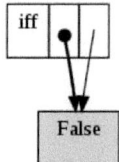

We still have a constructor term on the control and, accordingly, take another step along the bold arrow. We can then perform the unfolding on the function symbol we find at its end.

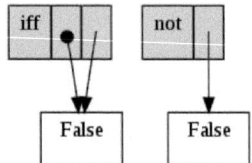

The remaining derivation repeats the illustrated patterns.

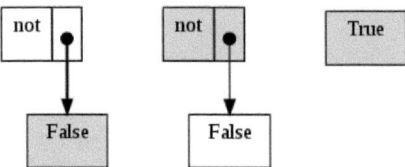

Now we know that we are finished because a constructor is on the control but no bold arrow leads to it.

As we could see description and notation is very dierent for calculi in the style examined here and term-graph rewriting. However, we hope that the reader could see that a close correspondence can be drawn even though the treatment here was rather informal. We turn back to proving the semantic equivalence of the two calculi introduced in this chapter.

4.5 Proving Soundness

This section contains several steps. A first observation is that employing the further flattening of ?-expressions $flat'(\cdot)$ does not influence the resulting values as expected. After that we define the mappings we need to prove that any derivation in $\Downarrow_5$ corresponds to a derivation in $\Downarrow_6$ (Section 4.5.1) and vice versa (Section 4.5.2). Section 4.6 summarizes the results in the terms of the value oriented semantics of Section 2.2.5.

As described, the first step is to note that the new version of flattening does only imply trivial changes in derivations.

Proposition 4.5.1 : $e \Downarrow \Delta : v \ in \ flat(\text{P}) \ i \quad : \quad e \Downarrow \Delta \cup \Delta' : v \ in \ flat'(\text{P})$

Proof. For simplicity suppose that both e_1, e_2 are not variables and contrast the two derivations

$$\frac{: \ e_i \Downarrow_5 \Delta : v}{: \ e_1 \ ? \ e_2 \Downarrow_5 \Delta : v}$$

and

$$\frac{\cup \ '[x_i \mapsto e_i, x_{3-i} \mapsto e_{3-i}] : x_i \Downarrow_6 \Delta \cup \ '[x_i \mapsto v, x_{3-i} \mapsto e_{3-i}] : v}{\cup \ '[x_i \mapsto e_i, x_{3-i} \mapsto e_{3-i}] : x_1 \ ? \ x_2 \Downarrow_6 \Delta \cup \ '[x_i \mapsto v, x_{3-i} \mapsto e_{3-i}] : v}{\cup \ ' : \mathsf{let} \ \{x_1 = e_1, x_2 = e_2\} \ \mathsf{in} \ x_1 \ ? \ x_2 \Downarrow_6 \Delta \cup \ '[x_i \mapsto v, x_{3-i} \mapsto e_{3-i}] : v}$$

4.5. PROVING SOUNDNESS

where $(x_1, x_2, e_1, e_2, x_1, x_2) = varArgs(e_1, e_2)$.
That the resulting heap is indeed of the given form is by definition of rule (Var) and Lemma 4.1.3 which is easily transferable from $\Downarrow_3$ to $\Downarrow_6$. The above consideration constitutes the only interesting case of a simple induction yielding the claim. □

4.5.1 From Uniform to Flat Uniform

In analogy to the family of mappings $\mathsf{gen}(\cdot)$ and $\mathsf{free}(\cdot)$ from the previous chapter we define a mapping from uniform configurations to flat uniform configurations.

Definition 4.5.2 *On Configurations*

$$norm(\,:\ e) = norm()\ \overline{\left[y_n \mapsto e'_n\right]} : e'$$

where let $\overline{\{y_n = e'_n\}}$ in $e' = norm(e)$.
On Heaps

$$norm(\emptyset) = \emptyset$$
$$norm(\,[\ x \mapsto e]) = norm()\ \overline{\left[y_n \mapsto e'_n\right]} [x \mapsto e']$$

where let $\overline{\{y_n = e'_n\}}$ in $e' = norm(e)$.

Likewise in analogy to Propostions 3.2.4 and 3.2.10 in the previous chapter we need a rather technical result about the relation of $norm(\cdot)$ and $flat'(\cdot)$.

Proposition 4.5.3 *For all uniform expressions* e *holds:*

$$norm(flat'(e)) = norm(e)$$

Proof. By definition in Proposition 4.3.2 $norm(e)$ is defined as fixed point of applying reduction rules to $flat'(e)$. A simple induction analogue to that for Proposition 3.2.4 shows that for all uniform expressions e holds $flat'(flat'(e)) = flat'(e)$. □

We are now ready to develop the constructions of derivations in $\Downarrow_6$ from derivations in $\Downarrow_5$.

Lemma 4.5.4 *Let* P *be a uniform program,* a *heap mapping to uniform expressions and* e *be a uniform expression. Then it holds that if* $:\ e \Downarrow_5 \Delta : v$ *in* P *then* $norm(\,:\ e) \Downarrow_6 norm(\Delta : v)$ *in* $norm(P)$.

By Proposition 4.5.1 we can use the mapping $flat'(\cdot)$ instead of $flat()$ in the following proof. In other words we will consider ?-expressions with variables only.

Proof. (Of Lemma 4.5.4) By induction on the structure of the proof tree.
Base cases:
(Val): We have

$$norm(\ :\ c(\overline{x_n}))\Downarrow_6 norm(\ :\ c(\overline{x_n})) = norm()\ :\ c(\overline{x_n})\Downarrow_6 norm()\ :\ c(\overline{x_n})$$

Inductive cases:
(Var): The induction hypothesis in this case is that if $:\ e\Downarrow_5 \Delta\ :\ v$ in P then $norm(\ :\ e)\Downarrow_6 norm(\Delta\ :\ v)$ in $norm(P)$. With this assumption we have to show that if $[\ x \mapsto e]:x\Downarrow_5 \Delta\ [x \mapsto v]:v$ in P then $norm([\ x \mapsto e]:x)\Downarrow_6 norm(\Delta\ [x \mapsto v]:v)$ in $norm(P)$. This claim holds because we have

$$\begin{array}{rl} & norm(\ :\ e)\Downarrow_6 norm(\Delta\ :\ v) \\ = & norm()\ \overline{[y_n \mapsto e'_n]}:e'\Downarrow_6 norm(\Delta\ ):v \\ \hline & norm()\ \overline{[y_n \mapsto e'_n]}[x \mapsto e']:x\Downarrow_6 norm(\Delta\ )[x \mapsto v]:v \\ = & norm([\ x \mapsto e]:x)\Downarrow_6 norm(\Delta\ [x \mapsto v]:v) \end{array}$$

where let $\overline{\{y_n = e'_n\}}$ in $e' = norm(e)$.
(Let): The induction hypothesis in this case is that if $[\ \overline{x_k \mapsto e_k}]:e\Downarrow_5 \Delta\ :v$ in P then $norm([\ \overline{x_k \mapsto e_k}]:e)\Downarrow_6 norm(\Delta\ :v)$ in $norm(P)$. With this assumption we have to show that if $:\text{let}\ \{\overline{x_k = e_k}\}$ in $e\Downarrow_5 \Delta\ :v$ in P then $norm(\ :\text{let}\ \{\overline{x_k = e_k}\}$ in $e)\Downarrow_6 norm(\Delta\ :v)$ in $norm(P)$ because we have

$$\begin{array}{rl} & norm(\ :\ \text{let}\ \{\overline{x_k = e_k}\}\ \text{in}\ e) \\ = & norm()\ \overline{[y_{kn_k} \mapsto e''_{kn_k}}, \overline{x_k \mapsto e''_k}, \overline{y_n \mapsto e'_n}]:e' \\ = & norm([\ \overline{x_k \mapsto e_k}]:e) \end{array}$$

where let $\overline{\{y_{kn_k} = e''_{kn_k}}, \overline{x_k = e''_k}, \overline{y_n \mapsto= e'_n}\}$ in $e' = norm(\text{let}\ \{\overline{x_k = e_k}\}\ \text{in}\ e)$.
(Or): The induction hypothesis in this case is that if $:\ x_i\Downarrow_5\Delta\ :v$ in P then $norm(\ :\ x_i)\Downarrow_6 norm(\Delta\ :v)$ in $norm(P)$ where $i \in \{1,2\}$. With this assumption we have to show that if $:\ x_1\ ?\ x_2\Downarrow_5\Delta\ :v$ in P then $norm(\ :\ x_1\ ?\ x_2)\Downarrow_6 norm(\Delta\ :v)$ in $norm(P)$. This claim holds because we have

$$\begin{array}{rl} & norm(\ :\ x_i)\Downarrow_6 norm(\Delta\ :v) \\ = & norm()\ :\ x_i\Downarrow_6 norm(\Delta\ :v) \\ \hline & norm()\ :\ x_1\ ?\ x_2\Downarrow_6 norm(\Delta\ :v) \\ = & norm(\ :\ x_1\ ?\ x_2)\Downarrow_6 norm(\Delta\ :v) \end{array}$$

(Match): The induction hypothesis in this case is that if $:\ x\Downarrow_5\Delta\ :c(\overline{y_m})$ in P then $norm(\ :\ x)\Downarrow_6 norm(\Delta\ :c(\overline{y_m}))$ in $norm(P)$ and if $\Delta\ :\text{flat}'(e)\Downarrow_5\ :v$ in P then $norm(\Delta\ :\text{flat}'(e))\Downarrow_6 norm(\ :v)$ in $norm(P)$ where $f(\overline{x_n}, c(\overline{y_m})) = e \in P$. With this assumption we have to show that if $f(\overline{x_n}, x)\Downarrow_5\ :v$ in P then $norm(\ :\ f(\overline{x_n}, x))\Downarrow_6 norm(\ :v)$ in $norm(P)$. This claim holds because

4.5. PROVING SOUNDNESS

we have

$$\begin{aligned}
&\quad norm(\sigma : x) \Downarrow_6 norm(\Delta : c(\overline{y_m})) \qquad\qquad norm(\Delta : \text{flat}'(e)) \Downarrow_6 norm(\sigma' : v) \\
&= norm(\sigma) : x \Downarrow_6 norm(\Delta) : c(\overline{y_m}) \quad = \quad norm(\Delta) \overline{[y_n \mapsto e'_n]} : e' \Downarrow_6 norm(\sigma' : v) \\
&\qquad\qquad\qquad norm(\sigma) : f(\overline{x_n}, x) \Downarrow_6 norm(\sigma' : v) \\
&\qquad\qquad = norm(\sigma : f(\overline{x_n}, x)) \Downarrow_6 norm(\sigma' : v)
\end{aligned}$$

where let $\overline{\{y_n = e'_n\}}$ in $e' = norm(e) = norm(\text{flat}'(e))$ by Proposition 4.5.3. □

In the next section we show how to construct derivations for uniform expressions from derivations employing flat uniform expressions.

4.5.2 From Flat Uniform to Uniform

The transformation examined in this chapter basically compresses derivations in the way that the heap updates of several steps in the $\Downarrow_5$-calculus are done in one step in $\Downarrow_6$-derivations. Therefore, we need an auxiliary result to see that a group of $\Downarrow_5$-steps for $\text{flat}'(e)$ arrives to a result comparable to the heap update of an application of (Match) in $\Downarrow_6$.

Proposition 4.5.5 *Let* $norm(\Gamma' : e') = \Gamma : e$ *where* e' *is a flat expression. Then in any derivation for a statement* $\Gamma' : e' \Downarrow_5 \Delta : v$ *we have that* $\Gamma' : e'$ *depends on* $\Gamma'' : e$ *such that* $norm(\Gamma'') = \Gamma$.

Proof. We define the body-let depth $bld(e)$ of an expression e as

$$bld(e) = \begin{cases} 1 + bld(e') & \text{, if } e = \text{let } \overline{\{x_k = e_k\}} \text{ in } e' \\ 0 & \text{, otherwise} \end{cases}$$

and proof the claim by induction on $bld(e')$.

Base Case, $bld(e') = 0$: In this case we have by definition $norm(\Gamma' : e') = norm(\Gamma') : e'$ which by assumption is equal to $\Gamma : e$. Therefore we can choose $\Gamma'' := \Gamma'$.

Inductive Case, $bld(e') = n + 1$: In this case we have $e' = \text{let } \overline{\{x_k = e_k\}}$ in e'' where $bld(e'') = n$. Therefore we can construct by induction hypothesis

$$\frac{\Gamma'\overline{[x_k \mapsto e_k]} : e'' \Downarrow_5 \Delta : v}{\Gamma' : \text{let } \overline{\{x_k = e_k\}} \text{ in } e'' \Downarrow_5 \Delta : v}$$

such that $\Gamma'\overline{[x_k \mapsto e_k]} : e'' \prec \Gamma'' : e$ and $norm(\Gamma'') = \Gamma$ for which we have

$$\begin{aligned}
&\Gamma : e &&\text{by assumption} \\
&= norm(\Gamma' : \text{let } \overline{\{x_k = e_k\}} \text{ in } e) &&\text{def } norm(\cdot) \\
&= norm(\Gamma') \overline{[y_{kn_k} \mapsto e''_{kn_k}]}, \overline{x_k \mapsto e''_k}, \overline{y_n \mapsto e'_n}] : e' &&\text{def } norm(\cdot) \\
&= norm(\Gamma'\overline{[x_k \mapsto e_k]} : e)
\end{aligned}$$

where let $\overline{\{y_{kn_k} = e''_{kn_k}\}}, \overline{x_k = e''_k}, \overline{y_n \mapsto = e'_n}\}$ in $e' = norm(\text{let } \overline{\{x_k = e_k\}}$ in $e)$. □

With this auxiliary result we can now turn to the construction of $\Downarrow_5$ derivations from derivations in the $\Downarrow_6$-calculus.

Lemma 4.5.6 *if* $\sigma : e \Downarrow_6 \Delta : v$ *then for any* $\sigma' : e'$ *with* $norm(\sigma' : e') = \sigma : e$ *there exists a* Δ' *with* $norm(\Delta') = \Delta$ *such that* $\sigma' : e' \Downarrow_5 \Delta' : v$

Proof. (Of Lemma 4.5.6) By induction on the structure of the proof tree.
Base cases:
(Val): We have

$$\frac{\sigma'' : c(\overline{x_n}) \Downarrow_5 \sigma'' : c(\overline{x_n})}{\sigma' : e' \Downarrow_5 \sigma'' : c(\overline{x_n})} \ldots \text{by Proposition 4.5.5}$$

Inductive cases:
(Var): The induction hypothesis in this case is that if $\sigma : e \Downarrow_6 \Delta : v$ then for any $\sigma' : e'$ with $norm(\sigma' : e') = \sigma : e$ there exists a Δ' with $norm(\Delta') = \Delta$ such that $\sigma' : e' \Downarrow_5 \Delta' : v$. With this assumption we have to show that if $\sigma[x \mapsto e] : x \Downarrow_6 \Delta[x \mapsto v] : v$ then for any $\sigma'[x \mapsto e'] : x$ with $norm(\sigma'[x \mapsto e'] : x) = \sigma[x \mapsto e] : x$ there exists a $\Delta'[x \mapsto v]$ with $norm(\Delta'[x \mapsto v]) = \Delta[x \mapsto v]$ such that $\sigma'[x \mapsto e'] : x \Downarrow_5 \Delta'[x \mapsto v] : v$. This claim holds because we have the vailidity of the construction

$$\frac{\sigma'' : e'' \Downarrow_5 \Delta'' : v}{\sigma''[x \mapsto e''] : x \Downarrow_5 \Delta''[x \mapsto v] : v} \ldots \text{by Proposition 4.5.5}$$
$$\sigma' : e' \Downarrow_5 \Delta''[x \mapsto v] : v$$

The assumption $norm(\sigma''[x \mapsto e'']) = \sigma[x \mapsto e]$ implies that $norm(\sigma'' : e'') = \sigma : e$ and, therefore, the construction is valid by induction hypothesis. Moreover, for the resulting heap we have $norm(\Delta''[x \mapsto v]) = norm(\Delta'')[x \mapsto v] = \Delta[x \mapsto v]$ as required.

(Or): The induction hypothesis in this case is that if $\sigma : x_i \Downarrow_6 \Delta : v$ then for any $\sigma' : x_i$ with $norm(\sigma' : x_i) = \sigma : x_i$ there exists a Δ' with $norm(\Delta') = \Delta$ such that $\sigma' : x_i \Downarrow_5 \Delta' : v$ where $i \in \{1,2\}$. With this assumption we have to show that if $\sigma : x_1 \text{ ? } x_2 \Downarrow_6 \Delta : v$ then for any $\sigma' : x_1 \text{ ? } x_2$ with $norm(\sigma' : x_1 \text{ ? } x_2) = \sigma : x_1 \text{ ? } x_2$ there exists a Δ' with $norm(\Delta') = \Delta$ such that $\sigma' : x_1 \text{ ? } x_2 \Downarrow_5 \Delta' : v$. This claim holds because we have the vailidity of the construction

$$\frac{\sigma'' : x_i \Downarrow_5 \Delta'' : v}{\sigma'' : x_1 \text{ ? } x_2 \Downarrow_5 \Delta'' : v} \ldots \text{by Proposition 4.5.5}$$
$$\sigma' : e' \Downarrow_5 \Delta'' : v$$

(Match): The induction hypothesis in this case is that if $\sigma : x \Downarrow_6 \Delta : c(\overline{y_m})$ then for any $\sigma' : x$ with $norm(\sigma' : x) = \sigma : x$ there exists a Δ' with $norm(\Delta') = \Delta$ such that $\sigma' : x \Downarrow_5 \Delta' : c(\overline{y_m})$ and if $\Delta\left[\overline{z_k \mapsto e_k}\right] : e \Downarrow_6 \Theta : v$ then for any $\Delta'\left[\overline{z_k \mapsto e'_k}\right] : e'$ with $norm(\Delta'\left[\overline{z_k \mapsto e'_k}\right] : e') = \Delta\left[\overline{z_k \mapsto e_k}\right] : e$ there exists a Θ' with $norm(\Theta') = \Theta$ such that $\Delta'\left[\overline{z_k \mapsto e'_k}\right] : e' \Downarrow_5 \Theta' : v$ where $f(\overline{x_n}, c(\overline{y_m})) = e' \in P$ and let $\{\overline{z_k = e_k}\}$ in $e = norm(e')$. With this assumption

4.6. SUMMARY

we have to show that if : $f(\overline{x_n}, x) \Downarrow_6$: v then for any Δ' : $f(\overline{x_n}, x)$ with $norm(\Delta' : f(\overline{x_n}, x)) = \Delta$: $f(\overline{x_n}, x)$ there exists a Δ' with $norm(\Delta') = \Delta$ such that $\Delta' : f(\overline{x_n}, x) \Downarrow_5 \Delta' : v$. This claim holds because we have

$$\cfrac{\Delta'' : x \Downarrow_5 \Delta''' : c(\overline{y_m}) \quad \cfrac{\cfrac{\Delta''' \left[z_k \mapsto e''_k \right] : e'' \Downarrow_5 \Delta'''' : v}{\Delta''' : \text{flat}'(e) \Downarrow_5 \Delta'''' : v} \text{... by Proposition 4.5.5}}{\cfrac{\Delta'' : f(\overline{x_n}, x) \Downarrow_5 \Delta'''' : v}{\Delta' : e' \Downarrow_5 \Delta'''' : v} \text{... by Proposition 4.5.5}}$$

As we have the equation $norm(\Delta''' : \text{flat}'(e)) = \Delta \left[z_k \mapsto e_k \right]$: e the construction is correct by induction hypothesis. □

4.6 Summary

In this chapter we have introduced a dierent form for programs which, in our opinion, proves to be more readable. In consequence we were able to simplify the syntactic structure of expressions which occur during evaluation (cf. Figure 4.3) and could reduce the calculus to four rules (cf. Figure 4.4). In addition we have given some more motivation by illustrating the relation to term-graph rewriting in Section 4.4. In this section we will summarize the obtained results in one comprehensive theorem which is formulated in the terms of the value oriented semantics of Section 2.3.

In the course of this chapter we have changed the syntax of expressions. Accordingly we need to adjust the definition of the value oriented semantics.

Definition 4.6.1

$$\llbracket e \rrbracket_6^P := \{ c(\overline{*(x_n)}) \mid \emptyset \left[\overline{x_k \mapsto e_k} \right] : e' \Downarrow_6 \Delta : c(\overline{x_n}) \}$$

where let $\{ \overline{x_k = e_k} \}$ in $e' = norm(e)$

Theorem 2

$$\llbracket e \rrbracket_3^P = \llbracket e \rrbracket_6^{\text{uf}(P)}$$

where

- $vc(P)$ *is the program* P *with* case-expressions *restricted to variable arguments (Proposition 4.1.4),*

- $\text{lift}_{\overline{1}(P')}(P')$ *is the program* P' *with all labeled* case-expressions *lifted (Corollary 4.1.11),*

- $uni(P'')$ *is the program* P'' *with all* case-expressions *replaced by calls to functions with matching (Proposition 4.2.2), and finally,*

CHAPTER 4. UNIFORM PROGRAMS

- $uf(\mathtt{P})$ *is an abbreviation for* $uni(lift_{\overline{1}(vc(P))}(vc(\mathtt{P})))$

In the development towards the calculus for flat uniform programs we have introduced several small transformations: restricting case-expressions to variable arguments (Proposition 4.1.4), then lifting nested case-expressions to new functions (Corollary 4.1.11), replacing case-expressions altogether by a call to the new function in a different calculus (Proposition 4.2.2), and, finally, also restricting ?-expressions to variable arguments (Proposition 4.5.1). When expressions are evaluated in the context of programs transformed in these ways the resulting heaps are changed. For example, there are more bindings in the heap when case- and ?-expressions are restricted to variable arguments and there are no case-expressions when these are replaced by calls to matching functions. The important point to note, however, is that the value extraction $\Delta^*()$ for the resulting heaps Δ, does *not* change for each of the transformations. These are simple consequences of the constructions principles introduced in the according proofs.

- When case- or ?-expressions are restricted to variable arguments, the additional bindings do not influence $\Delta^*()$ as they are only reachable via these case- or ?-expression. By Definition 2.2.5 the value extraction $\Delta^*()$ does not follow the arguments of such expressions.

- When nested case-expressions are lifted to new functions or when case-expressions are replaced by matching functions the resulting heaps may contain the according function symbols and the branches of case-expressions in the heap change. By definition 2.2.5 the value extraction treats case-expressions and function calls in the same way and does not consider the case-branches.

Proof. (Of Theorem 2)

We first show that for any heap and any variable x with $x \in dom() \Leftrightarrow x \in dom(norm())$ holds:

$$^*(x) = norm()\ ^*(x) \qquad (1)$$

We prove this claim by Noetherian induction on the size of , cf. Proposition 3.3.2.

Base Case, $|\ | = 0$ implies $= \emptyset$ as well as $norm() = \emptyset$ and the claim holds trivially.

Inductive Cases, suppose the claim holds for all heaps with a smaller size than . As programs do not contain free variables, the following case distinction is full.

If $x \notin dom()$ then by assumption $x \notin dom(norm())$ and we have $^*(x) = norm()\ ^*(x) = x$.

If $= '[x \mapsto y]$ then $x \neq y$ and we have $^*(x) = '^*(y)$ as well as $norm()\ ^*(x) = norm(\ ')[x \mapsto y]^*(x) = norm(\ ')^*(y)$ and the claim follows by induction hypothesis.

If $= '[x \mapsto c(\overline{x_n})]$ then $^*(x) = c(\overline{'^*(x_n)})$ and we have that $norm()\ ^*(x) =$

4.6. SUMMARY

$norm(\sigma')[x \mapsto c(\overline{x_n})]^*(\sigma x) = c(\overline{norm(\sigma')^*(x_n)})$ and the claim follows by induction hypothesis.

If $\sigma = \sigma'[x \mapsto e]$ where e is a function call, ?-expression or a case-expression then $\sigma^*(x) = x$ and $norm(\sigma)^*(\sigma x) = norm(\sigma')[x \mapsto e]^*(x) = x$

If $\sigma = \sigma'[x \mapsto \text{let } \{\overline{x_k = e_k}\} \text{ in } e]$ then $\sigma^*(x) = \sigma'[\overline{x_k \mapsto e_k}, x \mapsto e]^*(x)$ and $norm(\sigma) = norm(\sigma'[\overline{x_k \mapsto e_k}, x \mapsto e])$ and the claim follows again by induction hypothesis.

By Lemma 4.5.4 we have that $\emptyset : flat'(e) \Downarrow_5 \sigma : c(\overline{x_n})$ in P implies the existence of the derivation $\emptyset[\overline{x_k \mapsto e_k}] : e' \Downarrow_6 norm(\sigma) : c(\overline{x_n})$ such that let $\{\overline{x_k = e_k}\}$ in $e' = norm(e)$. By (1) we can therefore conclude:

$$\{c(\overline{\sigma^*(x_n)}) \mid \emptyset : flat'(e) \Downarrow_5 \sigma : c(\overline{x_n}) \text{ in P }\}$$
$$\subseteq \{c(\overline{\Delta^*(x_n)}) \mid \emptyset[\overline{x_k \mapsto e_k}] : e' \Downarrow_6 \Delta : c(\overline{x_n}) \text{ in P }\} \quad (2)$$

Likewise by Lemma 4.5.6 we have that $\emptyset[\overline{x_k \mapsto e_k}] : e' \Downarrow_6 norm(\sigma) : c(\overline{x_n})$ implies the existence of the derivation $\emptyset : flat'(e) \Downarrow_5 \sigma : c(\overline{x_n})$ in P whenever $norm(e) = \text{let } \{\overline{x_k = e_k}\}$ in e'. Therefore we can conclude for such e:

$$\{c(\overline{\Delta^*(x_n)}) \mid \emptyset[\overline{x_k \mapsto e_k}] : e' \Downarrow_6 \Delta : c(\overline{x_n}) \text{ in P }\}$$
$$\subseteq \{c(\overline{\sigma^*(x_n)}) \mid \emptyset : flat'(e) \Downarrow_5 \sigma : c(\overline{x_n}) \text{ in P }\} \quad (3)$$

With these facts the following equations hold.

$[\![e]\!]_3^P$
$= \{c(\overline{\sigma^*(x_n)}) \mid \emptyset : flat(e) \Downarrow_3 \sigma : c(\overline{x_n}) \text{ in P }\}$ Def 2.2.5
$= \{c(\overline{\sigma'^*(x_n)}) \mid \emptyset : flat(e) \Downarrow_3 \sigma' : c(\overline{x_n}) \text{ in P}' := vc(P)\}$ Prop 4.1.4
$= \{c(\overline{\sigma'^*(x_n)}) \mid \emptyset : flat(e) \Downarrow_3 \sigma' : c(\overline{x_n}) \text{ in P}'' := lift_{\overline{i}(P')}(P')\}$ Cor 4.1.11
$= \{c(\overline{\sigma''^*(x_n)}) \mid \emptyset : flat(e) \Downarrow_5 \sigma'' : c(\overline{x_n}) \text{ in } uni(P'')\}$ Prop 4.2.2
$= \{c(\overline{\sigma'''^*(x_n)}) \mid \emptyset : flat'(e) \Downarrow_5 \sigma''' : c(\overline{x_n}) \text{ in } flat'(uni(P))\}$ Prop 4.5.1
$= [\![e]\!]_5^P$ Def 2.2.5
$\subseteq \{c(\overline{\Delta^*(x_n)}) \mid \emptyset[\overline{x_k \mapsto e_k}] : e' \Downarrow_6 \Delta : c(\overline{x_n}) \text{ in } uf(P)\}$ (2)
$= [\![e]\!]_6^P$ Def 4.6.1
$\subseteq \{c(\overline{\sigma^*(x_n)}) \mid \emptyset : flat'(e) \Downarrow_5 \sigma : c(\overline{x_n}) \text{ in } uf(P)\}$ (3)
$= [\![e]\!]_5^P$ Def 2.2.5

□

The next chapter is dedicated to one of the main results of this work: the transformation of functional logic programs to functional programs preserving many important properties.

Chapter 5

Eliminating Non-Determinism

In Chapter 1 we have introduced lazy functional logic programming. We described that programming languages adhering to this paradigm extend the setting of lazy functional programming by non-deterministic choices, free variables and narrowing. In the previous chapters we have shown that these extensions can be stripped down to the existence of a non-deterministic choice operator (?) and that functional logic programs can be restricted to uniform programs.

In this chapter we will describe how lazy functional logic programs can be transformed to purely functional programs while fully preserving laziness and sharing. There have been many approaches to express logic computations in functional programs. Other existing approaches to simulate logic features in functional languages do, however, either not preserve laziness, i.e., they can only model strict logic programming like in Prolog or they reimplement sharing instead of employing the sharing of the host language. Lazy functional logic programming however, has interesting properties supporting a more declarative style of programming search without sacrificing e ciency.

We will present a technique to reduce all logic extensions to the single problem of generating unique identifiers. The impact of this reduction is a general scheme for compiling functional logic programs to lazy functional programs without side eects, see also the detailed motivation in Section 1.2.1.

One of the design goals is that the purely functional parts of a program should not suer from significant run-time overhead. The content of Sections 5.1 and 5.2 has been published as [Braßel and Fischer, 2008]. Central ideas of Section 5.3 are contained in [Braßel and Huch, 2007a] but have been revised considerably for the new transformation scheme.

5.1 Informal Presentation of the Transformation

The interaction of laziness and logic programming features — especially non-determinism — is not trivial both semantically, as well as operationally, i.e., from the point of view of an implementation. Current lazy functional logic programming languages have agreed on a model coined *call-time choice* that supports the intuition that variables are placeholders for *values* rather than possibly non-deterministic computations. An important consequence of this computational model is that a lazy (call-by-need) computation has the same results as an eager (call-by-value) computation of the same program (if the latter terminates). The according semantic distinctions have been introduced and illustrated in Sections 1.1.1.3 and 1.1.2, especially Section 1.1.2.3.

In this section we describe the problems of translating lazy functional logic programs and informally present the idea behind our solution. We first show that a naive encoding of non-determinism in a functional language either violates call-time choice or looses laziness (Section 5.1.1) and present our approach to correctly implement it (Section 5.1.2).

5.1.1 Naive Functional Encoding of Non-Determinism

In a first attempt, we might consider to represent non-deterministic values using lists [Wadler, 1985] and lift all operations to the list type.

Example 5.1.1 *Reconsider the code of Examples 1.1.3, 1.1.13 and 1.1.16. In the approach of [Wadler, 1985] the program that computes (selfEq coin) would be translated as follows.*

```
goal :: [Bool]
goal = selfEq coin

coin :: [Bool]
coin = [True,False]

not, selfEq :: [Bool]    [Bool]
not bs = [ False | True    bs ] ++
         [ True  | False   bs ]

selfEq bs = iff bs bs

iff :: [Bool]     [Bool]    [Bool]
iff xs ys = [ y | True    xs, y    ys ] ++
            [ y | False   xs, y    not ys ]
```

This translation does not adhere to call-time choice semantics because argument variables of functions denote possibly non-deterministic computations rather than values. For example, the argument bs *of* selfEq *represents all non-deterministic results of this argument and the function* iff *might choose dierent values for each of its arguments. Consequently, the result of evaluating* goal *is*
[True,False,False,True]

5.1. INFORMAL PRESENTATION OF THE TRANSFORMATION 101

which resembles a call-by-name derivation of the corresponding functional logic program rather than call-by-need, cf. Section 1.1.1.3.

In order to model call-time choice, we could translate all functions such that they take deterministic arguments and use the list monad to handle non-determinism.

Example 5.1.2 *The above example would be translated as follows (the definition of* coin *is unchanged):*

```
goal :: [Bool]
goal = do { b     coin; selfEq b }

not, selfEq :: Bool     [Bool]
not True  = return False
not False = return True

selfEq b = iff b b

iff :: Bool    Bool     [Bool]
iff True  b = return b
iff False b = not b
```

Here, the value of goal *is* [True,True] *as in a call-by-value derivation of a functional logic program, i.e., it corresponds to call-time choice.*

Unfortunately, the resulting program is strict, e.g., the call to coin is evaluated before passing its result to the function selfEq. Strictness can lead to unexpected non-termination and performance problems due to unnecessary evaluations. In lazy functional logic programming, unnecessary evaluation often means *unnecessary search*. The consequence may even be exponential overhead which is clearly unacceptable. We have seen in Example 1.1.18 that for programs in generate-and-test style such overhead can be significantly reduced by laziness.

With a naive approach, and also with sophisticated optimizations [Hinze, 2000, Kiselyov, 2005, Naylor et al., 2007], we have the choice between laziness and call-time choice, we cannot obtain both. In the following sections we present a transformation from functional logic to purely functional programs which does not produce monadic programs. Following the original publication of the presented transformation [Braßel and Fischer, 2008] a new approach succeeded in preserving laziness while targeting monadic functional programs [Fischer et al., 2009] with a reimplementation of sharing. We will discuss the dierences to the latter approach in the next chapter.

5.1.2 Combining Laziness and Call-Time Choice

In our approach to translating lazy functional logic programs we do not use lists to represent non-determinism. Instead, we introduce a new constructor Choice :: ID   a   a   a and use it to build trees of non-deterministic values.

Of course, a constructor of this type cannot be defined in Haskell, but in order to keep the description of our transformation as simple as possible, we do not consider types in the following. In an implementation we can introduce dierent choice constructors for every data type, as explained in Chapter 6.

The type ID in the first argument of Choice is an abstract type with the following signature:

```
type ID
instance Eq ID
initID :: ID
leftID, rightID :: ID    ID
```

The functions `leftID` and `rightID` compute unique identifiers from a given identifier and are used to pass unique identifiers to every part of the computation that needs them. In order to ensure that the generated identifiers are indeed unique, the shown functions need to satisfy specific properties:

- `leftID` and `rightID` must not yield the same identifier for any arguments,
- they never yield an identifier equal to `initID`, and
- both functions yield dierent results when given dierent arguments.

More formally, we can state that `leftID` and `rightID` have disjoint images that do not contain `initID`, and are both injective. Id est, that for all $i, j \in$ ID we have

$$\text{initID} \neq \text{leftID}(i) \;\land\; \text{initID} \neq \text{rightID}(i) \tag{5.1}$$

$$\text{leftID}(i) \neq \text{rightID}(j) \tag{5.2}$$

$$\text{leftID}(i) = \text{leftID}(j) \;\lor\; \text{rightID}(i) = \text{rightID}(j) \Rightarrow i = j \tag{5.3}$$

In this chapter we will use variables i, j to denote identifiers rather than natural numbers as we did in the remaining work. The property of the uniqueness of identifiers can be expressed as in the following proposition.

Proposition 5.1.3 *Let* $f_1, \ldots, f_n$ *and* $g_1, \ldots, g_n$ *be sequences of functions such that* $f_k, g \in \{\text{leftID}, \text{rightID}\}$ *for all* $1 \leq k \leq n$ *and* $1 \leq l \leq m$. *Then* $f_n \circ \ldots \circ f_1(\text{initID}) = g_m \circ \ldots \circ g_1(\text{initID})$ *implies* $n = m$ *and* $f_k = g_k$ *for all* $1 \leq k \leq n$.

Proof. Suppose there exist n, m such that there are sequences $f_1, \ldots, f_n$ and $g_1, \ldots, g_n$ with $f_n \circ \ldots \circ f_1(\text{initID}) = g_m \circ \ldots \circ g_1(\text{initID})$ and $n \neq m$ or $f_k \neq g_k$ for some $1 \leq k \leq n$. Then without loss of generality we can choose n to be the smallest such number. Now there are three cases:

1. $n > 0, f_n \neq g_m$:
   In this case there must be identifiers i, j such that $\text{leftID}(i) = \text{rightID}(j)$ contradicting 5.2.

5.1. INFORMAL PRESENTATION OF THE TRANSFORMATION

2. $n > 0, f_n = g_m$:
   By property 5.3 we have $f_{n-1}, \ldots, f_1(\texttt{initID}) = g_{m-1}, \ldots, g_1(\texttt{initID})$. Therefore, n would not be smallest.

3. $n = 0$:
   In this case there must be an identifier i such that $g_m(i) = \texttt{initID}$. Therefore we either have $\texttt{leftID}(i) = \texttt{initID}$ or $\texttt{rightID}(i) = \texttt{initID}$ contradicting Property 5.1.

□

Like in the above proposition we are only interested in those identifiers which can be generated by finite sequences of applications of the functions $\texttt{leftID}$ and $\texttt{rightID}$ to the identifier $\texttt{initID}$.

$$\texttt{ID} := \{f_n \circ \ldots \circ f_1(\texttt{initID}) \mid \overline{f_n} \in \{\texttt{leftID}, \texttt{rightID}\}, n \in \mathbb{N}_0\}$$

In other words a standard model of identifiers would be the objects freely generated from the signature $\{\texttt{initID}^0, \texttt{leftID}^1, \texttt{rightID}^1\}$.

A possible implementation of identifiers uses positive integers of unbounded size:

```
type ID = Integer   -- positive

initID :: ID
initID = 1

leftID, rightID :: ID    ID
leftID  i = 2 i
rightID i = 2 i + 1
```

This implementation satisfies the given properties for all positive integers. In fact, the choice of 1 in the definition of $\texttt{initID}$ is arbitrary—any positive integer would suffice. This implementation is not perfect because the generated identifiers grow rapidly and many integers might not be used as identifiers depending on how the functions $\texttt{leftID}$ and $\texttt{rightID}$ are used. However, it is purely functional and serves well as a prototype implementation. There are more efficient implementations [Augustsson et al., 1994] that make selected use of side effects without sacrificing compiler optimizations.

Unique identifiers are crucial in our approach to translate lazy functional logic programs because they allow to detect sharing of non-deterministic choices. If the result of a computation contains occurrences of **Choice** with the same identifier, the same alternative of both choices needs to be taken when computing the (functional logic) *values*[1] of this expression. In order to label non-deterministic choices with unique identifiers, we need to pass them to every position in the program that eventually performs a non-deterministic choice.

---

[1] We define the computation of functional logic values in Section 5.2.1.

Example 5.1.4 *As a first example, we consider the translation of* (selfEq coin) *in our approach:*

```
goal :: ID     Bool
goal i = selfEq (coin i)

coin :: ID     Bool
coin i = Choice i True False

not, selfEq :: Bool     Bool
not True            = False
not False           = True
not (Choice i x y)  = Choice i (not x) (not y)

selfEq b = iff b b

iff :: Bool     Bool     Bool
iff True            z = z
iff False           z = not z
iff (Choice i x y)  z = Choice i (iff x z) (iff y z)
```

We pass an identifier to the operations `goal` and `coin` because they either directly create a `Choice` or call an operation which does. The functions `selfEq`, `iff`, and `not` do not need an additional parameter. We only have to extend their pattern matching to handle choices. If a value constructed by `Choice` is demanded, we return a choice with the same identifier and reapply the function to the dierent alternatives to compute the alternatives of the result. With these definitions (`goal initID`) evaluates to the following result (assuming *initID* yields 1).

    Choice 1 (Choice 1 True False) (Choice 1 False True)

This result can be interpreted as `Choice 1 True True` because for all occurrences of `False` we would need to take once a left branch and once a right branch of a `Choice` labeled with `1`. In our approach, however, choices with the same label are constrained to take the same branch when computing non-deterministic results. The invalid branches of the inner choices are, hence, pruned away. As a result, we obtain call-time choice semantics without sacrificing laziness: `coin` is evaluated by `iff` — not before passing it to `selfEq`. Moreover, because of laziness the computations leading to the invalid results `False` are never evaluated (see Section 5.2.1).

Example 5.1.5 *A more complex example is the translation of* `permute` *(see Examples 1.1.12 and 1.1.18):*

```
permute :: ID    [a]     [a]
permute _ []              = []
permute i (x:xs)          = insert (leftID i) x (permute (rightID i) xs)
permute i (Choice il xs ys) = Choice il (permute i xs) (permute i ys)
```

5.2. FORMAL DEFINITION OF TRANSFORMATION

```
insert :: ID   a   [a]   [a]
insert i x []    = [x]
insert i x (y:ys) =
  Choice i (x:y:ys) (y : insert (rightID i) x ys)
insert i x (Choice il xs ys) =
  Choice il (insert i x xs) (insert i x ys)
```

Both functions take an identifier as additional argument because they either directly create a `Choice` *or call an operation which does and both functions make use of* `leftID` *and* `rightID` *to generate new identifiers that are passed down to sub computations.*

5.2 Formal Definition of Transformation

For the following, assume a given uniform program P over a signature . We assume that does not contain any of those symbols which we want to add as discussed in Section 5.1.2 These symbols are

$$_0 := \{\text{initID}^0, \text{leftID}^1, \text{rightID}^1, \text{Choice}^3, \text{hnf}^2\}$$

where the symbol `hnf` will be introduced in Section 5.2.1. In this section we define how to produce a (purely functional) program P' over a signature '.

One of the design goals of the transformation is that purely functional computations should be as e cient as possible. To achieve this we have to distinguish between purely functional and (potentially) non-deterministic operations. A necessary requirement for an operation to be non-deterministic is that it depends on the operation $?^2$. In other words, it either calls $?^2$ directly or calls a function depending on $?^2$. Formally, the set of non-deterministic operations N ⊆ is the smallest set such that

$$N := \{?^2\} \cup \{f \mid \exists l = r \in p(f) : \exists g(\overline{e_n}) \in sub(r) : g^n \in N \}$$

All elements of N are extended by an extra argument to form the new signature
' := $_{\text{ID}}$ ∪ {Choice^3} ∪   \ N ∪ {f^{n+1} | f^n ∈ N }.

One of the main concepts discussed in Section 5.1.2 is that each non-deterministic sub expression is extended by a *unique identifier* generated by `leftID`, `rightID` and `initID`. In the following it will be necessary to distinguish expressions evaluating to identifiers and expressions (possibly) evaluating to a value in the sense of the original program P.

Definition 5.2.1 *Let Var$_{\text{ID}}$ be an enumerable set of variables disjoint from Var and let* $_{\text{ID}}$ *be the signature defined as*

$$_{\text{ID}} := \{\text{initID}^0, \text{leftID}^1, \text{rightID}^1\}$$

Then the well typed expressions for the transformed version of program P are

106   CHAPTER 5. ELIMINATING NON-DETERMINISM

defined by the following production rules.

$$
\begin{align*}
\mathtt{i} ::= \ & \mathtt{x} & & \mathtt{x} \in \mathit{Var}_{\mathtt{ID}} \\
\mid \ & \mathtt{initID} \mid \mathtt{leftID}(\mathtt{i}) \mid \mathtt{rightID}(\mathtt{i}) \\
\mid \ & \mathtt{let}\ \{\overline{\mathtt{x}_n = \mathtt{i}_n}\}\ \mathtt{in}\ \mathtt{i} & & \overline{\mathtt{x}_n} \in \mathit{Var}_{\mathtt{ID}} \in \mathit{Var} \\
\mathtt{e} ::= \ & \mathtt{x} & & \mathtt{x} \in \mathit{Var} \\
\mid \ & \mathtt{s}(\overline{\mathtt{e}_n}) & & \mathtt{s} \in {}^{(n)}, \mathtt{s} \notin \mathrm{N} \\
\mid \ & \mathtt{f}(\mathtt{i}, \overline{\mathtt{e}_n}) & & \mathtt{f} \in {}^{(n)}, \mathtt{f} \in \mathrm{N} \\
\mid \ & ?(\mathtt{i}, \mathtt{e}_1, \mathtt{e}_2) \\
\mid \ & \mathtt{Choice}(\mathtt{i}, \mathtt{e}_1, \mathtt{e}_2) \\
\mid \ & \mathtt{let}\ \{\overline{\mathtt{x}_n = \mathtt{i}_n}, \overline{\mathtt{y}_m = \mathtt{e}_m}\}\ \mathtt{in}\ \mathtt{e} & & \overline{\mathtt{x}_n} \in \mathit{Var}_{\mathtt{ID}}, \overline{\mathtt{y}_m} \in \mathit{Var}
\end{align*}
$$

The set of terms produced by the rules for i *is called* ID-expressions *and will be denoted by* $E_{\mathtt{ID}}$. *The set of terms produced by the rules for* e *are called program expressions or* P-expressions *for short and will be denoted by* E_P.

In accordance to the above definition a well typed heap   is a mapping from $\mathit{Var} \cup \mathit{Var}_{\mathtt{ID}}$ to $E_P \cup E_{\mathtt{ID}}$ such that (x, e) $\in$, e $\in E_P$ imply x $\in \mathit{Var}$ and (y, i) $\in$, i$\in E_{\mathtt{ID}}$ imply y $\in \mathit{Var}_{\mathtt{ID}}$.

Without giving a new formal definition, we assume from now on that the transformations $\mathit{flat}'(\cdot)$ and $\mathit{norm}(\cdot)$ yield well typed results. This means in particular that any fresh variable introduced for an expression in E_P is in Var and any fresh variable introduced for an ID-expression is taken from $\mathit{Var}_{\mathtt{ID}}$.

Let i $\in E_{\mathtt{ID}}$ be an ID-expression. Then the function $\mathit{fresh}_n(\mathtt{i})$ generates an expression yielding a dierent identifier from   i for each natural number n. This is achieved by adding n times the function rightID and finally leftID.[2]

$$\mathit{fresh}_n(\mathtt{i}) = \mathtt{leftID}(\mathtt{rightID}^n(\mathtt{i}))$$

It is easy to see, given the properties of leftID, rightID, that for arbitrary n the identifiers $\mathit{fresh}_1(\mathtt{i}), \ldots, \mathit{fresh}_n(\mathtt{i})$ are pairwise dierent and also dierent from i, cf. Proposition 5.1.3. We need, however, a stronger property of $\mathit{fresh}_n(\mathtt{i})$, namely that also all identifiers generated by applying leftID, rightID to any of the $\overline{\mathit{fresh}_n(\mathtt{i})}$ will be dierent from any other. This is also implied by Proposition 5.1.3 but less obvious. We therefore define some convenient notation and prove this property explicitly.

Definition 5.2.2 *Let* i, j *be identifiers. We say that* j *is generated from* i, *in symbols* i $\preceq$ j, *i there is a finite sequence of functions* $\overline{\mathtt{f}_n} \in \{\mathtt{leftID}, \mathtt{rightID}\}$ *such that* $\mathtt{f}_n \circ \ldots \circ \mathtt{f}_1(\mathtt{i}) = \mathtt{j}$. *We say that* i *is independent from* j, *in symbols* i $\parallel$ j, *i we have neither* i $\preceq$ j *nor* j $\preceq$ i. *By* $\prec$ *we define the strict part of* $\preceq$, *i.e.* i $\prec$ j i   i $\preceq$ j *and* i $\neq$ j.

With this notation we can see that ID = $\{\mathtt{i} \mid \mathtt{initID} \preceq \mathtt{i}\}$. More importantly, we have:

---

[2] Note that we are quite wasteful in the generation of identifiers. We do so for simplicity; a transformation generating a minimal amount of calls to leftID and rightID is straightforward by counting non-deterministic sub terms.

5.2. FORMAL DEFINITION OF TRANSFORMATION

Proposition 5.2.3

a) The relation $\preceq$ is a partial order.

b) For any $i, i', j, j' \in \texttt{ID}$ we have that $i \parallel j$ and $i \preceq i'$ and $j \preceq j'$ imply $i' \parallel j'$.

Proof. a) A partial order is reflexive, transitive and antisymmetric. The relation $\preceq$ is reflexive because we can take the empty sequence of functions, i.e., $\overline{f_n}$ where n = 0, to generate any i from i. It is transitive as for any $i \preceq j$ and $j \preceq k$ we have that $j = f_n \circ \ldots \circ f_1(i)$ and $g_m \circ \ldots \circ g_1(j) = k$ we have $g_m \circ \ldots \circ g_1 \circ f_n \circ \ldots \circ f_1(i) = k$ and, thus, $i \preceq k$. Finally, we have to show that $\preceq$ is antisymmetric, i.e., for all i, j holds that $i \preceq j$ and $j \preceq i$ together imply $i = j$: By definition we have $\overline{f_n}, \overline{g_m} \in \{\texttt{leftID}, \texttt{rightID}\}$ such that $i = f_n \circ \ldots \circ f_1(\texttt{initID})$ and $j = g_m \circ \ldots \circ g_1(\texttt{initID})$. Furthermore, by definition of $\preceq$ we have $\overline{f'_{n'}}, \overline{g'_{m'}}$ such that

$$f'_{n'} \circ \ldots \circ f'_1 \circ f_n \circ \ldots \circ f_1(\texttt{initID}) = g_m \circ \ldots \circ g_1(\texttt{initID})$$
$$g'_{m'} \circ \ldots \circ g'_1 \circ g_m \circ \ldots \circ g_1(\texttt{initID}) = f_n \circ \ldots \circ f_1(\texttt{initID})$$

By Proposition 5.1.3 this implies that we have $\overline{f'_{n'}}, \overline{f_n} = \overline{g_m}$ and $n' + n = m$ as well as $\overline{g'_{m'}}, \overline{g_m} = \overline{f_n}$ and $m' + m = n$. This implies $n' = m' = 0$, $n = m$, $\overline{f_n} = \overline{g_m}$, and, all in all, $i = j$.

b) Suppose we have $i, i', j, j' \in \texttt{ID}$ we have $i \parallel j, i \preceq i', j \preceq j'$ but $i' \not\preceq j'$. Then we have two ways to generate j' from $\texttt{initID}$, namely the sequence of functions generating j' from j from $\texttt{initID}$ and the one generating j' from i' from i from $\texttt{initID}$. By the assumption $i \parallel j$ these sequences must be dierent which contradicts Proposition 5.1.3. □

The next definition covers the transformation of expressions. It adds expressions of type $\texttt{ID}$ to each call to an operation in N. The added expressions are all generated from a given ID-expression $i \in E_{\texttt{ID}}$.

Definition 5.2.4 (Adding Identifiers to Expressions)

$$tr(i, x) = x$$
$$tr(i, \texttt{let } \{\overline{x_n = e_n}\} \texttt{ in } e) = \texttt{let } \{\overline{x_n = tr(i_n, e_n)}\} \texttt{ in } tr(i_{n+1}, e)$$
$$tr(i, s(\overline{e_n})) = \begin{cases} s(\overline{tr(i_n, e_n)}) & , \text{ if } s^n \notin N \\ s(i_{n+1}, \overline{tr(i_n, e_n)}) & , \text{ if } s^n \in N \end{cases}$$

where

$$\overline{i_{n+1}} = \overline{fresh_{n+1}(i)}$$

The transformation ensures that every call to a potentially non-deterministic operation is extended by a unique identifier, as is the content of the next proposition.

Proposition 5.2.5 *Let e be an expression and $i \in Var_{\texttt{ID}}$ be a variable of type $\texttt{ID}$ and let $\{\overline{id_n}\}$ be the set of identifier expressions occurring in $tr(i, e)$. Then* *for any identifier* i *and the substitution* $\sigma = \{\mathtt{i} \mapsto \mathtt{i}\}$ *we have that the identifiers in* $\sigma(id_n)$ *are pairwise independent and each* e_j *occurs not more than once in* $tr(\mathtt{i}, e)$.

Proof. We first remark that for any $n \in \mathbb{N}_0$ we have by construction and Property 5.2.3.b) that $\sigma(\mathtt{i}) \prec \sigma(\mathit{fresh}_n(\mathtt{i}))$ and for any $m \in \mathbb{N}_0$ such that $n \neq m$ we also have $\sigma(\mathit{fresh}_n(\mathtt{i})) \parallel \sigma(\mathit{fresh}_m(\mathtt{i}))$.

We prove by induction on the structure of e that the identifiers $\overline{\sigma(id_n)}$ are pairwise independent, each occurs not more than once and for $\mathtt{j} \in \{\overline{\sigma(id_n)}\}$ we have $\mathtt{i} \prec \mathtt{j}$.

Base Case, $\mathtt{e} = \mathtt{x}$: The claim holds trivially since $\overline{\sigma(id_n)} = \varepsilon$.

Inductive cases,

$\mathtt{e} = \mathtt{let}\ \{\overline{\mathtt{x}_n = \mathtt{e}_n}\}$ in $\mathtt{e'}$: Suppose that the claim holds for all $\overline{\mathtt{e}_n}$ and $\mathtt{e'}$. Then it also holds for let $\{\overline{\mathtt{x}_n = \mathtt{e}_n}\}$ in $\mathtt{e'}$ since by the above remark the $\overline{\sigma(\mathit{fresh}_{n+1}(\mathtt{i}))}$ are all pairwise dierent and Proposition 5.2.3.b) ensures that the same holds for all identifiers generated from them. Moreover, if each appears at most once in the $\overline{\mathtt{e}_n}$ and $\mathtt{e'}$ then they also do in let $\{\overline{\mathtt{x}_n = \mathtt{e}_n}\}$ in $\mathtt{e'}$ as no identifier is introduced.

$\mathtt{e} = \mathtt{s}(\overline{\mathtt{e}_n})$: If $\mathtt{s} \notin \mathtt{N}$ the case is analog to that of let above. For $\mathtt{s} \in \mathtt{N}$ we have in addition that $\sigma(\mathit{fresh}_{n+1}(\mathtt{i}))$ is independent from all of the $\overline{\sigma(\mathit{fresh}_n(\mathtt{i}))}$ and can therefore not appear in any of the $\overline{\sigma(tr(\mathit{eid}, \mathtt{e}_n))}$. □

We are now ready to transform the rules defining an operation $\mathtt{f} \neq \mathtt{?}^2$. Each rule is transformed by an application of $tr(\mathtt{i}, \cdot)$ to both the left and the right-hand side of the rule where $\mathtt{i}$ is a fresh variable not occurring anywhere in p.[3] The definitions are extended by the additional rules to lift the Choice constructor (see Section 5.1.2).

$$tr(\mathtt{i}, \mathtt{p})(\mathtt{f}) := \left\{ \begin{array}{l} \overline{tr(\mathtt{i}, \mathtt{l}_n) = tr(\mathtt{i}, \mathit{flat}(\mathtt{r}_n))}, \\ \mathtt{f}(\overline{\mathtt{x}_m}, \mathtt{Choice}(\mathtt{x}, \mathtt{y}, \mathtt{z})) \\ = \mathtt{Choice}(\mathtt{x}, \mathtt{f}(\overline{\mathtt{x}_m}, \mathtt{y}), \mathtt{f}(\overline{\mathtt{x}_m}, \mathtt{z})) \end{array} \right\}, \quad \begin{array}{l} \mathtt{p}(\mathtt{f}) = \overline{\mathtt{l}_n = \mathtt{r}_n}, \\ \mathtt{f} \in F_\Sigma^{m+1} \end{array}$$

The transformed program is extended by the definitions of the external operations initID, leftID, rightID. Possible implementations were discussed in Section 5.1.2.

Later on the operation $?^2$ will be replaced by $?^3$ which is the only one to introduce the constructor Choice.

$$?(\mathtt{i}, \mathtt{x}, \mathtt{y}) = \mathtt{Choice}(\mathtt{i}, \mathtt{x}, \mathtt{y})$$

---

[3] That the right-hand side is also flattened happens for the purely technical reason to make the soundness prove in Section 5.3 more concise. Flattening does not impose any restriction on programs, as it can be easily seen that an expression can be evaluated in the context of a program P iff it can be evaluated in a flattened version of P. This is because the right-hand side of the program rules are flattened anyway when applying rule (fun) and flattening is idempotent, i.e., *flat*(*flat*(*e*)) = *flat*(*e*).

5.2. FORMAL DEFINITION OF TRANSFORMATION

Before we do so we first give an alternative definition as:

$$?(\texttt{i}, \texttt{x}, \texttt{y}) = \texttt{x} ? \texttt{y}$$

This gives us the chance to put in an intermediate step to show that the addition of identifiers does not influence the overall evaluation. With this intermediate step the complete proof of soundness is easier to comprehend. Accordingly, the next step is to map configurations with identifiers to ones without by simply eliminating every occurrence. This is the aim of the next definition and the following lemma.

Definition 5.2.6

$$\begin{array}{rcll}
noi(\texttt{x}) & = & \texttt{x} & \\
noi(\texttt{s}(\overline{\texttt{x}_n})) & = & \texttt{s}(\overline{\texttt{x}_n}) & \textit{if } \texttt{s} \notin N \\
noi(\texttt{f}(\texttt{x}, \overline{\texttt{x}_n})) & = & \texttt{f}(\overline{\texttt{x}_n}) & \textit{if } \texttt{f} \in N \\
noi(\texttt{x}_1 ? \texttt{x}_2) & = & \texttt{x}_1 ? \texttt{x}_2 & \\[4pt]
noi(\Gamma) & = & \{(\texttt{x}, noi(e)) \mid (\texttt{x}, e) \in \Gamma, \texttt{x} \notin Var_{\texttt{ID}}\} & \\[4pt]
noi(\Gamma : e) & = & noi(\Gamma) : noi(e) &
\end{array}$$

Lemma 5.2.7 *Let* P *be the transformed version of a program* P$'$ *and* $e \in E_P$ *be a* P *-expression and* Γ *a well typed heap. Then we have if* $\Gamma : e \Downarrow_6 \Delta : v$ *in* P *then* $noi(\Gamma : e) \Downarrow_6 noi(\Delta : v)$ *in* P$'$.

Proof. (Of Lemma 5.2.7) By induction on the structure of the proof tree.
Base cases:
(Val): We have

$$noi(\Gamma : c(\overline{\texttt{x}_n})) \Downarrow_6 noi(\Gamma : c(\overline{\texttt{x}_n})) = noi(\Gamma) : c(\overline{\texttt{x}_n}) \Downarrow_6 noi(\Gamma) : c(\overline{\texttt{x}_n})$$

Inductive cases:
(Var): The induction hypothesis in this case is that if $\Gamma : e \Downarrow_6 \Delta : v$ in P then $noi(\Gamma : e) \Downarrow_6 noi(\Delta : v)$ in P$'$. With this assumption we have to show that if $\Gamma[\texttt{x} \mapsto e] : \texttt{x} \Downarrow_6 \Delta[\texttt{x} \mapsto v] : v$ in P then $noi(\Gamma[\texttt{x} \mapsto e] : \texttt{x}) \Downarrow_6 noi(\Delta[\texttt{x} \mapsto v] : v)$ in P$'$. This claim holds because we have

$$\begin{array}{rl}
& noi(\Gamma : e) \Downarrow_6 noi(\Delta : v) \\
= & noi(\Gamma) : noi(e) \Downarrow_6 noi(\Delta) : v \\ \hline
& noi(\Gamma)[\texttt{x} \mapsto noi(e)] : \texttt{x} \Downarrow_6 noi(\Delta)[\texttt{x} \mapsto v] : v \\
= & noi(\Gamma[\texttt{x} \mapsto e] : \texttt{x}) \Downarrow_6 noi(\Delta[\texttt{x} \mapsto v] : v)
\end{array}$$

as by assumption $\texttt{x} \in E_P$ and $\Gamma[\texttt{x} \mapsto e]$ is well typed. Therefore e must also be in E_P.
(Or): The induction hypothesis in this case is that if $\Gamma : \texttt{x}_i \Downarrow_6 \Delta : v$ in P then $noi(\Gamma : \texttt{x}_i) \Downarrow_6 noi(\Delta : v)$ in P$'$ where $\texttt{i} \in \{1, 2\}$. With this assumption we have

to show that if Γ : x_1 ? $x_2 \Downarrow_6 \Delta$: v in P then $noi(\Gamma$: x_1 ? $x_2) \Downarrow_6 noi(\Delta$: v) in P′. This claim holds because we have

$$\begin{array}{c} noi(\Gamma : x_i) \Downarrow_6 noi(\Delta : v) \\ = noi(\Gamma) : x_i \Downarrow_6 noi(\Delta : v) \\ \hline noi(\Gamma) : x_1 \text{ ? } x_2 \Downarrow_6 noi(\Delta : v) \\ = noi(\Gamma : x_1 \text{ ? } x_2) \Downarrow_6 noi(\Delta : v) \end{array}$$

as x_i must be in Var.

(Match): The induction hypothesis in this case is that if Γ : $x \Downarrow_6 \Delta$: $c(\overline{y_m})$ in P then $noi(\Gamma$: $x) \Downarrow_6 noi(\Delta : c(\overline{y_m}))$ in P′ and if $\Delta [\overline{z_k \mapsto e_k}]$: $e \Downarrow_6 \Gamma$: v in P then $noi(\Delta [\overline{z_k \mapsto e_k}]$: $e) \Downarrow_6 noi(\Gamma$: v) in P′ where $f(\overline{x_n}, c(\overline{y_m})) = e' \in$ P and let $\{\overline{z_k = e_k}\}$ in $e = norm(e')$. With this assumption we have to show that if Γ : $f(\overline{x_n}, x) \Downarrow_6 \Gamma$: v in P then $noi(\Gamma$: $f(\overline{x_n}, x)) \Downarrow_6 noi(\Gamma$: v) in P′. This claim holds because we have

$$\left[\begin{array}{l} noi(\Gamma : f(\overline{x_n}, x)) \\ = noi(\Gamma) : f(\overline{x_n}, x) \\ \left[\begin{array}{l} noi(\Gamma : x) = noi(\Gamma) : x \\ \ldots \\ noi(\Delta : c(\overline{y_m})) = noi(\Delta) : c(\overline{y_m}) \\ noi(\Delta [\overline{z_k \mapsto e_k}] : e) = noi(\Delta) \left[\overline{a_j \mapsto noi(e'_j)} \right] : noi(e) \\ \ldots \\ noi(\Gamma : v) \end{array} \right] \\ noi(\Gamma : v) \end{array} \right.$$

whenever $f \notin N$ because, where by assumption about P and P′ we have let $\{\overline{a_j = noi(e'_j)}\}$ in $e = norm(noi(e))$ such that $\{\overline{a_j = noi(e'_j)}\} \subseteq \{\overline{z_k = e_k}\}$ and $f(\overline{x_n}, c(\overline{y_m})) = noi(e) \in $ P′.

And if $f \in N$ we have for some variable $i \in Var_{ID}$ and $e_i \in E_{ID}$:

$$\begin{array}{rl} & noi(\Gamma) : f(\overline{x_n}, x) \Downarrow_6 noi(\Gamma : v) \\ = & noi(\Gamma[\ i \mapsto e_i] : f(i, \overline{x_n}, x)) \Downarrow_6 noi(\Gamma : v) \end{array}$$

and by construction $f(i, \overline{x_n}, c(\overline{y_m}))) = e \in $ P i $f(\overline{x_n}, c(\overline{y_m}))) = noi(e) \in $ P′. □

In the other direction it is possible to add arbitrary identifiers as they are not yet considered during evaluation.

Lemma 5.2.8 *It holds that if* Γ : $e \Downarrow_6 \Delta$: v in P *then for all well typed* Γ' : e' *with* $noi(\Gamma') = \Gamma$ *and* $noi(e') = e$ *there exists a* Δ' *such that* $noi(\Delta') = \Delta$ *and* Γ' : $e' \Downarrow_6 \Delta'$: v *in* P′.

Proof. (Of Lemma 5.2.8) By induction on the structure of the proof tree.
Base cases:
(Val): We have Γ' : $c(\overline{x_n}) \Downarrow_6 \Gamma'$: $c(\overline{x_n})$ as $noi(e') = c(\overline{x_n})$ implies $e' = c(\overline{x_n})$.
Inductive cases:

5.2. FORMAL DEFINITION OF TRANSFORMATION

(Var): The induction hypothesis in this case is that if $\Gamma : e \Downarrow_6 \Delta : v$ in P then for all well typed $\Gamma' : e'$ with $noi(\Gamma') = \Gamma$ and $noi(e') = e$ there exists a Δ' such that $noi(\Delta') = \Delta$ and $\Gamma' : e' \Downarrow_6 \Delta' : v$ in P'. With this assumption we have to show that if $\Gamma[x \mapsto e] : x \Downarrow_6 \Delta[x \mapsto v] : v$ in P then for all well typed $\Gamma' : e'$ with $noi(\Gamma') = \Gamma[x \mapsto e]$ and $noi(e') = x$ there exists a Δ' such that $noi(\Delta') = \Delta[x \mapsto v]$ and $\Gamma' : e' \Downarrow_6 \Delta' : v$ in P'. This claim holds because we have

$$\frac{\Gamma' : e' \Downarrow_6 \Delta' : v}{\Gamma'[x \mapsto e'] : x \Downarrow_6 \Delta'[x \mapsto v] : v}$$

as $noi(e') = x$ implies $e'' = x$ and $noi(\Gamma'') = \Gamma[x \mapsto e]$ implies the existence of Γ', e' such that $\Gamma'' = \Gamma'[x \mapsto e']$ and $noi(\Gamma') = \Gamma$ and $noi(e') = e$. Furthermore, $noi(\Delta') = \Delta$ implies $noi(\Delta'[x \mapsto v]) = \Delta[x \mapsto v]$.

(Or): The induction hypothesis in this case is that if $\Gamma : x_i \Downarrow_6 \Delta : v$ in P then for all well typed $\Gamma' : e'$ with $noi(\Gamma') = \Gamma$ and $noi(e') = x_i$ there exists a Δ' such that $noi(\Delta') = \Delta$ and $\Gamma' : e' \Downarrow_6 \Delta' : v$ in P' where $i \in \{1,2\}$. With this assumption we have to show that if $\Gamma : x_1 ? x_2 \Downarrow_6 \Delta : v$ in P then for all well typed $\Gamma' : e'$ with $noi(\Gamma') = \Gamma$ and $noi(e') = x_1 ? x_2$ there exists a Δ' such that $noi(\Delta') = \Delta$ and $\Gamma' : e' \Downarrow_6 \Delta' : v$ in P'. This claim holds because we have

$$\frac{\Gamma' : x_i \Downarrow_6 \Delta' : v}{\Gamma' : x_1 ? x_2 \Downarrow_6 \Delta' : v}$$

as $noi(e') = x_1 ? x_2$ implies $e' = x_1 ? x_2$ and $noi(x_i) = x_i$.

(Match): The induction hypothesis in this case is that if $\Gamma : x \Downarrow_6 \Delta : c(\overline{y_m})$ in P then for all well typed $\Gamma' : e'$ with $noi(\Gamma') = \Gamma$ and $noi(e') = x$ there exists a Δ' such that $noi(\Delta') = \Delta$ and $\Gamma' : e' \Downarrow_6 \Delta' : c(\overline{y_m})$ in P' and if $\Delta\left[\overline{z_k \mapsto e_k}\right] : e \Downarrow_6 \Theta : v$ in P then for all well typed $\Delta' : e'$ with $noi(\Delta') = \Delta\left[\overline{z_k \mapsto e_k}\right]$ and $noi(e') = e$ there exists a Θ' such that $noi(\Theta') = \Theta$ and $\Delta' : e' \Downarrow_6 \Theta' : v$ in P' where $f(\overline{x_n}, c(\overline{y_m})) = e' \in P$ and let $\{\overline{z_k = e_k}\}$ in $e = norm(e')$. With this assumption we have to show that if $\Gamma : f(\overline{x_n}, x) \Downarrow_6 \Theta : v$ in P then for all well typed $\Gamma' : e'$ with $noi(\Gamma') = \Gamma$ and $noi(e') = f(\overline{x_n}, x)$ there exists a Θ' such that $noi(\Theta') = \Theta$ and $\Gamma' : e' \Downarrow_6 \Theta' : v$ in P'. This claim holds because we have

$$\frac{\Gamma' : x \Downarrow_6 \Delta' : c(\overline{y_m}) \quad \Delta'\left[\overline{z_k \mapsto e'_k}\right] : e' \Downarrow_6 \Theta' : v}{\Gamma' : f(\overline{x_n}, x) \Downarrow_6 \Theta' : v}$$

if $f \notin N$ as in this case $noi(e') = f(\overline{x_n}, x)$ implies $e' = f(\overline{x_n}, x)$ as well as $f(\overline{x_n}, c(\overline{y_m})) = e'' \in P'$ such that $norm(e'') = $ let $\{z_k = e'_k\}$ in $e' = e''$ where $noi(e'_k) = e_k$. Consequently, and because $noi(\Delta') = \Delta$, we have $noi(\Delta'\left[\overline{x_k \mapsto e'_k}\right]) = \Delta\left[\overline{x_k \mapsto e_k}\right]$ and, thus, the claim for Θ' follows by induction hypothesis.

And if $f \in N$ it holds that $noi(e') = f(\overline{x_n}, x)$ implies $e' = f(i, \overline{x_n}, x)$ for some variable $i \in Var_{ID}$ and we have

$$\frac{\Gamma' : x \Downarrow_6 \Delta' : c(\overline{y_m}) \quad \Delta'\left[\overline{z_k \mapsto e'_k}\right] : e' \Downarrow_6 \Theta' : v}{\Gamma' : f(i, \overline{x_n}, x) \Downarrow_6 \Theta' : v}$$

analogue to the case above.   □

According to the idea described in Section 5.1.2, the approach depends on the identifiers being unique. The next definition formalizes the required notion of uniqueness. The definition is followed by a proof that evaluations in the context of our approach to program transformation meet this requirement.

Definition 5.2.9 *We say that* $i \in Var_{ID}$ *is a* call-identifier *in the heap* $\quad$ *i there is an* $x \in dom()$ *such that* $(\quad x) = f(i, \overline{x_n})$ *where* $f \in N$.

A heap uniquely identifies *(calls to non-deterministic operations) i for all call identifiers* $i \neq j$ *in* $\quad$ *we have* $i \parallel j$. *We say that a configuration* $\quad$: $\quad$ e uniquely identifies i $\quad$ does and if e is of the form $f(i, \overline{x_n})$, $f \in N$ then i is independent from all call identifiers in$\quad$.

Lemma 5.2.10 *It holds that if* $\quad : \quad$ e *uniquely identifies then so does any configuration in* $\quad : \quad$ e $\Downarrow_6 \Delta \quad : v$.

Proof. (Of Lemma 5.2.10) By induction on the structure of the proof tree.
Base cases:
(Val): We have that in this case the claim holds trivially.
Inductive cases:
(Var): The induction hypothesis in this case is that if $\quad : \quad$ e uniquely identifies then so does any configuration in $\quad : \quad$ e $\Downarrow_6 \Delta \quad : v$. With this assumption we have to show that if $[\quad x \mapsto e] : x$ uniquely identifies then so does any configuration in $[\quad x \mapsto e] : x \Downarrow_6 \Delta [x \mapsto v] : v$. This claim holds because if $[\quad x \mapsto e]$ uniquely identifies then so does $\quad : \quad$ e and if Δ uniquely identifies then so does $\Delta [x \mapsto e]$ as v cannot be of the form $f(i, \overline{x_n})$ where $f \in N$.
(Or): The induction hypothesis in this case is that if $\quad : \quad x_i$ uniquely identifies then so does any configuration in $\quad : \quad x_i \Downarrow_6 \Delta \quad : v$ where $i \in \{1,2\}$. With this assumption we have to show that if $\quad : \quad x_1 ? x_2$ uniquely identifies then so does any configuration in $\quad : \quad x_1 ? x_2 \Downarrow_6 \Delta \quad : v$ which directly stems from the induction hypothesis.
(Match): The induction hypothesis in this case is that if $\quad : \quad x$ uniquely identifies then so does any configuration in $\quad : \quad x \Downarrow_6 \Delta \quad : c(\overline{y_m})$ and if $\Delta [\overline{z_k \mapsto e_k}] : $ e uniquely identifies then so does any configuration in $\Delta [\overline{z_k \mapsto e_k}] : $ e $\Downarrow_6 \quad : \quad v$ where $f(\overline{x_n}, c(\overline{y_m})) = e' \in P$ and let $\{\overline{z_k = e_k}\}$ in e $= norm(e')$. With this assumption we have to show that if $\quad : \quad f(\overline{x_n}, x)$ uniquely identifies then so does any configuration in $\quad : \quad f(\overline{x_n}, x) \Downarrow_6 \quad : v$. This claim holds because if $\quad : \quad f(\overline{x_n}, x)$ uniquely identifies then so does $\quad : \quad x$ and if Δ uniquely identifies then so does $\Delta [\overline{z_k \mapsto e_k}] : $ e by Proposition 5.2.5. Therefore, the claim directly stems from the induction hypothesis.   □

5.2.1 Head Normal Forms and Transformation of Goals

In Section 5.1.2 we have seen that the transformed program yields terms of the form Choice 1 (Choice 1 True False) (Choice 1 False True) where the only valid solution is True (computed in two dierent ways). In order to extract

5.2. FORMAL DEFINITION OF TRANSFORMATION

the correct values from such a term we need some representation of a mapping from identifiers to the set $\{1,2\}$ which is computable within the calculus. We assume that it is well known that such representations can be expressed in functional logic programming.[4] We will simply assume the existence of a suitable operation $\text{lookup}(\cdot,\cdot)$ which has two arguments: a) an identifier $\text{i} \in \text{ID}$ and b) a subset of $\text{ID} \times \{1,2\}$ which represents a function $\text{f} : \text{ID} \mapsto \{1,2\}$ and computes the result of f(i). For example $\text{lookup}(1,\{(1,2)\})$ should yield 2. In the following we will completely abstract from the implementation of $\text{lookup}(\cdot,\cdot)$ and assume in our derivations that any call to this operations is immediately replaced by the according result.

Assuming such an operation $\text{lookup}(\cdot,\cdot)$ we can now define a function to abstract the admissible values from a given tree of choices.

Definition 5.2.11 (Head Normal Form)
Let be a signature such that $C_\Sigma = \{\overline{c_m}\}$ with $c_k \in {}^{(n_k)}$ for $1 \leq k \leq m$. Then function **hnf** is defined by the following set of rules.

$$\begin{aligned}
\text{hnf}(\text{ch}, \mathcal{C}\text{hoice}(\text{i}, x_1, x_2)) &= \text{hnfLup}(\text{ch}, x1, x2, \text{lookup}(\text{i}, \text{ch})) \\
\text{hnf}(\text{ch}, c_1(\overline{x_{n_1}})) &= c_1(\overline{x_{n_1}}) \\
&\vdots \\
\text{hnf}(\text{ch}, c_m(\overline{x_{n_m}})) &= c_m(\overline{x_{n_m}}) \\
\text{hnfLup}(\text{ch}, x1, x2, 1) &= \text{hnf}(\text{ch}, x1) \\
\text{hnfLup}(\text{ch}, x1, x2, 2) &= \text{hnf}(\text{ch}, x2)
\end{aligned}$$

Example 5.2.12 (Head Normal Form)
For the example result of Section 5.1.2 we have for, e.g., $\text{ch} = \{(1,2)\}$:

$$\begin{aligned}
&\text{hnf}(\text{ch}, \mathcal{C}\text{hoice}(1, \mathcal{C}\text{hoice}(1, \text{T}, \text{F}), \mathcal{C}\text{hoice}(1, \text{F}, \text{T}))) \\
={}& \text{hnfLup}(\text{ch}, \mathcal{C}\text{hoice}(1, \text{T}, \text{F}), \mathcal{C}\text{hoice}(1, \text{F}, \text{T}), \text{lookup}(1, \text{ch})) \\
={}& \text{hnfLup}(\text{ch}, \mathcal{C}\text{hoice}(1, \text{T}, \text{F}), \mathcal{C}\text{hoice}(1, \text{F}, \text{T}), 2) \\
={}& \text{hnf}(\text{ch}, \mathcal{C}\text{hoice}(1, \text{F}, \text{T})) \\
={}& \text{hnfLup}(\text{ch}, \text{F}, \text{T}, \text{lookup}(1, \text{ch})) \\
={}& \text{hnfLup}(\text{ch}, \text{F}, \text{T}, 2) \\
={}& \text{hnf}(\text{ch}, \text{T}) \\
={}& \text{T}
\end{aligned}$$

Likewise the evaluation $\text{ch} = \{(1,1)\}$ will also yield T, as the reader might want to verify. Accordingly, there is no way to extract the value F from this term as discussed in Section 5.1.2.

Providing a set as argument to **hnf** is our way of abstracting from the search strategy. In Section 6.2 we will discuss how our approach can be connected to dierent search strategies. Until then we will refer to ch as *s set of choices* and assume that it provides a choice for any identifier coming up during evaluation.

---
[4] A naive implementation could use lists of pair along with the **Prelude** function **lookup**.

(Val) $\quad:\ c(\overline{x_n}) \Downarrow_? :\ c(\overline{x_n})$

(Var) $\dfrac{:\ e \Downarrow_? \Delta\ :\ v}{[\ x \mapsto e]\ :\ x \Downarrow_? \Delta\ [x \mapsto v]\ :\ v}$

(Match) $\dfrac{:\ x \Downarrow_? \Delta\ :\ c(\overline{y_m})\quad \Delta\ [\overline{z_k \mapsto e_k}]\ :\ e \Downarrow_?\ :\ v}{:\ f(\overline{x_n}, x) \Downarrow_?\ :\ v}$
where $f(\overline{x_n}, c(\overline{y_m})) = e' \in P$ and let $\{\overline{z_k = e_k}\}$ in $e = norm(e')$

Figure 5.1: Semantics without Nondeterminism

The astute reader might wonder why we restrict ourselves to *head* normal forms only, and not complete normal forms. A simple answer is that the calculi considered in this work yield head normal forms only. But this is only begging the question. The deeper reason is that complete normal forms do not bring any conceptually new insight, cf. the discussion by Hanus and Prehofer [1999]. If we would like to compute the normal form of e.g., a Peano number, cf. Example 1.1.14, we could define:

```
nf Z     = Z
nf (S x) = nf_S (nf x)

nf_S Z     = S Z
nf_S (S x) = S (S x)
```

It is easy to see that the eect of evaluating `nf(e)` for an expression e is that in order to yield a head normal form of this expression the complete normal form of e has to be evaluated.

There is a simple way of generalizing this scheme to arbitrary normal forms, even simpler when higher order operations can be used.

Having defined `hnf`, the final step of our transformation is to translate the goals given by the user, e.g., as the body of a function `goal` or on an interactive command line environment. For any set of choices ch the start expression for a given goal e is then `hnf(ch, tr(initID, e))`. In the next section we will prove that in this way we can indeed compute exactly the set of all values computable with the calculus of the previous chapter.

5.3 Proof of Soundness

Figure 5.1 shows the most condensed version of a natural semantics of this work. It is a simple first order functional calculus. In this section we show that this calculus can be used to compute the same results as the non-deterministic calculus of Figure 4.4, provided the program is transformed as defined above. Hence we turn to the formal comparison of evaluations in the context of a

5.3. PROOF OF SOUNDNESS

program with identifiers P and a version of this program in which a call to (?) introduces the constructor $Choice$. In Section 5.3.1 we will show that derivations with the $Choice$ constructor and hnf corresponds to an evaluation in the original calculus. In Section 5.3.2 we will show the dual result that any derivation in the original calculus employing non-deterministic choice can be reconstructed without non-determinism by employing hnf. To conclude Section 5.4 contains a summarizing theorem.

5.3.1 Correctness

In Example 5.2.12 we have seen that *sets of choices* are used to obtain values from terms containing the $Choice$ constructor. The next definition formalizes this idea for expressions and heaps. As noted in Section 5.2.1 we will assume that identifier variables are directly bound to identifiers during evaluation.

Definition 5.3.1 *Let* $e \in FUE$ *be a flat uniform expression,* *a flat uniform heap and* ch *be a set of choices. Then the mapping* $choose_{,ch}(e)$ *is defined by:*

$$choose_{,ch}(e) = \begin{cases} x_j & \text{if } e = Choice(i, x_1, x_2) \text{ and } ((\ i), j) \in ch \\ e & \text{otherwise} \end{cases}$$

When the heap is clear from the context we may omit it in $choose_{ch}(e)$. *This holds especially when* e *appears in a heap or configuration, as for a heap* $choose_{ch}(\ )$ *is defined by*

$$choose_{ch}(\ ) := \{(x, choose_{,ch}(e)) \mid (x, e) \in\ \}$$

and for a configuration $\ :\ e\ choose_{ch}(\ :\ e)$ *is defined* $choose_{ch}(\ :\ e)$ *to be equal to* $choose_{ch}(\ ):\ choose_{,ch}(e)$.

We say that a program P *is* a programm with identifiers i it is the result of transforming some original program P_0 by the transformation defined in the previous section, i.e. i we have $P = tr(i, P_0)$.

Let P be a program with identifiers. Then the program $detQM(P)$ is P with a redefinition of (?) to:

$$?(i, x, y) = \text{Choice}(i, x, y)$$

The proof of correctness takes several steps. We will first examine derivations without the $Choice$ constructor. Then study the behavior of a transformed program in the presence of $Choice$ and finally add the evaluation to head normal form by hnf. Accordingly, our first lemma states that any "conventional value", i.e., a value rooted by any constructor but $Choice$ derived in the $\Downarrow_7$-calculus is also obtained in the original $\Downarrow_6$ calculus.

Lemma 5.3.2 *Let* P' *be a program with identifiers, let* $P = detQM(P')$ *and let* v *be a value not of the form* $Choice(x, y, z)$. *Then we have that* $\ :\ e \Downarrow_7 \Delta\ :\ v$ *in* P *implies* $choose_{ch}(\ :\ e) \Downarrow_6 choose_{ch}(\Delta\ :\ v)$ *in* P' *for any set of choices* ch.

116   CHAPTER 5. ELIMINATING NON-DETERMINISM

Proof. (Of Lemma 5.3.2) By induction on the structure of the proof tree.
Base cases:
(Val): We have : $c(\overline{x_n}) \Downarrow_7$: $c(\overline{x_n})$ in P implies $choose_{ch}($: $c(\overline{x_n})) \Downarrow_6$ $choose_{ch}($: $c(\overline{x_n}))$ in P'=$choose_{ch}()$: $c(\overline{x_n}) \Downarrow_6 choose_{ch}()$: $c(\overline{x_n})$).
Inductive cases:
(Var): The induction hypothesis in this case is that : $e \Downarrow_7 \Delta$: v in P implies $choose_{ch}($: e$) \Downarrow_6 choose_{ch}(\Delta$: v) in P'. With this assumption we have to show that [$x \mapsto e$] : $x \Downarrow_7 \Delta$ [$x \mapsto v$] : v in P implies $choose_{ch}($ [$x \mapsto e$] : x) $\Downarrow_6$ $choose_{ch}(\Delta$ [$x \mapsto v$] : v) in P'. This claim holds because we have

$$\frac{choose_{ch}(: \text{ e}) \Downarrow_6 choose_{ch}(\Delta : v)}{= choose_{ch}() : choose_{ch}(e) \Downarrow_6 choose_{ch}(\Delta) : v}$$

$$= \frac{choose_{ch}()[\ x \mapsto choose_{ch}(e)] : x \Downarrow_6 choose_{ch}(\Delta)[x \mapsto v] : v}{choose_{ch}([\ x \mapsto e] : x) \Downarrow_6 choose_{ch}(\Delta[x \mapsto v] : v)}$$

(Match): The induction hypothesis in this case is that : $x \Downarrow_7 \Delta$: $c(\overline{y_m})$ in P implies $choose_{ch}($: x) $\Downarrow_6 choose_{ch}(\Delta$: $c(\overline{y_m}))$ in P' and $\Delta \ [\overline{z_k \mapsto e_k}]$: $e \Downarrow_7$: v in P implies $choose_{ch}(\Delta \ [\overline{z_k \mapsto e_k}]$: e) $\Downarrow_6 choose_{ch}($: v) in P' where $f(\overline{x_n}, c(\overline{y_m})) = e' \in P$ and let $\{\overline{z_k = e_k}\}$ in $e = norm(e')$. With this assumption we have to show that : $f(\overline{x_n}, x) \Downarrow_7$: v in P implies $choose_{ch}($: $f(\overline{x_n}, x)) \Downarrow_6 choose_{ch}($: v) in P'. This claim holds because we have

$$\begin{bmatrix} choose_{ch}(: \ f(\overline{x_n}, x)) \\ = choose_{ch}() : \ f(\overline{x_n}, x) \\ \begin{bmatrix} choose_{ch}(: \ x) = choose_{ch}() : \ x \\ \ldots \\ choose_{ch}(\Delta : c(\overline{y_m})) = choose_{ch}(\Delta) : c(\overline{y_m}) \\ choose_{ch}(\Delta \ [\overline{z_k \mapsto e_k}] : e) = choose_{ch}(\Delta) \left[\overline{z_k \mapsto choose_{ch}(e_k)}\right] : choose_{ch}(e) \\ \ldots \\ choose_{ch}(: \ v) \end{bmatrix} \\ choose_{ch}(: \ v) \end{bmatrix}$$

because $c(\overline{y_m})$ can not be of the form $Choice(x, y, z)$ or otherwise we would also have that v is also of that form by definition of the transformation $tr(\cdot, \cdot)$. □

The appearance of a $Choice$ constructor on the control during derivation can be interpreted as referring to two possible continuations which are at the moment suspended. In this sense the next lemma states that resuming any of the two suspended continuations leads to correct values.

Lemma 5.3.3 *Let* P *be a program with identifiers and let* ch *be a set of choices and* $Choice(j, x_1, x_2)$ *be such that* $choose_{ch}(Choice(j, x_1, x_2)) = x_i$. *Then* : $e \Downarrow_7 \Delta'$: $Choice(j, x_1, x_2)$ *and* $choose_{ch}(\Delta')$: $x_j \Downarrow_6 \Delta$: v *imply* $choose_{ch}($: e) $\Downarrow_6 \Delta$: v *where the first derivation is in the context of program* $detQM(P)$, *the latter in the context of* P.

5.3. PROOF OF SOUNDNESS

Note that in the following proof we omit P and $detQM(\text{P})$ since it should be clear from the context which program is meant, respectively.

Proof. (Of Lemma 5.3.3) By induction on the structure of the proof tree.

Base cases:

(Val): We have : $c(\overline{x_n}) \Downarrow_7 \Delta'$: Choice(j, x_1, x_2) and $choose_{ch}(\Delta')$: $x_j \Downarrow_6 \Delta$: v imply $choose_{ch}(: c(\overline{x_n})) \Downarrow_6 \Delta$: v because : $c(\overline{x_n})$ must in this case be equal to Δ' : Choice(j, x_1, x_2) and therefore $choose_{ch}(: c(\overline{x_n})) = choose_{ch}(\Delta')$: x_j.

Inductive cases:

(Var): The induction hypothesis in this case is that : $e \Downarrow_7 \Delta'$: Choice(j, x_1, x_2) and $choose_{ch}(\Delta')$: $x_j \Downarrow_6 \Delta$: v imply $choose_{ch}(: e) \Downarrow_6 \Delta$: v. With this assumption we have to show that $[x \mapsto e]$: $x \Downarrow_7 \Delta'$: Choice(j, x_1, x_2) and $choose_{ch}(\Delta')$: $x_j \Downarrow_6 \Delta [x \mapsto v]$: v imply $choose_{ch}([x \mapsto e] : x) \Downarrow_6 \Delta [x \mapsto v]$: v. This claim holds because we have that $[x \mapsto e]$: $x \Downarrow_7 \Delta'$: Choice(j, x_1, x_2) implies : $e \Downarrow_7 \Delta'$: Choice(j, x_1, x_2) and therefore we can construct by assumption:

$$\frac{choose_{ch}(: e) \Downarrow_6 \Delta : v}{= choose_{ch}() : choose_{ch}(e) \Downarrow_6 \Delta : v}$$

$$\frac{choose_{ch}()[x \mapsto choose_{ch}(e)] : x \Downarrow_6 \Delta [x \mapsto v] : v}{= choose_{ch}([x \mapsto e] : x) \Downarrow_6 \Delta [x \mapsto v] : v}$$

(Match): The induction hypothesis in this case is that : $x \Downarrow_7 \Delta'$: Choice(j, x_1, x_2) and $choose_{ch}(\Delta')$: $x_j \Downarrow_6 \Delta$: $c(\overline{y_m})$ imply $choose_{ch}(: x) \Downarrow_6 \Delta$: $c(\overline{y_m})$ and $\Delta [\overline{z_k \mapsto e_k}]$: $e \Downarrow_7 \quad '$: Choice(j, x_1, x_2) and $choose_{ch}(\quad ')$: $x_j \Downarrow_6 \quad$: v imply $choose_{ch}(\Delta [\overline{z_k \mapsto e_k}] : e) \Downarrow_6 \quad$: v where $f(\overline{x_n}, c(\overline{y_m})) = e' \in \text{P}$ and let $\{\overline{z_k = e_k}\}$ in $e = norm(e')$. With this assumption we have to show that : $f(\overline{x_n}, x) \Downarrow_7 \quad '$: Choice(j, x_1, x_2) and $choose_{ch}(\quad ')$: $x_j \Downarrow_6 \quad$: v imply $choose_{ch}(: f(\overline{x_n}, x)) \Downarrow_6 \quad$: v. This claim holds because we have of the following case distinction:

Case 1, : $f(\overline{x_n}, x) \Downarrow_7 \quad$: v is of the form

$$\frac{: x \Downarrow_7 \Delta : c(\overline{y_m}) \quad \Delta [\overline{z_k \mapsto e_k}] : e \Downarrow_7 \quad : \text{Choice}(j, x_1, x_2)}{: f(\overline{x_n}, x) \Downarrow_7 \quad : \text{Choice}(j, x_1, x_2)}$$

Then by Lemma 5.3.2 we have $choose_{ch}(: x) \Downarrow_6 choose_{ch}(\Delta : c(\overline{y_m}))$ and, therefore, we can construct by assumption:

$$\begin{bmatrix} choose_{ch}(: f(\overline{x_n}, x)) \\ = choose_{ch}() : f(\overline{x_n}, x) \\ \begin{bmatrix} choose_{ch}(: x) = choose_{ch}() : x \\ \ldots \\ choose_{ch}(\Delta : c(\overline{y_m})) = choose_{ch}(\Delta) : c(\overline{y_m}) \\ choose_{ch}(\Delta [\overline{z_k \mapsto e_k}] : e) = choose_{ch}(\Delta) [\overline{z_k \mapsto choose_{ch}(e_k)}] : choose_{ch}(e) \\ \ldots \\ : v \end{bmatrix} \\ : v \end{bmatrix}$$

Case 2, : $\mathtt{f}(\overline{\mathtt{x}_n},\mathtt{x}) \Downarrow_7$: v is of the form

$$\Downarrow_7 \left[\begin{array}{l} : \mathtt{f}(\overline{\mathtt{x}_n},\mathtt{x}) \\ \Downarrow_7 \left[\begin{array}{l} : \mathtt{x} \\ \ldots \\ \Delta': \mathrm{Choice}(\mathtt{j},\mathtt{x}_1,\mathtt{x}_2) \\ \Delta'[\mathtt{a}_1 \mapsto \mathtt{f}(\overline{\mathtt{x}_n},\mathtt{x}_1)][\mathtt{a}_2 \mapsto \mathtt{f}(\overline{\mathtt{x}_n},\mathtt{x}_2)] : \mathrm{Choice}(\mathtt{j},\mathtt{a}_1,\mathtt{a}_2) \\ \Delta'[\mathtt{a}_1 \mapsto \mathtt{f}(\overline{\mathtt{x}_n},\mathtt{x}_1)][\mathtt{a}_2 \mapsto \mathtt{f}(\overline{\mathtt{x}_n},\mathtt{x}_2)] : \mathrm{Choice}(\mathtt{j},\mathtt{a}_1,\mathtt{a}_2) \end{array} \right] \\ \Delta'[\mathtt{a}_1 \mapsto \mathtt{f}(\overline{\mathtt{x}_n},\mathtt{x}_1)][\mathtt{a}_2 \mapsto \mathtt{f}(\overline{\mathtt{x}_n},\mathtt{x}_2)] : \mathrm{Choice}(\mathtt{j},\mathtt{a}_1,\mathtt{a}_2) \end{array} \right]$$

We first note that $choose_{ch}(\mathrm{Choice}(\mathtt{j},\mathtt{x}_1,\mathtt{x}_2)) = \mathtt{x}_i$ implies

$$choose_{ch}(\mathrm{Choice}(\mathtt{j},\mathtt{a}_1,\mathtt{a}_2)) = \mathtt{a}_i$$

Now we additionally assume existence of the derivation

$$choose_{ch}(\Delta')[\mathtt{a}_1 \mapsto \mathtt{f}(\overline{\mathtt{x}_n},\mathtt{x}_1)][\mathtt{a}_2 \mapsto \mathtt{f}(\overline{\mathtt{x}_n},\mathtt{x}_2)] : \mathtt{a}_i \Downarrow_6 \ : \ \mathtt{v}$$

We take a closer look at the latter derivation.

$$\Downarrow_6 \left[\begin{array}{l} \Delta'[\mathtt{a}_1 \mapsto \mathtt{f}(\overline{\mathtt{x}_n},\mathtt{x}_1)][\mathtt{a}_2 \mapsto \mathtt{f}(\overline{\mathtt{x}_n},\mathtt{x}_2)] : \mathtt{a}_i \\ \Downarrow_6 \left[\begin{array}{l} \Delta'[\mathtt{a}_{3-i} \mapsto \mathtt{f}(\overline{\mathtt{x}_n},\mathtt{x}_{3-i})] : \mathtt{f}(\overline{\mathtt{x}_n},\mathtt{x}_j) \\ \Downarrow_6 \left[\begin{array}{l} \Delta'[\mathtt{a}_{3-i} \mapsto \mathtt{f}(\overline{\mathtt{x}_n},\mathtt{x}_{3-i})] : \mathtt{x}_j \\ \ldots \\ \Delta\,[\mathtt{a}_{3-i} \mapsto \mathtt{f}(\overline{\mathtt{x}_n},\mathtt{x}_{3-i})] : \mathtt{c}(\overline{\mathtt{y}_m}) \\ \Delta\,[\mathtt{a}_{3-i} \mapsto \mathtt{f}(\overline{\mathtt{x}_n},\mathtt{x}_{3-i})][\overline{\mathtt{x}_k \mapsto \mathtt{e}_k}] : \mathtt{e} \\ \Downarrow_6 \\ \ldots \\ [\ \mathtt{a}_{3-i} \mapsto \mathtt{f}(\overline{\mathtt{x}_n},\mathtt{x}_{3-i})] : \mathtt{v} \end{array} \right] \\ [\ \mathtt{a}_{3-i} \mapsto \mathtt{f}(\overline{\mathtt{x}_n},\mathtt{x}_{3-i})] : \mathtt{v} \end{array} \right] \\ [\ \mathtt{a}_{3-i} \mapsto \mathtt{f}(\overline{\mathtt{x}_n},\mathtt{x}_{3-i})][\mathtt{a}_i \mapsto \mathtt{v}] : \mathtt{v} \end{array} \right]$$

where $\mathtt{f}(\overline{\mathtt{x}_n},\mathtt{c}(\overline{\mathtt{y}_m})) = \mathtt{e}' \in det(P)$ and $norm(\mathtt{e}')$=let $\{\overline{\mathtt{x}_k = \mathtt{e}_k}\}$ in e. The binding of $\mathtt{a}_{3-i}$ is not altered in the Derivation by Observation 2.2.4.3 since $\mathtt{a}_{3-i}$ is not reachable from $\mathtt{x}_j$. By Lemma 4.1.3 $\Delta'[\mathtt{a}_{3-i} \mapsto \mathtt{f}(\overline{\mathtt{x}_n},\mathtt{x}_{3-i})] : \mathtt{x}_j \Downarrow \Delta\,[\mathtt{a}_{3-i} \mapsto \mathtt{f}(\overline{\mathtt{x}_n},\mathtt{x}_{3-i})] : \mathtt{c}(\overline{\mathtt{y}_m})$ implies $\Delta' : \mathtt{x}_j \Downarrow \Delta : \mathtt{c}(\overline{\mathtt{y}_m})$. And, therefore, we can construct as required:

$$\Downarrow_6 \left[\begin{array}{l} choose_{ch}() : \ \mathtt{f}(\overline{\mathtt{x}_n},\mathtt{x}) \\ \Downarrow_6 \left[\begin{array}{l} choose_{ch}() : \ \mathtt{x} \\ \ldots \\ \Delta \ : \mathtt{c}(\overline{\mathtt{y}_m}) \\ \Delta \ [\overline{\mathtt{x}_k \mapsto \mathtt{e}_k}] : \mathtt{e} \end{array} \right] \\ \Downarrow_6 \\ \ldots \\ : \mathtt{v} \end{array} \right]$$
$: \mathtt{v}$

□

5.3. PROOF OF SOUNDNESS

We can now put the observations of Lemmas 5.3.2 and 5.3.3 together and prove the desired fact about evaluation to head normal form. Recall that we abstract from the implementation (and evaluation) of `lookup`.[5]

Lemma 5.3.4 *Let* P *be a program with identifiers and let* Δ *be heap such that* $\Delta(x_{ch}) = ch$. *Then*

$$\Delta : \mathtt{hnf}(x_{ch}, x_e) \Downarrow_7 \Delta' : v$$

implies

$$choose_{ch}(\Delta : x_e) \Downarrow_6 choose_{ch}(\Delta' : v)$$

where the first derivation is in the context of program $detQM(\mathtt{P})$, *the latter in the context of* P.

Note that in the following proof we again omit P and $detQM(\mathtt{P})$ since it should be clear from the context which program is meant, respectively.

Proof. By Induction on the number c of calls to `hnf` in the whole derivation.
Base Case, $c = 1$:
In this case the derivation is, by definition of `hnf`, of the following form.

$$\frac{\Delta : x_e \Downarrow_7 \Delta' := \Delta'[x_e \mapsto v] : v \quad \Delta' : v \Downarrow_7 \Delta' : v}{\Delta : \mathtt{hnf}(x_{ch}, x_e) \Downarrow_7 \Delta' : v}$$

Therefore, we get by Lemma 5.3.2 $choose_{ch}(\Delta : x_e) \Downarrow_6 choose_{ch}(\Delta' : v)$.
Inductive Case $c \Rightarrow c+1$:
In this case the derivation is, by definition of `hnf`, of the following form.

$$\Downarrow_7 \left[\begin{array}{l} \Delta : \mathtt{hnf}(x_{ch}, x_e) \\ \Downarrow_7 \left[\begin{array}{l} \Delta : x_e \\ \ldots \\ \Delta'' := \Delta'[x_e \mapsto \mathrm{Choice}(x_1, x_2, i)] : \mathrm{Choice}(x_1, x_2, i) \\ \Delta'' : \mathtt{hnfLup}(x_{ch}, x_1, x_2, j) \end{array} \right\} D_1 \\ \Downarrow_7 \left[\begin{array}{l} \Delta'' : j \\ \Delta'' : j \\ \Downarrow_7 \left[\begin{array}{l} \Delta'' : \mathtt{hnf}(x_{ch}, x_j) \\ \ldots \\ \Delta' : v \end{array} \right\} D_2 \right. \\ \Delta' : v \end{array} \right. \\ \Delta' : v \end{array} \right.$$

For the sub derivation D_2 we conclude by induction hypothesis the existence of the derivation $choose_{ch}(\Delta'') : x_j \Downarrow_6 choose_{ch}(\Delta') : v$. By Lemma 5.3.3 this derivation together with derivation D_1 allows to conclude the existence of $choose_{ch}(\Delta) : x_e \Downarrow_6 choose_{ch}(\Delta') : v$. □

---

[5] A formal justification for this abstraction is given with Lemma 4.1.3.

(Val) $\quad$: $c(\overline{x_n}) \Downarrow_8$: $c(\overline{x_n}) \mid \emptyset$

(Var) $\dfrac{\quad : e \Downarrow_8 \Delta : v \mid ch}{[\, x \mapsto e\,] : x \Downarrow_8 \Delta\, [x \mapsto v] : v \mid ch}$

(Or) $\dfrac{\quad : e_i \Downarrow_8 \Delta : v \mid ch}{\quad : ?(j, e_1, e_2) \Downarrow_8 \Delta : v \mid \{(j,i)\} \cup ch}$ $\quad$ where $i \in \{1,2\}$

(Match) $\dfrac{\quad : x \Downarrow_8 \Delta : c(\overline{y_m}) \mid ch \quad \Delta\, [\overline{z_k \mapsto e_k}] : e \Downarrow_8 : v \mid ch'}{\quad : f(\overline{x_n}, x) \Downarrow_8 : v \mid ch \cup ch'}$
$\quad$ where $f(\overline{x_n}, c(\overline{y_m})) = e' \in P$ and let $\{\overline{z_k = e_k}\}$ in $e = norm(e')$

Figure 5.2: Recording the choices made in a derivation

5.3.2 Completeness

Like in the completeness proof of Chapter 3 we will not directly map derivations in $\Downarrow_7$ to those in $\Downarrow_6$. Rather, we also need an intermediate conservative extension which provides information about derivations in $\Downarrow_6$. In this case the information concerns the non-deterministic choices taken during evaluation. Whenever we have an application of (Or) we need to record whether e_1 or e_2 was chosen like this:

(Or) $\dfrac{\quad : e_i \Downarrow_8 \Delta : v \mid ch}{\quad : ?(j, e_1, e_2) \Downarrow_8 \Delta : v \mid \{(j,i)\} \cup ch}$ $\quad$ where $i \in \{1,2\}$

Note that we use the identifier given as additional parameter to (?). Accordingly we discard the rule
$$?(i, x, y) = x\, ?\, y$$
from the program and use the ternary $?(\cdot, \cdot, \cdot)$ symbol directly as a primitive for non-deterministic disjunction instead of $?(\cdot, \cdot)$. The remaining rules of Figure 5.2 do not change this additional information with the exception of (Match) which yields the union of the information of its sub computations. The complete conservative extension is depicted in Figure 5.2. Altogether the rules compute a set of choices along with the evaluation. This set of choices will then be used as parameter for `hnf`.

The proof of completeness consists of two steps. We first show that the order of evaluation of the last argument of a matching function can be altered in a certain sense. This is important for resuming suspended computations.

Lemma 5.3.5 *For a matching function* f *the existence of the two derivations*

$$: hnf(x_{ch}, x_e) \Downarrow_7 \Delta : v'$$

5.3. PROOF OF SOUNDNESS

and

$$\Delta\,[x_f \mapsto f(\overline{x_n},x_e)] : h\mathrm{nf}(x_{\mathrm{ch}},x_f) \Downarrow_7\ :\ v$$

implies the existence of the derivation

$$[\,x_f \mapsto f(\overline{x_n},x_e)] : h\mathrm{nf}(x_{\mathrm{ch}},x_f) \Downarrow_7\ :\ v.$$

Note that the latter two derivations dier in the heap of the in-configuration.

Proof. We assume the existence of the two derivations : $h\mathrm{nf}(x_{\mathrm{ch}},x_e) \Downarrow_7 \Delta\ :\ v'$ and $\Delta\,[x_f \mapsto f(\overline{x_n},x_e)] : h\mathrm{nf}(x_{\mathrm{ch}},x_f) \Downarrow_7\ :\ v$ and prove the claim by Induction on the number c of calls to $h\mathrm{nf}(\cdot,\cdot)$ in the first of these derivations.

Base Case, c = 1:
In this case the derivations are, by definition of **hnf**, of the following forms, respectively.

$$= \frac{\dfrac{':e \Downarrow_7 \Delta'\,:\,c(\overline{y_m})}{'[x_e \mapsto e]:x_e \Downarrow_7 \Delta := \Delta'\,[x_e \mapsto c(\overline{y_m})]\,:\,c(\overline{y_m})}\qquad \Delta\,:\,c(\overline{y_m}) \Downarrow_7 \Delta\,:\,c(\overline{y_m})}{:\ h\mathrm{nf}(x_{\mathrm{ch}},x_e) \Downarrow_7 \Delta\,:\,c(\overline{y_m})}$$

and

$$\frac{\dfrac{\dfrac{\Delta\,:\,x_e \Downarrow_7 \Delta\,:\,c(\overline{y_m})\qquad \Delta\,[\overline{x_k \mapsto e_k}]:e \Downarrow_7\ '' :v'}{\Delta\,:\,f(\overline{x_n},x_e) \Downarrow_7\ '' :v'}}{\Delta\,[x_f \mapsto f(\overline{x_n},x_e)] : x_f \Downarrow_7\ ' := ''\,[x_f \mapsto v']:v'}\qquad ':e' \Downarrow_7\ :\ v}{\Delta\,[x_f \mapsto f(\overline{x_n},x_e)] : h\mathrm{nf}(x_{\mathrm{ch}},x_f) \Downarrow_7\ :\ v}$$

where $f(\overline{x_n},c(\overline{y_m})) = e' \in P$ and let $\{\overline{x_k = e_k}\}$ in $e = norm(e')$. Therefore, we can construct the derivation

$$\frac{\dfrac{\dfrac{:\,x_e \Downarrow_7 \Delta\,:\,c(\overline{y_m})\qquad \Delta\,[\overline{x_k \mapsto e_k}]:e \Downarrow_7\ '' :v'}{:\,f(\overline{x_n},x_e) \Downarrow_7\ '' :v'}}{[\,x_f \mapsto f(\overline{x_n},x_e)] : x_f \Downarrow_7\ ' := ''\,[x_f \mapsto v']:v'}\qquad ':e' \Downarrow_7\ :\ v}{[\,x_f \mapsto f(\overline{x_n},x_e)] : h\mathrm{nf}(x_{\mathrm{ch}},x_f) \Downarrow_7\ :\ v} \quad (*)$$

Inductive Case, c ⇒ c + 1:
We assume that the derivation $:\ h\mathrm{nf}(x_{\mathrm{ch}},x_e) \Downarrow_7 \Delta\ :\ v'$ contains c + 1 calls to the function $h\mathrm{nf}(\cdot,\cdot)$ where $c \geq 1$. The derivation must then, by definition of

$hnf(\cdot,\cdot)$, be of the following form.

$$
\Downarrow_7 \left[
\begin{array}{l}
: hnf(x_{ch}, x_e) \\
\Downarrow_7 \left[
\begin{array}{l}
\Downarrow_7 \left[
\begin{array}{l}
= \quad '[x_e \mapsto e] : x_e \\
\quad ' : e \\
\ldots \\
\Delta'' : Choice(x_1, x_2, i)
\end{array}
\right. \\
\Delta' := \Delta''[x_e \mapsto Choice(x_1, x_2, i)] : Choice(x_1, x_2, i) \\
\Delta' : hnfLup(x_{ch}, x_1, x_2, j)
\end{array}
\right\} D_1 \\
\Downarrow_7 \left[
\begin{array}{l}
\Downarrow_7 \left[
\begin{array}{l}
\Delta' : j \\
\Delta' : j
\end{array}
\right. \\
\Downarrow_7 \left[
\begin{array}{l}
\Delta' : hnf(x_{ch}, x_j) \\
\ldots \\
\Delta : c(\overline{y_m})
\end{array}
\right. \\
\Delta : c(\overline{y_m})
\end{array}
\right. \\
\Delta : c(\overline{y_m})
\end{array}
\right\} D_2
$$

Here, the sub derivation D_2 contains c calls to $hnf(\cdot,\cdot)$. Therefore, the induction hypothesis allows to conclude the existence of the derivation $\Delta'[a_j \mapsto f(\overline{x_n}, x_e)] : hnf(x_{ch}, a_j) \Downarrow_7 \; : \; v$ which is of the form $(*)$ constructed above.

With this we can construct

$$
\Downarrow_7 \left[
\begin{array}{l}
[\; x_f \mapsto f(\overline{x_n}, x_e)] : hnf(x_{ch}, x_f) \\
\Downarrow_7 \left[
\begin{array}{l}
[\; x_f \mapsto f(\overline{x_n}, x_e)] : x_f \\
\Downarrow_7 \left[
\begin{array}{l}
: f(\overline{x_n}, x_e) \\
\Downarrow_7 \left[
\begin{array}{l}
: x_e \\
\ldots \\
\Delta' : Choice(x_1, x_2, i)
\end{array}
\right.
\end{array}
\right\} D_1 \\
\Delta' : Choice(x_1, x_2, i) \\
\Downarrow_7 \left[
\begin{array}{l}
\Delta'' := \Delta'[a_1 \mapsto f(\overline{x_n}, x_1), a_2 \mapsto f(\overline{x_n}, x_2)] : Choice(a_1, a_2, i) \\
\Delta'' : Choice(a_1, a_2, i)
\end{array}
\right. \\
\Delta := \Delta''[x_f \mapsto Choice(a_1, a_2, i)] : Choice(a_1, a_2, i) \\
\Delta : hnfLup(x_{ch}, a_1, a_2, j)
\end{array}
\right. \\
\Downarrow_7 \left[
\begin{array}{l}
\Delta : j \\
\Delta : j
\end{array}
\right. \\
\Downarrow_7 \left[
\begin{array}{l}
\Delta : hnf(x_{ch}, a_j) \\
\ldots \\
: v
\end{array}
\right\} \text{def } hnfLup, \text{ induction hypothesis} \\
: v
\end{array}
\right.
$$

$\square$

The last step of this section is the proof of completeness. Any derivation in the calculus employing non-determinism can be reconstructed as a deterministic derivation.

5.3. PROOF OF SOUNDNESS

Lemma 5.3.6 *It holds that for a program with identifiers* P *the existence of the derivation*

$$: \text{e} \Downarrow_8 \Delta : \text{v} \mid \text{ch}$$

implies that the derivation

$$[\ x_e \mapsto \text{e}]\,[x_{ch} \mapsto \text{ch}] : \text{hnf}(x_{ch}, x_e) \Downarrow_7 \Delta\,[x_e \mapsto \text{v}]\,[x_{ch} \mapsto \text{ch}] : \text{v}$$

exists in $detQM(\text{P})$.

Again we omit to explicitly name the programs P and $detQM(\text{P})$ in the proof.

Proof. (Of Lemma 5.3.6) By induction on the structure of the proof tree.
Base cases:
(Val): We have for $:\ c(\overline{x_n}) \Downarrow_8 :\ c(\overline{x_n}) \mid \emptyset$:

$$\Downarrow_7 \left[\begin{array}{l} [\ x_{ch} \mapsto \emptyset]\,[x_e \mapsto c(\overline{x_n})] : \text{hnf}(x_{ch}, x_e) \\ \Downarrow_7 \left[\begin{array}{l} [\ x_{ch} \mapsto \emptyset]\,[x_e \mapsto c(\overline{x_n})] : x_e \\ \Downarrow_7 \left[\begin{array}{l} [\ x_{ch} \mapsto \emptyset] : c(\overline{x_n}) \\ [\ x_{ch} \mapsto \emptyset] : c(\overline{x_n}) \end{array} \right. \\ [\ x_{ch} \mapsto \emptyset]\,[x_e \mapsto c(\overline{x_n})] : c(\overline{x_n}) \end{array} \right. \\ [\ x_{ch} \mapsto \emptyset]\,[x_e \mapsto c(\overline{x_n})] : c(\overline{x_n}) \end{array} \right.$$

Inductive cases:
(Var): The induction hypothesis in this case is that the existence of the derivation

$$: \text{e} \Downarrow_8 \Delta : \text{v} \mid ch$$

implies that the derivation

$$[\ x_e \mapsto \text{e}]\,[x_{ch} \mapsto ch] : \text{hnf}(x_{ch}, x_e) \Downarrow_7 \Delta\,[x_e \mapsto \text{v}]\,[x_{ch} \mapsto ch] : \text{v}$$

exists. With this assumption we have to show that the existence of the derivation

$$[\ x \mapsto \text{e}] : x \Downarrow_8 \Delta\,[x \mapsto \text{v}] : \text{v} \mid ch$$

implies that the derivation

$$[\ x \mapsto \text{e}]\,[x_e \mapsto x]\,[x_{ch} \mapsto ch] : \text{hnf}(x_{ch}, x_e) \Downarrow_7 \Delta\,[x \mapsto \text{v}]\,[x_e \mapsto \text{v}]\,[x_{ch} \mapsto ch] : \text{v}$$

exists. This claim holds because we have that from

$$\Downarrow_7 \left[\begin{array}{l} [\ x_{ch} \mapsto ch]\,[x_e \mapsto \text{e}] : \text{hnf}(x_{ch}, x_e) \\ \Downarrow_7 \left[\begin{array}{l} [\ x_{ch} \mapsto ch]\,[x_e \mapsto \text{e}] : x_e \\ \Downarrow_7 \left[\begin{array}{l} [\ x_{ch} \mapsto ch] : \text{e} \\ \ldots \\ \Delta\,[x_{ch} \mapsto ch] : \text{v} \end{array} \right. \\ \Delta\,[x_{ch} \mapsto ch]\,[x_e \mapsto \text{v}] : \text{v} \end{array} \right. \\ \Delta\,[x_{ch} \mapsto ch]\,[x_e \mapsto \text{v}] : \text{v} \end{array} \right.$$

we can construct

$$\Downarrow_7 \left[\begin{array}{l} [\, x \mapsto e] \, [x_{ch} \mapsto ch] \, [x_e \mapsto x] : \mathtt{hnf}(x_{ch}, x_e) \\ \Downarrow_7 \left[\begin{array}{l} [\, x \mapsto e] \, [x_{ch} \mapsto ch] \, [x_e \mapsto x] : x_e \\ \Downarrow_7 \left[\begin{array}{l} [\, x \mapsto e] \, [x_{ch} \mapsto ch] : x \\ \Downarrow_7 \left[\begin{array}{l} [\, x_{ch} \mapsto ch] : e \\ \ldots \\ \Delta \, [x_{ch} \mapsto ch] : v \end{array}\right. \\ \Delta \, [x \mapsto v] \, [x_{ch} \mapsto ch] : v \end{array}\right. \\ \Delta \, [x \mapsto v] \, [x_{ch} \mapsto ch] \, [x_e \mapsto v] : v \end{array}\right. \\ \Delta \, [x \mapsto v] \, [x_{ch} \mapsto ch] \, [x_e \mapsto v] : v \end{array}\right.$$

(Or): The induction hypothesis in this case is that the existence of the derivation

$$: \; e_i \Downarrow_8 \Delta : v \mid ch$$

implies that the derivation

$$[\, x_e \mapsto e_i] \, [x_{ch} \mapsto ch] : \mathtt{hnf}(x_{ch}, x_e) \Downarrow_7 \Delta \, [x_e \mapsto v] \, [x_{ch} \mapsto ch] : v$$

exists where $i \in \{1,2\}$. With this assumption we have to show that the existence of the derivation

$$: \; ?(j, e_1, e_2) \Downarrow_8 \Delta : v \mid \{(j, i)\} \cup ch$$

implies that the derivation

$$[\, x_e \mapsto ?(j, e_1, e_2)] \, [x_{ch} \mapsto \{(j, i)\} \cup ch] : \mathtt{hnf}(x_{ch}, x_e) \Downarrow_7 \Delta \, [x_e \mapsto v]$$

exists. This claim holds because we have that from

$$\Downarrow_7 \left[\begin{array}{l} [\, x_{ch} \mapsto ch] \, [x_e \mapsto e_i] : \mathtt{hnf}(x_{ch}, x_e) \\ \Downarrow_7 \left[\begin{array}{l} [\, x_{ch} \mapsto ch] \, [x_e \mapsto e_i] : x_e \\ \Downarrow_7 \left[\begin{array}{l} [\, x_{ch} \mapsto ch] : e_i \\ \ldots \\ \Delta \, [x_{ch} \mapsto ch] : v \end{array}\right. \\ \Delta \, [x_{ch} \mapsto ch] \, [x_e \mapsto v] : v \end{array}\right. \\ \Delta \, [x_{ch} \mapsto ch] \, [x_e \mapsto v] : v \end{array}\right.$$

5.4. SUMMARY

we can construct

$$\Downarrow_7 \begin{bmatrix} \Downarrow_7 \begin{bmatrix} \Downarrow_7 \begin{bmatrix} [x_{ch} \mapsto \{(j,i)\} \cup ch][x_e \mapsto ?(j,e_1,e_2)] : \text{hnf}(x_{ch}, x_e) \\ [x_{ch} \mapsto \{(j,i)\} \cup ch][x_e \mapsto ?(j,e_1,e_2)] : x_e \\ \Downarrow_7 \begin{bmatrix} [x_{ch} \mapsto \{(j,i)\} \cup ch] : ?(j,e_1,e_2) \\ \Downarrow_7 \begin{bmatrix} [x_{ch} \mapsto \{(j,i)\} \cup ch] : \text{Choice}(j,e_1,e_2) \\ [x_{ch} \mapsto \{(j,i)\} \cup ch] : \text{Choice}(j,e_1,e_2) \end{bmatrix} \\ \Delta\, [x_{ch} \mapsto \{(j,i)\} \cup ch] : \text{Choice}(j,e_1,e_2) \end{bmatrix} \\ [x_{ch} \mapsto \{(j,i)\} \cup ch][x_e \mapsto \text{Choice}(j,e_1,e_2)] : \text{Choice}(j,e_1,e_2) \\ [x_{ch} \mapsto \{(j,i)\} \cup ch][x_e \mapsto \text{Choice}(j,e_1,e_2)] : \text{hnfLup} \\ \Downarrow_7 \begin{bmatrix} [x_{ch} \mapsto \{(j,i)\} \cup ch][x_e \mapsto \text{Choice}(j,e_1,e_2)] : i \\ [x_{ch} \mapsto \{(j,i)\} \cup ch][x_e \mapsto \text{Choice}(j,e_1,e_2)] : i \\ [x_{ch} \mapsto \{(j,i)\} \cup ch][x_e \mapsto \text{Choice}(j,e_1,e_2)] : \text{hnf}(x_{ch}, e_i) \end{bmatrix} \\ \Downarrow_7 \quad \ldots \\ \Delta : v \end{bmatrix} \\ \Delta : v \end{bmatrix} \\ \Delta\, [x_{ch} \mapsto \{(j,i)\} \cup ch][x_e \mapsto v] : v \end{bmatrix}$$

(Match): The induction hypothesis in this case is that the existence of the derivation

$$: x \Downarrow_8 \Delta : c(\overline{y_m}) \mid ch$$

implies that the derivation

$$[x_e \mapsto x][x_{ch} \mapsto ch] : \text{hnf}(x_{ch}, x_e) \Downarrow_7 \Delta\, [x_e \mapsto c(\overline{y_m})][x_{ch} \mapsto ch] : c(\overline{y_m})$$

exists and the existence of the derivation

$$\Delta\, [\overline{z_k \mapsto e_k}] : e \Downarrow_8 \ : \ v \mid ch'$$

implies that the derivation

$$\Delta\, [\overline{z_k \mapsto e_k}][x_e \mapsto e][x_{ch} \mapsto ch'] : \text{hnf}(x_{ch}, x_e) \Downarrow_7 [x_e \mapsto v][x_{ch} \mapsto ch'] : v$$

exists where $f(\overline{x_n}, c(\overline{y_m})) = e' \in P$ and let $\{\overline{z_k = e_k}\}$ in $e = norm(e')$. With this assumption we have to show that the existence of the derivation

$$: f(\overline{x_n}, x) \Downarrow_8 \ : \ v \mid ch \cup ch'$$

implies that the derivation

$$[x_e \mapsto f(\overline{x_n}, x)][x_{ch} \mapsto ch \cup ch'] : \text{hnf}(x_{ch}, x_e) \Downarrow_7 [x_e \mapsto v][x_{ch} \mapsto ch \cup ch'] : v$$

exists by Lemma 5.3.5. □

5.4 Summary

The following theorem summarizes the adequacy of the transformation from functional logic to functional programs developed in this chapter.

Definition 5.4.1

$$[\![e]\!]_7^P := \{\alpha(\overline{{}^*_{ch}(x_n)}) \mid \exists ch : {}_0 : \mathtt{hnf}(x_{ch}, x_e) \Downarrow_7 : \alpha(\overline{x_n})\}$$

where

$$\mathtt{let}\ \{\overline{x_k = e_k}\}\ \mathtt{in}\ e'\ {}_0 := norm(e) := \emptyset\, [\overline{x_k \mapsto e_k}, x_e \mapsto e', x_{ch} \mapsto ch]$$

$${}^*_{ch}(x) := choose_{ch}()\ {}^*(x)$$

Theorem 3

$$[\![e]\!]_3^P = [\![e]\!]_7^{dQM(P)}$$

where

$$det(\mathtt{P}) := tr(\mathtt{i}, uf(\mathtt{P}))$$
$$dQM(\mathtt{P}) := detQM(det\,\mathtt{P})$$

Proof.

$$\begin{aligned}
& [\![e]\!]_3^P \\
=\ & [\![e]\!]_6^{uf(P)} && \text{Theorem 2} \\
\subseteq\ & [\![e]\!]_6^{det(P)} && {}^*(x) = noi()\ {}^*(x)\ \text{and Lem 5.2.7} \\
\subseteq\ & [\![e]\!]_6^{uf(P)} && {}^*(x) = noi()\ {}^*(x)\ \text{and Lem 5.2.8} \\
=\ & [\![e]\!]_8^{det(P)} && \text{extension from } \Downarrow_6 \text{ to } \Downarrow_8 \text{ is conservative} \\
=\ & \{\alpha(\overline{{}^*(x_n)}) \mid \emptyset\, [\overline{x_k \mapsto e_k}] : e' \Downarrow_8 : \alpha(\overline{x_n}) \mid ch\ \text{in}\ det(\mathtt{P})\} && \text{Def 4.6.1} \\
\subseteq\ & \{\alpha(\overline{{}^*_{ch}(x_n)}) \mid \exists ch : {}_0 : \mathtt{hnf}(x_{ch}, x_e) \Downarrow_7 : \alpha(\overline{x_n})\ \text{in}\ dQM(\mathtt{P})\} && \text{Lem 5.3.6} \\
=\ & [\![e]\!]_7^{dQM(P)} && \text{Def 5.4.1} \\
\subseteq\ & \{\alpha(\overline{{}^*_{ch}(x_n)}) \mid \exists ch : {}_0 : e' \Downarrow_6\ {}_{ch} : \alpha(\overline{x_n})\ \text{in}\ det(\mathtt{P})\} \\
& && \text{Def } {}_0,\ \text{Def 5.3.1, Prop 4.3.2, Lem 5.3.4} \\
\subseteq\ & [\![e]\!]_6^{det(P)} && \text{Def 4.6.1}
\end{aligned}$$

where

$$\mathtt{let}\ \{\overline{x_k = e_k}\}\ \mathtt{in}\ e'\ {}_0 = norm(e) := \emptyset\, [\overline{x_k \mapsto e_k}, x_e \mapsto e', x_{ch} \mapsto ch]$$

$\square$

This proof finishes the formal treatment of the transformation from functional logic to purely functional programs. The remaining chapter of this work is dedicated to the demonstration that the examined approach is practically relevant. As we will see, our transformation yields programs which can be compiled to machine code which is quite e cient when compared to existing compilation systems for the functional logic programming language Curry.

Chapter 6

Advanced Topics and Benchmarks

In this chapter we will compare an implementation of our approach to existing compilation systems for the functional logic language Curry [Hanus (ed)., 2006]. Along with testing system performance we will discuss how features available in dierent systems can be integrated into the approach presented in this work. Furthermore, the studied benchmarks will reveal opportunities for optimizations both of the presented translation scheme and that of the related systems.

The compilation systems to be compared in this chapter are given in Figure 6.1. For comparing performance on purely functional programs in Section 6.1 we will also take the Glasgow Haskell Compiler GHC[1] into account. Systems employing the GHC as part of the compilation process are tested with and without full optimization, cf. Figure 6.1. The GHC system employed for our approach and that of [Fischer et al., 2009, Braßel et al., 2010] was version `6.12.1`. All benchmarks have been taken on a computer with an Intel(R) Core(TM)2 Duo CPU E8400 @ 3.00GHz and 4 GB of memory running Debian Linux. A run-time measurement given as "×" means that the program could not be fully executed in the available memory.

In the following the reader should be aware that the presented code is *Haskell code* added to the programs *after transformation*. In order to present the actual implementation, some details treated in abstract way before need to be dealt with more concretely, in this chapter. In Section 5.1.2, for example, we have introduced a constructor `Choice :: ID` a a a in order to transform non-deterministic programs to purely functional ones. We have noted back then that such a constructor cannot be defined in Haskell. Instead we need to define a simple type class.

```
class NonDet a where
    choiceCons :: ID    a    a    a
```

---

[1] http://www.haskell.org/ghc

GHC	Glasgow Haskell Compiler
ID	Our approach employing identifiers
CM	Curry Monad [Fischer et al., 2009, Braßel et al., 2010]
MCC	The Münster Curry Compiler [Lux and Kuchen, 1999] in Version 0.9.10
PAKCS	The Portland Aachen Kiel Curry System [Hanus et al., 2010] in Version 1.9.2(9)
+	with optimization (-O2)
-	without optimization (-O0)

Figure 6.1: The systems compared

This declaration allows us to:

- declare a different `Choice` constructor for each transformed Curry type and
- map the function `choiceCons` to that constructor in instance declarations, allowing for a uniform interface for transformed programs.

Example 6.0.2 (Instances of Class `NonDet`)
Creating instances for class `NonDet` is straight forward. Consider the following two types declarations in Curry.

```
data Bool    = False | True
data List a  = Nil   | Cons a (List a)
```

The corresponding declarations in Haskell will be:

```
data Bool    = False | True
             | Choice_Bool ID Bool Bool

data List a = Nil | Cons a (List a)
            | Choice_List ID (List a) (List a)

instance NonDet Bool      where choiceCons = Choice_Bool
instance NonDet (List a)  where choiceCons = Choice_List
```

Note that these definitions shadow Haskell definitions. Whenever we need to refer to Haskell's original definitions we will use qualification, e.g., `Prelude.True`.

The implementation of different logic features examined in this chapter will require a stepwise extension of class `NonDet`.

We will discuss different features of functional logic programs separately. First we will talk about purely functional programs (Section 6.1) followed by examining the implementation of search strategies (Section 6.2). In Section 6.3 we will extend the setting by representing finitely failing computations and Section 6.4 we discuss the advantage of sharing across non-determinism which is a feature of our approach. Section 6.5 gives a more elaborate discussion of recursive let-bindings. Section 6.6 shows how our implementation can be extended to feature state-of-the-art approaches to encapsulated search. Section 6.7 discusses a way to reintroduce free variables, which are then extended for constraints (Section 6.8). In Section 6.9 we will examine drawbacks of our approach with regard to memory consumption. Finally, Section 6.10 discusses an approach to debugging of declarative programs.

6.1 Functional Programs

The translation scheme proposed in the given work is optimized towards a fast execution of the functional parts of the programs. Therefore, measuring performance on purely functional programs is an interesting topic. The programs measured in this section are taken from the "no-fib"-benchmark suite for Haskell programs [Partain, 1992].

6.1.1 First-Order Programs

The first program we consider is a simple recursive function given by the following definition. It employs sharing and will run many iterations for the calls given in Figure 6.2.

```
tak :: Int     Int     Int     Int
tak x y z = if mynot(y < x) then z
            else tak (tak (x-1) y z)
                     (tak (y-1) z x)
                     (tak (z-1) x y)
```

systems	tak 24 16 8	tak 27 16 8	tak 33 17 8
GHC+	0.01	0.04	1.02
ID-	0.12	0.41	11.05
ID+	0.08	0.31	8.10
CM-	7.18	24.98	×
CM+	5.34	19.53	×
MCC	0.42	1.54	40.36
PAKCS	11.30	40.50	1089.39

Figure 6.2: Benchmarks for first-order program `tak`

The results reveal mainly that the reimplementation of sharing necessary for the approach CM is very costly while the translation of functional programs to Prolog in PAKCS naturally shows the considerable overhead of interpretation.

6.1.2 Higher-Order Programs

We consider two higher-order programs in this section. The first is the computation of prime numbers by the well known sieve of Eratosthenes.

```
isdivs :: Int     Int     Bool
isdivs n x = mod x n /= 0
```

```
the_filter :: [Int]    [Int]
the_filter (n:ns) = filter (isdivs n) ns

primes :: [Int]
primes = map head (iterate the_filter (iterate (+1) 2))
```

The second program is a search problem and will serve for future reference for benchmarking the logic extensions of Curry. The program computes the number of solutions for the well known n queens problem.

```
queens nq = length (gen nq)
  where
    gen :: Int    [[Int]]
    gen n = if n==0
            then [[]]
            else [ (q:b) | b    gen (n-1), q    [1..nq], safe q 1 b]

safe :: Int    Int    [Int]    Bool
safe _ _ []      = True
safe x d (q:l) = x /= q && x /= q+d && x /= q-d && safe x (d+1) l
```

The results for computing the 12569th and 24001st prime number as well as the number of solutions for posing queens on a board of size 10 and 12 are given in Figure 6.3.[2]

systems	primes !! 12569	primes !! 24001	queens 10	queens 12
GHC+	2.98	18.06	0.02	0.72
ID-	138.95	577.88	0.94	33.57
ID+	47.51	217.75	0.28	11.28
CM-	×	×	17.69	×
CM+	×	×	14.58	×
MCC	13.71	55.40	0.62	22.80
PAKCS	695.19	×	14.02	502.06

Figure 6.3: Benchmarks for higher-order programs `primes` and `Queens`

It is apparent that our approach does not perform as well as expected. What is the reason for this slowdown? We come to the cause of the problem when reconsidering the discussion of higher-order programs in Section 1.1.1.2, especially Example 1.1.8. There we have shown how higher-order programs can be transformed to first-order programs by introduction of a function `apply`. The important insight to understand the slowdown for higher-order programs is that this function `apply` has to be treated as dependent on the operation (?). As `apply` potentially calls any operation present in the program it especially calls every non-deterministic one. Therefore, `apply` and—in consequence—every higher-order function has to be extended by a new argument and the operations `leftID`

---
[2] Note that for fairness of comparison we have used the standard definitions of functions from the Curry Prelude instead of the one shipped with **GHC**.

6.1. FUNCTIONAL PROGRAMS

and `rightID` have to be added everywhere to generate fresh identifiers. And although we do not really use defunctionalization in our compilation scheme, the conceptual necessity to add identifiers to all higher-order calls sticks. This explains the considerable overhead.

Example 6.1.1 (Transforming Higher-Order) *Reconsider the definition of* `map` *from Example 1.1.5.*

```
map :: (a      b)     List a    List b
map f Nil            = Nil
map f (Cons x xs)    = Cons (apply f x) (map f xs)
```

For this operation we generate the following code.

```
map :: NonDet b    Func a b    List a    ID    List b
map f Nil          i = Nil
map f (Cons x xs) i =
  let il = leftID i
      ir = rightID i
  in Cons (apply x1 x3 il) (map f xs ir)
map f (Or j x y)  i = Or j (map f x i) (map f y i)
```

Here, the type `Func a b` *is the extension of the type* `a    b` *to allow non-deterministic choice as discussed at the beginning of this chapter.*[3]

```
data Func a b = Func (a    ID    b)
              | Func_Choice ID (Func a b) (Func a b)
```

The function `apply` *is defined by:*

```
apply :: NonDet b    Func a b    a    ID    b
apply (Func f) s x = f s x
apply (Func_Choice r f1 f2) s x =
  choiceCons r (apply f1 s x) (apply f2 s x)
```

The use of higher-order operations is central for the declarative programming paradigm. Therefore, an approach to improve the situation is important. We make use of a simple observation to speed up higher-order computations. The observation is that while higher-order features are often used in functional logic programs the operations applied in a higher-order fashion are seldom non-deterministic *on the higher-order level.* Therefore, it is well worth the additional code to have *two versions* of any higher-order operation: one translated with the scheme examined in the previous chapter and the other assuming that all higher-order arguments are evaluate to a function object *deterministically.*

Example 6.1.2 *For the definition of* `map` *(cf. Example 6.1.1 above) we generate an additional version (with a prefix* `d_` *for deterministic) as follows.*

---

[3] As a side note it is more convenient for the higher-order translation to add identifiers as a last argument rather than as first.

```
d_map  :: (a        b)      List a      List b
d_map f Nil              = Nil
d_map f (Cons x xs)      = Cons (d_apply f x) (d_map f xs)
d_map f (Or i x y)       = Or i (d_map f x) (d_map f y)
```

Here, the function `d_apply` is simply defined as:

```
d_apply :: (a       b)      a       b
d_apply f x = f x
```

Note that the arguments *of a partial application may still be non-deterministic. For example, the call "*map (+coin) [1,2,3]*" can be translated using* `d_map`. *Only the much rarer case that the evaluation to the function itself is non-deterministic has to introduce the overhead. For example, the translation of* "*map ((+0) ? (+1))*" *has to employ* map *as defined in Example 6.1.1. In our experience the latter use of higher-order together with non-determinism is very rare in Curry programs. Therefore, in most cases the code duplication is immediately remedied by the elimination of dead code done during optimization.*

A simple analysis of the arguments of a given function call can give a useful approximation when it is safe to use the deterministic version of a higher-order operation. With this optimization the results for the examples of this section improve considerably as shown in Figure 6.4 where IDHO is short for our approach employing the described improvement.

systems	primes !! 12569	primes !! 24001	queens 10	queens 12
GHC+	2.98	18.06	0.02	0.72
ID-	138.95	577.88	0.94	33.57
ID+	47.51	217.75	0.28	11.28
IDHO-	8.81	44.51	0.17	7.52
IDHO+	3.94	25.78	0.12	5.24
CM-	×	×	17.69	×
CM+	×	×	14.58	×
MCC	13.71	55.40	0.62	22.80
PAKCS	695.19	×	14.02	502.06

Figure 6.4: Benchmarks for improved higher-order program `primes` `Queens`

We feel that the improvements are so encouraging that in the remainder of this chapter we will always measure run times for the programs improved for higher-order computation.

6.2 Collecting Sets of Choices

In the previous chapter we have thoroughly examined the evaluation of transformed programs assuming a given set of choices. But where does such a set of choices come from? Normally, a computation will not be provided with a complete set of choices up front but will rather construct such a set during the

6.2. COLLECTING SETS OF CHOICES

course of evaluation. The method of constructing sets of choices will in the following be referred to as a *search operation*. In this section we develop concrete implementations of three well known search strategies, namely depth-first, breadth-first, and iterative depth-first search. In addition we will examine a parallel search strategy based on concurrency features of the GHC.

The operation $hnf(\cdot, \cdot)$ (cf. Section 5.2.1) can be seen as a first rudimentary search operation. Recall that this operation was provided with some means to look up information corresponding to identifiers. This information was used whenever the evaluation to head normal form encountered a `Choice`-constructor. The impact of the information was to continue the evaluation either with the left or the right sub expression of the `Choice`-constructor. For technical simplicity, in the previous chapter we were content with encoding the information as the numbers 1 and 2, respectively. In this chapter we will make full use of Haskell and encode the information as the following enumeration type.

```
data Choice = ChooseLeft | ChooseRight | NoChoice
```

In order to preserve the soundness results obtained in the previous chapter any search operation must behave towards `ChooseLeft` and `ChooseRight` as $hnf(\cdot, \cdot)$ does towards 1 and 2, respectively. The last alternative `NoChoice`, however, marks the extension of $hnf(\cdot, \cdot)$ to a full search operation. Whenever no information corresponding to the encountered identifier is available the search operation will make a new choice and manage the selection of the current set of choices.

As we have remarked in the previous chapter dierent implementations of the type `ID` of identifiers are possible. Our first approach implements identifiers as *memory cells* (of the Haskell type `IORef`). This choice is lead by considerations with regard to e ciency both where time and memory are concerned.

```
newtype ID = ID (IORef Choice)
```

With this definition the current "set of choices" is simply the set of values contained in the memory cells allocated for identifiers. We provide two operations to manage the information about a set of choices.

```
lookupChoice :: ID      IO Choice
lookupChoice (ID ref) = readIORef ref

setChoice :: ID     Choice    IO ()
setChoice (ID ref) c = writeIORef ref c
```

The type class `NonDet` was introduced at the beginning of this chapter to obtain a uniform interface to *construct* non-deterministic choices. We will now extend this type class to uniformly allow deconstruction. For this we encode the information whether a given value is a non-deterministic choice or a deterministic value (in head normal form[4]) by the Haskell data type `Try`.

---
[4] We have discussed in Section 5.2.1 how complete normal forms can be computed by employing evaluation to head normal form.

134   CHAPTER 6. ADVANCED TOPICS AND BENCHMARKS

```
data Try a = Val a | Choice ID a a

class NonDet a where
  ...
  try :: a    Try a
```

Generating instances for the extension of class NonDet is straightforward.

Example 6.2.1 (Implementation of try) *Reconsider the definitions of Example 6.0.2. The declarations for the functions try can be given as:*

```
instance NonDet Bool where
  ...
  try (Choice_Bool i x y) = Choice i x y
  try x = Val x

instance NonDet (List a) where
  ...
  try (Choice_List i x y) = Choice i x y
  try x = Val x
```

To give a first impression how the operations on identifiers and try work together we consider how to print all values of a given expression according to depth-first search.

Example 6.2.2 (Printing Values, Depth First)

```
printValsDFS :: (Show a,NonDet a)    Try a    IO ()
printValsDFS (Val v)            = print v
printValsDFS (Choice i x1 x2) = lookupChoice i >>= choose
  where
    choose ChooseLeft  = printValsDFS (try x1)
    choose ChooseRight = printValsDFS (try x2)
    choose NoChoice    = do newChoice ChooseLeft  x1
                            newChoice ChooseRight x2

    newChoice j x = do setChoice i j
                       printValsDFS (try x)
                       setChoice i NoChoice
```

When no choice has yet been made for identifier i *(i.e., the result of calling* (lookupChoice i) *is* NoChoice*), the operation* printValsDFS *will first follow the left (*x1*) and then the right sub expression (*x2*) of the* Choice*-constructor. Note, that in this case the choice has to be reset to* NoChoice *after each recursive call to* printValsDFS*.*

With regard to applications it will not be enough to simply print all values of a search. Rather we would like to obtain each value in an on-demand fashion. For this it is convenient to define a new list structure which is able to yield monadic values on demand.

6.2. COLLECTING SETS OF CHOICES

```
data MList m a = MCons a (m (MList m a)) | MNil
```

As usual such a list is either empty (`MNil`) or contains a value of type `a` along with the remaining list (`MCons`). The remaining list, however, is an argument of the higher-kind type parameter `m`. For example a non-empty list of type `MList IO Int` will contain a number and an `IO`-action to yield a new (possibly empty) list.

We only give the type signature of the according operations on monadic lists as the implementation is simple.

```
mnil   :: Monad m    m (MList m a)
mcons  :: Monad m    a   m (MList m a)   m (MList m a)
(+++)  :: Monad m    m (MList m a)   m (MList m a)   m (MList m a)
(|<)   :: Monad m    m (MList m a)   m ()   m (MList m a)
```

As the reader might expect `mnil` and `mcons` are used to construct empty and non-empty monadic lists, respectively while (+++) concatenates two given monadic lists. Operation |< adds a monadic action of type `m ()` to the end of the list. The search operations will yield lists in the `IO` monad such that the following abbreviation will be handy.

```
type IOList a = MList IO a
```

Example 6.2.3 (Printing Values of Monadic Lists) *Printing all values in a monadic list can be defined as*

```
printVals :: Show a    IOList a    IO ()
printVals MNil                    = return ()
printVals (MCons x getRest) = print x >> getRest >>= printVals
```

We will consider the implementation of different search strategies in separate sub sections. Firstly, we will look at the programs used for benchmarking, which are simple variants of Examples 1.1.12 and 1.1.18. The difference for both programs is that the evaluation of `insert` does not produce failing computations as these will not be introduced before the next section.

Example 6.2.4 (Permutations With and Without Sharing)
Definition of `insert` *for program* `perm`:

```
insert x [] = [x]
insert x (y:ys) = x:y:ys
insert x (y:ys) = y : insert x ys
```

Definition of `insert` *for program* `permSh`:

```
insert x [] = [x]
insert x (y:ys) = x:y:ys ? y : insert x ys
```

The definition of `permute` *is for both programs:*

```
permute [] = []
permute (x:xs) = insert x (permute xs)
```

The dierence between the programs `permSh` and `perm` seems negligible: the first calls operation (?) where the other employs two separate rules to express the non-deterministic choice. Semantically, both definitions can be easily seen to be equivalent. In our approach both are transformed in exactly the same way since we treat (?) as the primitive for non-deterministic choice. We will see, however, that drastic dierences ensue for the run-times of the two versions in most of the other approaches. The reason for these eects is that the definition of `insert` by (?) seems to make a sharing for `x`, `y` and `xs` necessary where the definition by two separate rules makes the fact obvious that no sharing is needed. For the present examination the results should support the claim that reusing the sharing of the host language can be profitable for e ciency. In addition, the examples seem to suggest that even the simplest of sharing analysis could drastically improve the run times of some of the related approaches.

6.2.1 Depth-First Search

With the representation of monadic lists it is straight forward to define a search operation employing depth-first search.

```
searchDFS :: NonDet a    Try a      IO (IOList a)
searchDFS (Val v)                 = mcons v mnil
searchDFS (Choice i x1 x2) = lookupChoice i >>= choose
  where
    choose ChooseLeft   = searchDFS (try x1)
    choose ChooseRight  = searchDFS (try x2)
    choose NoChoice     = newChoice ChooseLeft  x1 +++
                          newChoice ChooseRight x2

    newChoice c x = do setChoice i c
                       searchDFS (try x) |< setChoice i NoChoice
```

Figure 6.5 shows the result of benchmarking permutations employing depth-first search.[5]

6.2.2 Breadth-First Search

The PAKCS system does not allow to influence the search strategy and relies on depth-first search as provided by the Prolog host language. In our approach breadth-first search can be defined as follows.

```
searchBFS :: NonDet a    Try a     IO (IOList a)
searchBFS x = bfs [] [] (return ()) (return ()) x
  where
```

---

[5]For CM we have used a monad based on functional lists. In PAKCS and MCC we used the primitive `findall` to measure the time for pure depth-first search without failing computations, e.g.:
```
dfsSearch = findall goal0
goal0 x = x=:=perm [1 .. 9]
```

6.2. COLLECTING SETS OF CHOICES

systems	perm [1..9]	perm [1..10]	permSh [1..9]	permSh [1..10]
IDHO-	0.60	6.61	0.60	6.61
IDHO+	0.21	2.44	0.21	2.44
CM-	0.93	9.50	15.20	189.37
CM+	0.77	7.75	18.52	230.28
MCC	0.44	4.56	0.44	4.63
PAKCS	6.07	61.19	7.36	78.17

Figure 6.5: Benchmarks for depth-first search

```
bfs xs ys _   reset (Val v)       = reset >> mcons v (next xs ys)
bfs xs ys set reset (Choice i x y) = set >> lookupChoice i >>= choose
  where
    choose ChooseLeft  = bfs xs ys (return ()) reset (try x)
    choose ChooseRight = bfs xs ys (return ()) reset (try y)
    choose NoChoice    = do
      reset
      next xs ((newSet ChooseLeft , newReset, x) :
               (newSet ChooseRight, newReset, y) : ys)

    newSet c = set   >> setChoice i c
    newReset = reset >> setChoice i NoChoice

next [] []                     = mnil
next [] ((set,reset,y):ys)     = bfs ys [] set reset (try y)
next ((set,reset,x):xs) ys     = bfs xs ys set reset (try x)
```

Note that the strategy needs to ensure that all IORefs are set before looking up a value and that the memory cells are reset whenever a change of context occurs.

Figure 6.6 shows the result of benchmarking permutations employing breadth-first search. For CM we have used the level monad[6] and for MCC we used the primitive try to implement breadth-first search analogously as follows:

```
bfsSearch :: [a     Success]     [a]
bfsSearch = bfs [] []
  where
    bfs xs ys []        = next xs ys
    bfs xs ys [v]       = unpack v : next xs ys
    bfs xs ys (x:y:zs) = next xs (x:y:zs ++ ys)

    next [] []       = []
    next [] (y:ys) = bfs ys [] (try y)
    next (x:xs) ys = bfs xs ys (try x)
```

---

[6]available under http://hackage.haskell.org/package/level-monad

systems	perm [1..9]	perm [1..10]	permSh [1..9]	permSh [1..10]
IDHO-	1.17	18.18	1.17	18.18
IDHO+	0.45	7.38	0.45	7.38
CM-	0.93	10.08	14.36	176.15
CM+	0.76	7.45	14.87	189.77
MCC	0.69	10.41	0.73	11.58

Figure 6.6: Benchmarks for breadth-first search

6.2.3 Iterative Depth-First Search

Iterative depth-first search (IDFS) is the idea to explore the search space in a depth-first manner but only up to a given bound. This bound is increased step-wise until no more solutions are to be found (which is not always known, naturally). The strategy combines the good memory behavior of depth-first search with the completeness of breadth-first search while having a proportional impact on run-time, only. We mainly include the examination of this strategy here because it could not be implemented correctly with our former approach [Braßel and Huch, 2009].

For IDFS we still want to compute lists of values. During evaluation, however, we need to distinguish the case that a list ended because there were no more values to be found or because we have hit the depth boundary. For this purpose we define a list with two dierent constructors for an empty list.

```
data DoubleNil a = a :< DoubleNil a | Abort | NoMore
```

The concatenation of two double-nil lists (++<) has to mind that `Abort` needs to have precedence over `NoMore`.

```
(++<) :: DoubleNil a   DoubleNil a   DoubleNil a
Abort      ++< NoMore = Abort
(x :< xs) ++< ys      = x :< (xs ++< ys)
nil        ++< ys     = ys
```

We extend double-nil lists to a monad minding that finding a single value via `return` means that there are no more values to be found.

```
instance Monad DoubleNil where
  return x =  x :< NoMore

  Abort    >>= _ = Abort
  NoMore   >>= _ = NoMore
  (x :< xs) >>= g = g x ++< (xs >>= g)
```

A run of iterative depth-first search maps a given boundary to a double-nil list. We declare instances of this definition for the classes `Monad` and `MonadPlus`.

```
newtype IterDFS a = IterDFS (Int   DoubleNil a)

instance Monad IterDFS where
  return x = IterDFS (λ n   if n<stepIDFS then return x else NoMore)
```

6.2. COLLECTING SETS OF CHOICES

```
    IterDFS f >>= g = IterDFS (λ n    join $ do
                                      x ← f n
                                      let IterDFS g' = g x
                                      return (g' n))

instance MonadPlus IterDFS where
  mzero = IterDFS (λ _    NoMore)
  IterDFS f 'mplus' IterDFS g =
    IterDFS (λ n   if   n>0
                   then let n'=n-1 in f n' +< g n'
                   else Abort)
```

Finally, the iteration is controlled by:

```
runIterDFS :: IterDFS a    [a]
runIterDFS (IterDFS f) = collect 0 (f 0)
  where
    collect n NoMore       = []
    collect n Abort        = let n'=n+stepIDFS in collect n' (f n')
    collect n (x :< xs) = x : collect n xs
```

The constant `stepIDFS` is considered to be a global parameter for the search strategy. For our benchmarks we have used `stepIDFS=10`.

The definitions given above are used to benchmark the CM system. The code for MCC and our approach transfers the same basic idea to use the `try` primitive and an adaption of monadic lists, respectively.

Figure 6.7 shows the result of benchmarking permutations employing iterative depth-first search.

systems	perm [1..9]	perm [1..10]	permSh [1..9]	permSh [1..10]
IDHO-	1.05	15.31	1.05	15.31
IDHO+	0.25	5.36	0.25	5.36
CM-	1.46	15.51	16.96	×
CM+	1.14	12.30	×	×
MCC	1.92	23.53	2.09	24.32

Figure 6.7: Benchmarks for iterative depth-first search

6.2.4 Parallel Search

In conjunction with the CM system a monad based on search trees[7] has been developed on which a parallel search employing GHC concurrency is defined.[8]

The idea to use `IORefs` to model sets of choices cannot be used for the concurrent case as dierent threads might need to access the same identifier at the same time. Using thread-safe memory cells like `MVars` would inhibit

---

[7]Available at http://hackage.haskell.org/package/tree-monad
[8]Available at http://hackage.haskell.org/package/parallel-tree-search

the parallelism since every thread would need to lock all variables it depends on. Therefore, every thread needs its own set of choices and we introduce a representation without side eects. For this we use integers as identifiers and search trees to store information about choices.

```
type ID = Integer
type SetOfChoices = Map ID Choice
```

In analogy to the monadic actions defined above for `IORefs` we define the following operations to manage sets of choices:

```
lookupChoice' :: SetOfChoices   ID       Choice
lookupChoice' set i =
  maybe NoChoice id (Data.Map.lookup i set)

setChoice' :: SetOfChoices    ID     Choice    SetOfChoice
setChoice' set i NoChoice = Data.Map.insert i c set
```

Using these operations the following code lifts the values produced by our approach to any monad conforming to the `MonadPlus` protocol. We will make good use of the abstraction of this definition later on in Section 6.6.

```
searchMPlus :: (NonDet a, MonadPlus m)    SetOfChoices    Try a    m a
searchMPlus _ Fail            = mzero
searchMPlus _ (Val v)         = return v
searchMPlus set (Choice i x y) = choose (lookupChoice' set i)
  where
    choose ChooseLeft  = searchMPlus set (try x)
    choose ChooseRight = searchMPlus set (try y)
    choose NoChoice    = searchMPlus (pick ChooseLeft)  (try x)
               'mplus' searchMPlus (pick ChooseRight) (try y)

    pick = setChoice' set i
```

Parallel search can be employed in our approach and the CM system only. Figure 6.8 shows the result of benchmarking permutations employing parallel search.

systems	perm [1..9]	perm [1..10]	permSh [1..9]	permSh [1..10]
IDHO-	0.38	4.28	0.38	4.28
IDHO+	0.36	3.98	0.36	3.98
CM-	0.99	10.14	14.73	182.47
CM+	0.77	8.01	14.18	176.49

Figure 6.8: Benchmarks for parallel search

6.3 Failing Computations

Non-determinism is only one means to model search in (functional-)logic programs. Another one is (finite) failure. Unlike in functional programs, where

6.3. FAILING COMPUTATIONS

failing computations are considered programming errors, a functional logic programmer uses incomplete patterns or guards to restrict search. For example, the `sort` function introduced in Example 1.1.18 uses a guard that fails for unsorted lists in order to constrain the set of results to sorted permutations of the input.

In order to model failing computations we introduce an additional special constructor `Failure`—both to each transformed data declaration and to class `NonDet`.

```
class NonDet a where
    ...
    failCons :: a
```

Example 6.3.1 (Adding Failure to Data Declarations)
Reconsider the definitions of Example 6.0.2. The declarations are extended for representing failure as:

```
data Bool   = False | True
            | Choice_Bool ID Bool Bool
            | Fail_Bool

data List a = Nil | Cons a (List a)
            | Choice_List ID (List a) (List a)
            | Fail_List

instance NonDet Bool where
    ...
    failCons = Fail_Bool

instance NonDet (List a) where
    ...
    failCons = Fail_List
```

Similar to the special rules for `Choice`, every pattern matching needs to be extended with a rule for `Failure`. For example, consider the transformed version of `sort` from Example 4.2.1[9]:

```
sort :: ID      List Int    List Int
sort i l = guard (sorted p) p where p = permute i l

guard :: Bool     a      a
guard True                 z = z
guard (Choice_Bool i x y) z = Choice i (guard x z) (guard y z)
guard _                   _ = consFail

sorted :: List Int    Bool
sorted Nil                    = True
sorted (Cons m xs)            = sorted2 m xs
sorted (Choice_List i x y) = consChoice i (sorted x) (sorted y)
```

---
[9]We omit the definitions of ($\leq$) and (`&&`).

```
sorted _                         = consFail

sorted2 :: Int      List Int     Bool
sorted2 m Nil                    = True
sorted2 m (Cons n ns)            = m ≤ n && sorted (Cons n ns)
sorted2 m (Choice_List i x y)   = consChoice i (sorted2 m x) (sorted2 m y)
sorted2 _ _                      = consFail
```

We introduce a function `guard` to express guards in functional logic programs. This function returns its second argument if the first argument is `True`. Additionally, we add a default case for all patterns that have not been matched to every function to return `consFail` in case of a pattern match error and to propagate such errors. In order to extend our implementation of failures to include more informative error messages like, e.g., proposed by Hanus [2007a], one would a) add arguments to the constructors representing failure and b) change the new rules to attach such information.

For the benchmarks we use the program for permutation sort as given in Example 1.1.18. In addition we examine the following variant of permutation sort where the result of `permute` is not shared and the function `sorted` yields its argument if it is sorted and fails otherwise. As we will see, this variant has a considerable eect on the run-times which behaves dierently in the examined systems.

Example 6.3.2 (Variant of Permutation Sort)

```
sort' :: [Int]      [Int]
sort' l = sorted (permute l)

sorted :: [Int]     [Int]
sorted []         = []
sorted [x]        = [x]
sorted (m:n:ns) | m ≤ n = m : sorted (n:ns)
```

Figure 6.9 shows the result of computing values for both variants of permutation sort of the two expressions `sort (2 : [15..1])` and `sort (2 : [20..1])`.

As we see there is a considerable speedup for every system with the exception of the MCC, which proves able to produce nearly identical run-times for both examples. Comparing the translation schemes for the two examples could therefore bring additional insights in possible improvements.

6.4 Sharing Across Non-Determinism

Sharing across non-determinism is the ability of a given compilation system to compute *deterministic expressions* at most once, regardless of the non-deterministic choices involved. For example, we could expect that the time for evaluating the expressions `e1=primes !! 1000` and `e2=let x=e1 in x ? x` should be roughly the same. (The cost to find the 1000th prime number makes the cost

6.4. SHARING ACROSS NON-DETERMINISM

systems	sort (2:[15..1])	sort (2:[20..1])
IDHO-	0.93	39.33
IDHO+	0.48	20.34
CM-	2.02	82.79
CM+	2.09	85.52
MCC	0.58	26.12
PAKCS	3.13	122.57

systems	sort' (2:[15..1])	sort' (2:[20..1])
IDHO-	0.80	34.78
IDHO+	0.37	16.39
CM-	1.57	61.62
CM+	1.29	52.98
MCC	0.58	26.16
PAKCS	2.42	95.78

Figure 6.9: Benchmarks for computing with failures

to establish a single choice point negligible.) For all of the examined systems with the exception of our approach, however, evaluating e2 takes double the time of evaluating e1. This is because e1 is *evaluated twice* during the course of evaluation in the other systems. As even comparably e cient functional logic algorithms can induce a number of choices, the eect on the resulting run-times can be considerable and hard to predict, especially in combination with laziness.

Example 6.4.1 (Sharing Across Non-Determinism) *Reconsider the definitions from Sections 6.1.2 and 6.3. For these definitions we measured run times for the following goals.*

```
goal0 = [primes!!800, primes!!801, primes!!802, primes!!803]
goal1 = sort' [6143, 6151, 6163, 6173]
goal2 = sort' [primes!!800, primes!!801, primes!!802, primes!!803]
```

systems	goal0	goal1	goal2
IDHO-	0.03	0.00	0.03
IDHO+	0.02	0.00	0.02
CM-	13.13	0.00	121.28
CM+	11.72	0.00	102.28
MCC	0.20	0.00	2.27
PAKCS	9.55	0.01	95.06

Figure 6.10: Benchmarks sharing across non-determinism

As the results in Figure 6.10 indicate any of the examined systems can sort a list with four elements within milliseconds (goal1). If the same list is, how-

ever, given as an unevaluated expression (goal2) the evaluation takes considerably longer than simply computing that list deterministically (goal0). For our approach, however, the equation t(goal2) = t(goal0) + t(goal1) holds (with negligible deviation).

The consequence of Example 6.4.1 is that without this kind of sharing programmers have to avoid using non-determinism for functions that might be applied to expensive computations. But in connection with *laziness* a programmer cannot know which arguments are already computed because evaluations are suspended until their value is demanded. Hence, the connection of laziness with logic search always threatens to perform with the considerable slowdown discussed above. Thus, sadly, when looking for possibilities to improve efficiency, the programmer in a lazy functional logic language is well advised to either try to eliminate the logic features he might have employed or to strictly evaluate expressions prior to each search. Both alternatives show that he still follows either the functional or the logic paradigm but cannot profit from a seamless integration of both. Therefore, sharing across non-determinism is a crucial ingredient when aiming at the seamless integration of both paradigms of declarative programming.

How is sharing across non-determinism achieved in our approach? To understand the effect it should be enough to examine the evaluation of the two expressions e1 and e2 from above in some detail.

Example 6.4.2 (Achieving Sharing Across Non-Determinism)
Our transformation produces the following Haskell code for e1 *and* e2.[10]

```
e1 :: C_Int
e1 = primes !! C_Int 1000

e2 :: ID    C_Int
e2 i = let x = e1 in (x ? x) i
```

Here C_Int *is a wrapper we need to add choice and fail constructors to integers.*

```
data C_Int = C_Int Integer
           | Int_Choice ID C_Int C_Int
           | Int_Fail
```

The evaluation of e2 *can be sketched as follows, cf. Section 1.1.1.3.*

```
e2 = let x = e1 in (x ? x) i
   = let x = e1 in choiceCons i x x
   = let x = e1 in Int_Choice i x x
   ...
   = let x = 7927 in Int_Choice i x x
   = Int_Choice i 7927 7927
```

Thus, the achievement of sharing across non-determinism is a direct consequence of employing the sharing of the host language Haskell.

---
[10] We assume the optimization for higher-order programs discussed in Section 6.1.2.

6.5. RECURSIVE LET BINDINGS

With regard to related work a different approach to formalize sharing deterministic computations across non-deterministic branches is called *bubbling* [Antoy et al., 2006a]. Bubbling is defined as a graph rewriting technique and the call-time choice semantics is realized by manipulating the graph globally. We, in contrast, do only the local manipulation of lifting or-nodes and realize call-time choice by storing branching information and comparing or-references later on. Our approach definitely speeds up deterministic computations in comparison, putting the whole overhead on branching. Unfortunately, there is no mature implementation of bubbling for us to compare with yet. We will come back to a more detailed discussion of bubbling in Section 6.10.2.

6.5 Recursive let bindings

In Section 2.3.1 we have introduced and discussed a change of the semantics with regard to [Albert et al., 2005]. As we have seen the change effects the semantics with regard to recursive let structures whose evaluation induces non-determinism. In this section we will examine this issue deeper giving further justification for our choice of semantics.

When restricting the discussion to *functional* languages, recursive let bindings can be defined in terms of other language features. The defining law for them is the following equation, which is used to introduce the meaning of recursive let [Peyton Jones, 1987, p42]:

$$\text{letrec } \{x = e\} \text{ in } e' := \text{let } \{x = \text{fix}(\lambda x.e)\} \text{ in } e'$$

where `fix f=f (fix f)`. In other words, recursive bindings can be eliminated by introduction of recursive function definitions.[11] Incidentally, the original version of semantics from [Albert et al., 2005] is constructed such that this law also holds in functional *logic* languages. Indeed, the evaluation of the expression let {x = T ? case x of {T ↦ F }} in x as introduced in Section 2.3.1 behaves exactly as if we had defined an *operation* x=T ? case x of {T ↦ F } in the program and would simply evaluate the expression x(), i.e., a call to that operation. In this view, the original version of the semantics seems preferable. (Even if, as we have seen in the quote in Section 2.3.1, this was not the reason to define it thus.) With our version of semantics, however, recursive let bindings cannot be eliminated from the program without considering its semantics. They introduce a new entity for which, as a side remark, a denotational semantics is hard to be obtained. This point is illustrated by the following example adapted from [Schmidt-Schauß et al., 2009].[12]

Example 6.5.1 (Recursive let is a New Entity) *Consider the following operation definitions.*

---

[11] For a recent work on a more elaborated elimination scheme for functional languages see [Siegel, 2008].

[12] My thanks to Jan Christiansen who brought this example to my notice.

146 CHAPTER 6. ADVANCED TOPICS AND BENCHMARKS

```
False !> e = e

list1 xs = False : null xs !> [False]
list2 xs = null xs !> [False,True]
list3 xs = False : null xs !> [True]

nd1 xs = list1 xs ? list2 xs
nd2 xs = nd1 xs    ? list3 xs
```

With regard to any possible input the operations nd1 *and* nd2 *behave the same, namely, either yield* False:⊥ *when the argument* xs *diverges or fails or yield* [False,False] ? [False,True] *when the argument* xs *evaluates to a non-empty list in finitely many steps. The situation changes, however, when the operations are called in a recursive context like this:*

```
goal0 = let xs = nd1 xs in xs
goal1 = let xs = nd2 xs in xs
```

In this context a fair search will yield only the value [False,False] *for* goal0 *and* [False,False] ? [False,True] *for* goal1 *as the ambitious reader could verify by the rules given in Chapter 2. This means that any denotational approach would have to assign a dierent semantics to* nd1 *and* nd2 *in order to faithfully reflect recursive* let *bindings.*

By now the reader might wonder whether the original definition of the rules might be better after all because it would allow the elimination of recursive let bindings. However, as we will see next this conception would render many transformations incorrect. Especially, this would eect transformations which seem natural and are employed by any Curry system in use today.[13]

Example 6.5.2 (Transforming let **Bindings)** *Consider the following five expressions:*

```
expr1 = let xs = (0?1) : xs
            ys = head xs : ys in  head xs + head ys

expr2 = let xs = let x=0?1 in x : xs
            ys = head xs : ys in  head xs + head ys

expr3 = let x  = 0?1
            xs = x : xs
            ys = head xs : ys in  head xs + head ys

expr4 = let x  = 0?1
            xs = x : xs
            ys = x : ys in  head xs + head ys

expr5 = let x  = 0?1     in
```

---

[13] I thank Holger Siegel for the examples and the fruitful discussion of the recursive let bindings in Curry and Haskell.

6.5. RECURSIVE LET BINDINGS

```
let xs = x : xs in
let ys = x : ys in  head xs + head ys
```

As the reader may verify, all five expressions evaluate to the same values, namely 0 or 2 with the rules of Figure 2.1. And so they should, since the dierences from one expression to the other are all covered by well known equivalences. These equivalences are widely considered to hold also for functional logic languages – both on a theoretical level and on the implementation level. Especially, expr2 *and* expr3 *on the one hand as well as* expr4 *and* expr5 *are identified by all major Curry implementations by mapping them to the same intermediate code. The step from* expr1 *to* expr2 *is a standard* let *introduction step like those used by the flat operation. In a calculus for the manipulation of* let *expressions for functional logic languages [López-Fraguas et al., 2007], this step corresponds to the rewrite rule "**(LetIn)**". From* expr2 *to* expr3 *we have another standard transformation step called "**(Flat)**" [López-Fraguas et al., 2007]. From* expr3 *to* expr4 *we have an inlining of the* deterministic *operation* head*. Such a step is also considered valid in the known approaches to functional logic computations. Finally, from* expr4 *to* expr5 *we get by breaking up the (hierarchically ordered)* let *bindings. Such a step is especially often used by compilers in order to minimize complex binding groups. The let calculus [López-Fraguas et al., 2007] does feature binding groups larger than one* let $\{\overline{x_k = e_k}\}$ *in* e *only "as a short cut for"* let $\{x_1 = e_1\}$ *in* ...in let $\{x_k = e_k\}$ *in* e *[López-Fraguas et al., 2007, page 200] which documents how strongly the authors feel that the step from* expr4 *to* expr5 *preserves semantics.*

However, with the definition of recursive let *bindings by recursive functions, e.g., by employing* fix*, the expressions* expr1 *and* expr5 *have a dierent meaning. Beginning with* expr5*, we get the according expression*

```
expr5' = let x  = 0?1    in
         let xs = fix (λ xs    x : xs) in
         let ys = fix (λ ys    x : ys) in head xs + head ys
```

With a bit of lambda lifting and the introduction of recursive functions we get the following equivalent first order program:

```
expr5' = let x  = 0?1 in head (xs x) + head (ys x)
xs x = x : xs x
ys x = x : ys x
```

It can be seen that by call-time choice semantics the expression expr5' *can only be evaluated to the values* 0 *and* 2 *since "there is always the same choice for"* x*. But what about the two bindings in* expr1 *which are in the same binding group? Shall we introduce two functions* xs *and* ys *for them, implicitly assuming that* expr1 *is equivalent to the following expression?*

```
expr1_b = let xs = (0?1) : xs    in
          let ys = head xs : ys in  head xs + head ys
```

In this case we get

```
expr1' = head xs + head ys
xs = (0?1) : xs
ys = head xs : ys
```

For this program it is easy to see that `expr1` also evaluates to 1, since there are separate choices for (0?1) in each unfolding of the operation xs.

All in all the example illustrates that transformations used in many Curry systems like hierarchically ordering binding groups would no longer be valid when recursive let bindings could be replaced by recursive operations.

After all we have seen the best option might be to disallow recursive let bindings in functional logic languages altogether. However, the concept of such bindings has proven useful in functional languages both in terms of expressiveness and e ciency. The most prominent example is the generation of regular numbers (also known as Hamming Numbers) which we will use as one of the benchmarks in this section. Therefore, a good compromise might be to allow recursive let bindings for expressions only which do not depend on the operation (?), i.e., such expressions which are sure to be deterministic.

The first benchmarks of this section feature both a purely functional and a functional logic program employing recursive let bindings.

Example 6.5.3 (Benchmark Regular Numbers)

```
reg n = let h = 1 : (map (2 ) h 'union'
                     (map (3 ) h 'union' map (5 ) h))
        in h !! n

union :: [Int]    [Int]     [Int]
union (a:as) (b:bs)
      | a < b    = a : union      as  (b:bs)
      | a == b   = a : union      as      bs
      | otherwise = b : union (a:as)     bs
```

The second benchmark makes use of Curry's logic features within a recursive let binding.

Example 6.5.4 (Benchmark Non-Deterministic Swap)
The operation `replace` exchanges any element of a given list by a given value and yields the new list along with the element which was replaced.

```
replace :: a   [a]    ([a],a)
replace x (y:ys) = (x:ys,y) ? (y:zs,z)
   where
      (zs,z) = replace x ys
```

The operation `swap` makes use of a recursive binding to swap two elements of a given list [Erkök, 2002].

```
swap :: [Int]    [Int]
swap xs = let (ys,y) = replace z xs
              (zs,z) = replace y ys in zs
```

6.6. ENCAPSULATED SEARCH

Thus, a call to `swap` *yields non-deterministically all possibilities to exchange elements in that list (including exchanging an element by itself).*

`swap [1..3] = [1,2,3] ? [2,1,3] ? [3,2,1] ? [1,3,2]`

Depending on the search strategy some of the results may be computed more than once.

Figure 6.11 shows the results of benchmarking the illustrated programs. For `reg` we have added the GHC to the systems as the program is purely functional. The benchmark could not be executed by the MCC since it does not provide numbers of arbitrary size. The CM approach does not feature recursive `let` bindings at all.

systems	`reg 50000`	`reg 100000`	`swap [1..100]`	`swap [1..200]`
GHC+	0.02	0.05	—	—
IDHO+	0.42	0.85	0.10	0.90
MCC	—	—	0.18	1.24
PAKCS	1.34	2.72	4.29	34.28

Figure 6.11: Benchmarks recursive let

6.6 Encapsulated Search

In Section 6.2 we have seen how the set of values of a possibly non-deterministic computation can be collected and accessed. There, the intention was to provide operations programmed *in Haskell* which were to be added to the transformed programs. *Encapsulated search* is an extension of a functional logic programming language which allows to access such values from *within the functional logic program*. In our case this means that encapsulated search enables the Curry programmer to access the set of all possible values of a given expression in his Curry program. Encapsulated search is employed whenever dierent values of one expression have to be related in some way, e.g., to compute the minimal value of a given expression and in a more structured setting also to formulate a search strategy.

Regarding related work Lux [1999] was the first to describe an approach to the implementation of encapsulated search for lazy functional logic languages. The described approach was integrated in the MCC compilation system. Later, as described by Lux [2004], an alternative implementation with the same operational behavior was examined and compared to the first implementation.

A theoretic treatment of constructive approaches to negation as failure in lazy functional logic languages is developed in the series of articles López-Fraguas and Sánchez-Hernández [2000, 2002, 2004], Sánchez-Hernández [2006]. The first of these papers, López-Fraguas and Sánchez-Hernández [2000], extends the setting of lazy functional logic languages to a rewriting logic with failure. In López-Fraguas and Sánchez-Hernández [2002] a narrowing relation is developed for this approach and programs are extended such that the user can express operations in a set-like way. The whole theory is extended to a wider range of programs in the article López-Fraguas and Sánchez-Hernández [2004] and, finally, an experimental step towards the implementation of the approach is given with Sánchez-Hernández [2006]. From our point of view the latter implementation seems similar with regard to the operational behavior of encapsulated search in the MCC. A more elaborated comparison between the approaches does, however, not exist to date.

In Braßel et al. [2004b] several problems of encapsulated search in functional logic languages are discussed and the existing implementations are divided in two basic categories, *strong* and *weak* encapsulation. These two categories will be explained in more detail in Section 6.6.2. Here it suces to know that the approaches mentioned so far fall under the category "weak". Braßel et al. [2004b] argue that from the application point of view a dierent approach to encapsulated search as given de facto in Prolog and the PAKCS system for Curry is desirable. The problem with this dierent approach, (strong encapsulation), was, however, that existing systems back in 2004 did lack a declarative operational semantics; the results depended on the order of evaluation.

The article by Braßel and Huch [2007a] presented the first approach to strong encapsulation which did not depend on the order of evaluation. In the same year Antoy and Braßel [2007] presented an analysis of the problems of weak encapsulation on base of term graph rewriting. One of the aims of the latter work was to argue that a weak encapsulating view on programs is also important in many application cases and that in the long run a mix of both approaches might be needed.

The most recent contribution to the ongoing discussion is given by Antoy and Hanus [2009]. There, a proposal for a syntactic extension of functional logic programming is made. The idea is to provide the programmer with an approach to encapsulated search which is more intuitive and predictable. The article also contains a formalism based on term graph rewriting to show that the approach – like all the others mentioned above with the exception of Antoy and Braßel [2007] – does indeed not depend on the order of evaluation. The article gives only basic ideas about how to implement the approach.

In this section we present the first implementation which combines the advantages of Braßel and Huch [2007a] with the one presented in Antoy and Hanus [2009]. In Section 6.6.1 we will show how to implement a solution to the problems discussed in Braßel et al. [2004b]. Section 6.6.2 presents how to implement the approach of Antoy and Hanus [2009]. In both sections we will also examine benchmarks for the presented implementations.

6.6.1 Primitives to Provide Encapsulated Search

Operations to provide encapsulated search come in dierent flavors. The first family of operations we consider computes a list of values for a given argument. For each search strategy S there may be one such operation which we will denote by `allValues`S and which is of type `a` `[a]`.

6.6. ENCAPSULATED SEARCH

Example 6.6.1 (Encapsulated Search with `allValues`) *In the context of the program of Example 6.5.4 we have*

```
nub (sort (allValuesDFS (swap [1,2,3])))
 = [[1,2,3],[1,3,2],[2,1,3],[3,2,1]]
```

where `nub` *eliminates duplicates in a given list. The operations* `allValues`S *should provide the list of values lazily. This is important in those cases in which there are infinitely many possible values. For example, an operation to yield all natural numbers could be defined as follows, see also Example 1.1.19.*

```
nat = 0 ? 2 nat ? 2 nat+1
```

Any strict implementation of any `allValues`S *would diverge when applied to* `nat`. *A lazy operation* `allValuesDFS` *(employing depth-first search) will only compute a subset of the natural numbers for this definition, typically 0,2,4,6,8 ... whereas* `allValuesBFS` *would eventually yield any natural number (as long as the memory su ces).*

In principle, the main idea to implement encapsulated search has already been introduced in Section 6.2.4. There, in order to improve the possible parallelism of the dierent threads for parallel search we introduced a pure data structure `SetOfChoices` to collect choices instead of the `IORefs` employed before. Especially, we have presented the function

```
searchMPlus :: (NonDet a, MonadPlus m)    SetOfChoices    Try a    m a
```

which computes the possible values of a given expression for a given instance of `MonadPlus`. Thus, all we have to do to implement `allValuesDFS` is to provide the according instance declarations for Curry lists (cf. Example 6.0.2).

```
instance Monad List where
  return x = Cons x Nil

  Nil      >>= _ = Nil
  Cons x xs >>= f = append (f x) (xs >>= f)

instance MonadPlus List where
  mzero = Nil
  mplus = append
```

Then we can formulate `allValuesDFS` as:

```
allValuesDFS :: NonDet a    a    List a
allValuesDFS x = searchMPlus empty (try x)
```

For breadth-first search we can reuse the level monad we have employed for the CM approach, cf. Section 6.2.2.

```
level :: NonDet a    a    FM.FMList a
level x = searchMPlus empty (try x)
```

We only need to convert the results to Curry lists.

152 CHAPTER 6. ADVANCED TOPICS AND BENCHMARKS

```
allValuesBFS :: NonDet a    a    FM.FMList a
allValuesBFS x = Data.Foldable.foldr Cons Nil (level x)
```

It is also possible to let the Curry programmer define the search strategy by different traversals of a representation of the search space. For this we first define the type representing *search trees* as proposed in Braßel et al. [2004b].

```
data SearchTree a = Value a
                 | Or (SearchTree a) (SearchTree a)
                 | Fail
```

Note that, in contrast to the type Try defined above in Section 6.2, SearchTree is a recursive type.

Again we only need to provide the according monad instances to use this data structure for encapsulation.

```
instance Monad SearchTree where
  return = Value

  Fail    >>= _ = Fail
  Value x >>= f = f x
  Or x y  >>= f = Or (x >>= f) (y >>= f)

instance MonadPlus SearchTree where
  mzero = Fail
  mplus = Or
```

With this we can define:

```
searchTree :: NonDet a    a    SearchTree a
searchTree x = searchMPlus empty (try x)
```

Different search strategies can now be defined *in the Curry program* as tree traversals. We only give the definition of depth-first search. See [Braßel and Huch, 2007b] for a definition of breadth-first search (bf).

```
df :: SearchTree a    [a]
df (Value v) = [v]
df (Or t1 t2) = df t1 ++ df t2
df Fail      = []
```

Finally, note that the approach for parallel search presented in Section 6.2.4 can also be employed for encapsulated search as it does not rely on I/O operations.

To benchmark our approach to encapsulated search we reevaluate the examples of Section 6.2. This allows to directly relate the performance to the results employing the primitive top-level search which is not accessible for the Curry programmer.

Note that the encapsulated variant of breadth-first search is indeed faster than the top-level search defined in Section 6.2.2. The reason is that the level monad is more sophisticated than our implementation of breadth-first search.

6.6. ENCAPSULATED SEARCH

search operation	perm [1..9]	perm [1..10]
allValuesDFS	0.35	3.86
allValuesBFS	0.46	5.08
df searchTree	0.38	4.16
bf searchTree	1.18	12.50

Figure 6.12: Benchmarks for encapsulated search

6.6.2 Set Functions

Braßel et al. [2004b] distinguish two versions of encapsulated search: strong and weak encapsulation. When allValues is an operation to provide strong encapsulation then for any expression e and any context C the evaluation of the sub expression allValues(e) within that context, i.e., in C [allValues(e)], does *not induce non-deterministic branching*. An operation providing weak encapsulation, in contrast, might induce non-determinism if applied to expressions declared "outside" of the encapsulation.[14] Moreover, in a *declarative* version of strong encapsulation the value of the (sub) expression allValues(e) does not depend on the context.

Example 6.6.2 (Weak and Strong Encapsulation)
The operation findall :: (a   Success)   [a] *is a primitive of the MCC to provide weak encapsulation. For a given expression* e *the template*

    findall (λ y   y=:=e)

provides weak encapsulation similar to the operation allValuesDFS *from the previous section. We call this a "template" as the surrounding context has to be textually copied wherever it is to be used in a program. A definition like*

    weakAllValuesDFS e = findall (λ y   y=:=e)

would not behave as desired. Now consider the following example expressions.

    goal0 = allValuesDFS (let x=0?1 in x)
    goal1 = let x=0?1 in allValuesDFS x

    goal2 = findall (λ y   let x=0?1 in y=:=x)
    goal3 = let x=0?1 in findall (λ y   y=:=x)

For these we have goal0=goal1=goal2=[0,1]. *For* goal3, *however, we have a non-deterministic evaluation to* [0] *or* [1]. *The reason is that* x *is defined "outside" of the weak encapsulation.*

Finally, in a declarative *version of strong encapsulation the expression* goal4 *as defined by*

    goal4 = let x=0?1 in (x,allValuesDFS x)

---

[14]We will employ the notion of inside/outside of an encapsulation informally here. The interested reader is referred to Antoy and Braßel [2007], Antoy and Hanus [2009] for a formal treatment.

should evaluate to (0,[0,1]) ? (1,[0,1]) *no matter in what order the arguments of the tuple are evaluated.*

Braßel et al. [2004b] argue that the strong encapsulation view is to be preferred for two reasons: 1. It is sometimes necessary to ensure that a given expression does not induce non-determinism, e.g., when printing values in the I/O monad. 2. The implications of distinguishing the inside/outside of encapsulation is too hard to understand such that even experts have difficulty predicting the outcome of relatively simple definitions.

Later works by Antoy and Braßel [2007], Antoy and Hanus [2009] argue, however, that the behavior of weak encapsulation is also important to formulate many logic programs in an expressive way. In answer to the two reasons above this means that some operation for strong encapsulation is necessary but that we need syntactic extensions to make programs using weak encapsulation better understandable. The latter answer leads to the introduction of set functions. For a given operation `f` the corresponding set function `f_set` is an operation to compute with the sets of all values possibly yielded by `f`. In accordance to call-time choice semantics the non-determinism induced by evaluating the arguments of `f_set` is treated as if the evaluation happened before the application of `f_set`.

Example 6.6.3 (Set Functions)
A reformulation of the goals of Example 6.6.2 with set functions could look like this:

```
fun0   = let x=0?1 in x
fun1 x = x

goal2 = fun0_set
goal3 = let x=0?1 in fun1_set x
```

For these definitions it seems more natural that `goal2` *should evaluate to* {0,1} *whereas* `goal2` *evaluates to* {0} *or* {1}.

Another point emphasized by Antoy and Hanus [2009] is that the results of encapsulation should not be lists but feature a set-like interface rather. If the results should be enlisted, they need to be yielded in accordance with a total order. From all the operations on sets proposed by Antoy and Hanus [2009] we will use only the test whether a given set is empty.

```
isEmpty :: Values a   Bool
```

Note that the same interface could be used for strong encapsulating operations as discussed in the previous section. The type `Values` is in our setting declared as:

```
data Values a = Values [a]
              | Choice_Values ID (Values a) (Values a)
              | Fail_Values
```

Accordingly, the test of emptiness can be defined by:

6.6. ENCAPSULATED SEARCH

```
isEmpty (Values xs) = if null xs then True else False
```

Note that the `True` and `False` are the once defined in Example 6.0.2, not Haskell's `Prelude.True` and `Prelude.False`. The operation `isEmpty` has to be extended by further rules in correspondence with our translation scheme.

```
isEmpty (Values xs)             = if null xs then True else False
isEmpty (Choice_Values i x y)   = choiceCons i (isEmpty x) (isEmpty y)
isEmpty _                       = failCons
```

For the internal (Haskell) implementation we also need the following constructors of sets.

```
empty :: Values a
empty = Values []

insert :: a   Values a    Values a
insert x (Values xs) = Values (x:xs)

union :: Values a    Values a    Values a
union (Values xs) (Values ys) = Values (merge xs ys)
   where merge []     ys = ys
         merge (x:xs) ys = x : merge ys xs
```

These constructors also need to be extended by rules treating `Choice_Values` and failure but we omit these schematic cases here. More interesting is that our definition makes no attempt to manage duplicate entries as might be expected for a representation of sets. This is necessary to obtain "maximal laziness" for the implementation, e.g., in order to not loose completeness because of evaluating possibly undefined expressions.

It is straight forward to give instances of the type class `Monad` for the type `Values`.

```
instance Monad Values where
   return x = insert x empty
   Values xs >>= f = foldr union empty (map f xs)

instance MonadPlus Values where
   mzero = empty
   mplus = union
```

With these instance declarations we could also use `Values` to introduce a set based operation of the `allValues`-family as discussed in the previous section. We now turn to extend this construct to implement weak encapsulation. As basic considerations for implementing set functions Antoy and Hanus [2009] suggest in examples and pictures that expressions should be tagged to mark whether they are inside or outside of encapsulation. They also put forward the idea that these marks should be attributes of the computed values, especially. An important point, however, is that it should be possible to *nest* set functions, i.e., employ the set function of operations which in turn call other set functions. With this possibility a simple flag inside/outside would not su ce. The idea to put the information to *values* is questionable since values are often referenced from dierent contexts, in other words they tend to be inside as well as outside of a given context so to speak. In our approach each set function is provided with a unique identifier in order to allow nested encapsulation. Instead of values we will tag the *choice constructors* with these identifiers, more specifically, we extend the type ID to carry the tag information. Fortunately, generating unique identifiers for set functions does not need any additional infrastructure. We can simply employ the IDs we have introduced to identify non-deterministic choices.

Our extension of the data type ID looks as follows. (For simplicity we again use integers to identify, not IORefs.)

```
data ID = ID [Integer] Integer
```

The additional list of Integers denotes those encapsulations for which the according choice constructor should be considered as "outside", i.e., it identifies those calls to set functions in which the choice constructor appeared at argument position. In the following we will call this information "cover" information as it "hides" a choice constructor from being encapsulated. For additional operations we need a constructor and a selector to retrieve this information and add to or delete from it as well as an additional selector for the original identifier.

```
covered :: ID     [Integer]
covered (ID is _) = is

mkInt :: ID    Integer
mkInt (ID _ i) = i

mkID :: Integer    ID
mkID = ID []

addCover :: Integer    ID    ID
addCover j (ID is i) = ID (j:is) i

deleteCover :: Integer    ID    ID
deleteCover i (ID is j) = ID (Data.List.delete i is) j
```

In order to add cover information to arbitrary data structures we need the operation cover. For simplicity, cover is defined here for simple data types only. For complex data structures, cover needs to decent into all arguments. This could be achieved by either introducing a new type class or using generic programming features as shipped with GHC.

```
cover :: NonDet a    ID    a    a
cover capsID x = cov (try x)
  where
    cov Fail          = failCons
    cov (Val x)       = x
    cov (Choice i x y) = choiceCons (addCover capsID i)
                                    (cov (try x))
                                    (cov (try y))
```

6.6. ENCAPSULATED SEARCH

The main extension of the setting to integrate weak encapsulation is the definition of an extended variant of the function `searchMPlus`.[15] The dierences to the original definition are:

- There is an additional parameter `capsID` of type `Integer` which identifies the current capsule.

- When a choice constructor is encountered, we check whether `capsID` is present in the list of covered identifiers. If so the non-determinism has to "escape" the capsule. If not the choices are connected via `mplus` as in the original definition.

- Therefore, for the given instance of `MonadPlus m` it must now be possible to yield non-deterministic choices *of the resulting monadic values*. This is ensured by an additional class context `NonDet (m a)`.

The complete definition looks as follows.

```
searchMPlusND :: (MonadPlus m, NonDet a, NonDet (m a))
   Integer    SetOfChoices    Try a    m a
searchMPlusND _ _ Fail        = mzero
searchMPlusND _ _ (Val v)     = return v
searchMPlusND capsID set (Choice i x y)
  | elem capsID (covered i) = choiceCons (deleteCover capsID i)
                                          (search set (try x))
                                          (search set (try y))
  | otherwise              = choose (lookupChoice' set i)
  where
    choose ChooseLeft   = search set (try x)
    choose ChooseRight  = search set (try y)
    choose NoChoice     = search (pick ChooseLeft)  (try x)
              `mplus` search (pick ChooseRight) (try y)

    pick = setChoice' set i

    search = searchMPlusND capsID
```

There is only one piece left to obtain our aim. We need to address how to define the set functions themselves. Set functions are introduced to our setting via a family of predefined operations, one for each arity. We only show the definition for arity 0 and 1, from which the remaining definitions can be deduced in a straight forward way.

```
set0 :: (NonDet res)     res     ID     Values res
set0 x i = searchMPlusND (mkInt i) Data.Map.empty (try x)

set1 :: (NonDet a,NonDet res)   (a  ID  res)    a    ID    Values res
set1 f x i = let res = f (cover i x) (leftID i)
             in searchMPlusND (mkInt i) Data.Map.empty (try res)
```

---
[15] The original definition is to be found in Section 6.2.4.

Note that the argument x is covered with the given ID which is the identifier of the current capsule.

Example 6.6.4 (Implementation of Set Functions) *Reconsider the definitions of Example 6.6.3. The functions corresponding to* fun0, fun1 *can be defined as:*

```
fun0_set   = set0 fun0
fun1_set x = set1 fun1 x
```

With these definitions it should be clear from the explanations of the previous section that goal2=fun0_set *evaluates to* {0,1}. *For* goal3 *we have the following equations where* (mkID 7) *is chosen arbitrarily to be dierent from* 0/1:

```
goal3 (mkID 7)
 = let x=(0?1) (mkID 7) in fun1_set x (leftID (mkID 7))
 = fun1_set ((0?1) (mkID 7)) (leftID (mkID 7))
 = set1 fun1 ((0?1) (mkID 7)) (leftID (mkID 7))
 = set1 fun1 (Choice (ID [] 7) 0 1) (mkID 14)

 = searchMPlusND 14 empty
       (try (fun1 (cover 14 (Choice (ID [] 7) 0 1)) (leftID (mkID 14))))

 = searchMPlusND 14 empty
       (try (fun1 (Choice (ID [14] 7) 0 1) (mkID 28)))

 = searchMPlusND 14 empty (Choice (ID [14] 7) 0 1)

 = Choice_Set (ID [] 7) (searchMPlusND 14 empty (try 0))
                        (searchMPlusND 14 empty (try 1))

 = Choice_Set (ID [] 7) (return 0) (return 1)
 = Choice_Set (ID [] 7) (Set [0]) (Set [1])
```

The result is the expected representation of {0} ? {1}.

For benchmark we choose an example adapted from Antoy and Braßel [2007].

Example 6.6.5 (Queens with (Weak) Encapsulation)
The problem of computing the number of possibilities to place queens on an n × n *chessboard without capture has been used for benchmarking higher-order functional programs in Section 6.1.2. We now present a dierent version adapted from Antoy and Braßel [2007] which makes use of the fact that it is easier to state when a position is unsafe, i.e., one queen captures another, than to express that a position is safe. Therefore, all possibilities for capture can be tested non-deterministically and encapsulated search can be employed to see whether one of these tests was successful. Before presenting the concise formulation we need two small auxiliary operations.*

```
memberWithRest :: [a]      (a,[a])
memberWithRest (x:xs) = (x,xs) ? memberWithRest xs
```

6.6. ENCAPSULATED SEARCH

```
memberWithIndex :: [a]     (a,Int)
memberWithIndex xs = mwi 0 xs
  where
    mwi i (x:xs) = (x,i) ? mwi (i+1) xs
```

The operation `memberWithRest` *yields any member of a given list as well as the remaining list. Operation* `memberWithIndex` *also yields any member of a list but along with its index. Both operations can be chained together to yield two members of a given list along with their distance.*[16]

```
membersWithDelta :: [a]     (a,Int,a)
membersWithDelta l = case memberWithRest l of
                       (x,xs)    case memberWithIndex xs of
                                   (y,i)    (x,i,y)
```

With this operation the queens problem can be expressed concisely as:

```
queens n = safe (perm (list 1 n))

safe p | isEmpty (unsafe_set p) = p

unsafe l = capture (membersWithDelta l)
  where
    capture (i,z,j) | abs (i-j)-1 == z = success
```

For the tested systems the operation `unsafe_set` *has to be expressed dierently. In the MCC the operation has to be expressed as*

```
unsafe_set l = findall (λ x     x=:=unsafe l)
```

and the function `isEmpty` *has to be defined as the* `null` *test on normal lists. For our approach and PAKCS we have:*

```
unsafe_set l = set1 unsafe l
```

Note, however, that the implementation in PAKCS is incomplete as it strictly evaluates arguments the arguments of a set function before application.

The results of benchmarking `queens` for boards of sizes 8 and 9 and are depicted in Figure 6.13.

systems	queens 8	queens 9
IDHO+	0.85	13.56
MCC	0.17	1.72
PAKCS	5.76	60.14

Figure 6.13: Benchmarks for narrowing

---

[16]Note that this operations can be expressed m uch more concisely using *function patterns* Antoy and Hanus [2005] as: `membersWithDelta ((x:xs)++(y:_)) = (x,length xs,y)`

6.7 Free Variables Revisited

In Section 3.2 we have obtained the result that free variables can be replaced by generator functions. This result formed the base of the implementation so far. One shortcoming of the result is, however, that it holds with regard to free variables used in context only. As stated by Lemma 3.2.6 there is a dierence with regard to free variables evaluated at top level. For example, evaluating the Curry expression `let x free in x :: Bool` does not induce non-determinism while the corresponding expression `let x=generateBool in x` does, as it yields `True ? False`. In this section we eliminate this last shortcoming for our implementation.

All that is needed to obtain our aim is the possibility to distinguish non-determinism induced by operation (?) from the one induced by generating operations. We do so by extending the declaration of identifier.[17]

```
data ID = ID      Ref
        | FreeID  Ref
```

We assume that the operations `initID`,`leftID`,`rightID` yield identifiers with the constructor `ID`.

The family of operations `generate` is provided by a new type class.

```
class NonDet a    Generatable a where
   generate :: ID    a
```

Instances of this class add the constructor `FreeID` to the choices.

Example 6.7.1 (Instances of Class `Generatable`**)**
Defining instances of class `Generatable` *is a straight forward implementation of the scheme discussed in Section 3.2.*[18]

```
freeID (ID i) = FreeID i

instance Generatable Bool where
  generate i = Bool_Choice (freeID i) False True

instance Generatable Peano where
  generate i = let r = rightID i in
    Peano_Choice (freeID i) 0 (S (generate r))

instance Generatable a    Generatable (List a) where
  generate i = let l = leftID i
                   r = rightID i
    in List_Choice (freeID i) Nil (Cons (generate l) (generate r))
```

---

[17] Note that this extension is orthogonal to the one discussed in the previous chapter. We discuss a different extension for simplicity, only, instead of combining both extensions in this section.

[18] Recall that the type for Peano numbers is given by `data Peano=0|S Peano`, cf. Example 1.1.14.

6.7. FREE VARIABLES REVISITED

Now the only aspect left to model is *narrowing*, i.e., the crossover from free variable to a non-deterministic choice. For this we introduce the following simple operation:

```
narrow :: ID    ID
narrow (FreeID r) = ID r
narrow x          = x
```

This operation is inserted in the transformation scheme for pattern matching, cf. Section 5.2. The original definition

$$f(\overline{x_m}, \text{Choice}(x, y, z)) = \text{Choice}(x, f(\overline{x_m}, y), f(\overline{x_m}, z))$$

is replaced by

$$f(\overline{x_m}, \text{Choice}(x, y, z)) = \text{Choice}(\text{narrow}(x), f(\overline{x_m}, y), f(\overline{x_m}, z))$$

Example 6.7.2 (Free Variables and Narrowing) *Consider the two goals*

```
goal0, goal1 :: Bool
goal0 = let x free in x
goal1 = let x free in not x
```

The function **not** *is now translated as:*

```
not True  = False
not False = True
not (Bool_Choice i x y) = consChoice (narrow i) (not x) (not y)
```

Therefore, the evaluation of the two goals is as follows, where for simplicity we assume identifiers to be integers.

```
goal0 (ID 1) = (generate 1 :: Bool)
             = Bool_Choice (FreeID 1) False True

goal1 (ID 1) = not (generate 1 :: Bool)
             = not (Bool_Choice (FreeID 1) False True)
             = Bool_Choice (narrow (FreeID 1)) (not False) (not True)
             = Bool_Choice (ID 1) True False
```

With this example it should be clear that free variables can be distinguished from other non-determinism by the run-time system.

For benchmarks we have chosen the definitions to solve the simple equations by narrowing introduced in Example 1.1.15.

```
half :: Peano    Peano
half y | equal (add x x) y = x where x free

toPeano :: Int    Peano
toPeano n = if n==0 then 0 else S (toPeano (n-1))
```

Figure 6.14 shows the result of solving the equations for 10000 and 20000. The CM compiling system does not feature free variables yet.

systems	half (toPeano 10000)	half (toPeano 20000)
IDHO+	2.38	9.40
MCC	3.50	16.93
PAKCS	94.21	403.03

Figure 6.14: Benchmarks for narrowing

6.8 Adding Constraints

One of the most successful paradigms in the field of logic programming is called *programming with constraints*. Indeed, the paradigm is so influential that many people regard logic programming languages like Prolog as a sub class of programming languages with constraints, cf. Hofstedt and Wolf [2007]. In this section we integrate constraints into our setting by implementing *unification*, i.e., the problem to find a substitution σ such that for two given t, t' we get $\sigma(t) = \sigma(t')$, if such a σ exists. Obviously, the concept of unification is easier when the considered terms are of a simple data type like Bool. Therefore, we partition this chapter in two according sub sections. For simplicity, we omit the topic of integrating an *occur check*, i.e., to render unifications like, e.g., x=:=S x as unsatisfiable.

6.8.1 Unifying Simple Data Types

We first illustrate the operational behavior of unification in Curry by example.

Example 6.8.1 (Unification) *In Curry it is possible to extend the defining rules of operations by constraints, i.e., expression of the predefined type* Success. *There is only a single constructor of this type, cf. 1.1.1, such that expressions either evaluate to this constructor or fail. The operation to compute a unification is* (=:=) :: a a Success *and we could write for example:*

    f x y | x=:=y = x

With this definition of f all of the following expressions should evaluate to True, binding all free variables x,y to True in the evaluation process.

    goal0 = let x free in f True x
    goal1 = let x free in f x True
    goal2 = let x,y free in f True (f x y)

The evaluation of the following expression, in contrast, should lead to a failure:

    goal3 = let x,y free in f (f (f x y) False) True

In order to extend our setting by constraints we need one additional constructor guardCons :: Constraint a   a of every possible type. We introduce this constructor by extending the type class NonDet.

6.8. ADDING CONSTRAINTS

```
class NonDet a where
   ...
   guardCons :: Constraint   a    a
```

Along with the type class we also need to extend the definition of `Try` in order to enable general deconstruction of values. The deconstruction is also supported by the auxiliary operation `tryChoice`

```
data Try a = Val a | Choice ID a a | Free ID a a | Guard Constraint a

tryChoice :: ID    a    a    Try a
tryChoice i@(ID _)      = Choice
tryChoice i@(FreeID _) = Free
```

Example 6.8.2 (Adding Guards to Data Declarations)
Reconsider the definitions of Example 6.3.1. The declarations are extended to add guards:

```
data Bool  = False | True | ...
           | Guard_Bool Constraint Bool Bool

data List a = Nil | Cons a (List a) | ...
            | Guard_List Constraint (List a) (List a)

instance NonDet Bool where
   ...
   guardCons = Guard_Bool

   try (Choice_Bool i x y) = tryChoice i xy
   try (Guard_Bool c e)    = Guard c e
   ...

instance NonDet (List a) where
   ...
   guardCons = Guard_List

   try (Choice_List i x y) = tryChoice i xy
   try (Guard_List c e)    = Guard c e
   ...
```

The transformation scheme is altered such that guards, too, are lifted. More precisely, in analogy to the translation rule

$$f(\overline{x_m}, \texttt{Choice}(x, y, z)) = \texttt{Choice}(\texttt{narrow}(x), f(\overline{x_m}, y), f(\overline{x_m}, z))$$

from the previous section we have in addition

$$f(\overline{x_m}, \texttt{Guard}(x_c, x_e)) = \texttt{Guard}(x_c, f(\overline{x_m}, x_e))$$

Example 6.8.3 (Lifting Guards)
The transformed definition of operation `sorted` *as shown in Section 6.3 is extended like thus:*

```
sorted :: List Int     Bool
sorted Nil                   = True
sorted (Cons m xs)           = sorted2 m xs
sorted (Choice_List i x y)   = consChoice (narrow i) (sorted x) (sorted y)
sorted (Guard_List c e)      = guardCons c (sorted e)
sorted _                     = consFail
```

The considerations up to now are valid for extending our approach for any kind of constraints. The next step is to model the constraints needed to implement unification. For this we have to consider which class of constraints can be solved with *local* information and which require *global* information. With regard to unification it is clear that constraints like `True=:=True` or `True=:=False` can be reduced to `Success` or `failCons`, respectively, without global information. In general, any unification which involves only ground terms can be treated this way. Global information is only needed in two cases,

a) binding one free variable to another and

b) binding a free variable to a ground term.

Binding a variable to a ground term of a simple type like `Bool` means that we need to add a `Choice` which *must correspond to the definition of* `generate` for that type as introduced in the previous section. We will illustrate this by example.

Example 6.8.4 *Reconsider the definition of* `generate` *from Example 6.7.1.*

```
instance Generatable Bool where
    generate i = Bool_Choice (freeID i) False True
```

In order to bind the variable identified by `freeID i` *to the ground term* `False` *we need to add the choice* `ChooseLeft` *for* i *to our set of choices and for* `True` *we add* `ChooseRight`, *respectively. The case that the given type has more than two constructors or that his constructors have arguments is treated in the next section.*

The representation of constraints in our setting needs to allow an association of identifiers with choices. In other words, it must be translated to what we store in our sets of choices. For the second case which cannot be decided locally, i.e., binding a free variable to another, we need a way to associate the identifiers of two free variables. In extension to what we have seen before it is a natural idea to represent the information by extending the type `Choice`.

```
data Choice = NoChoice | ChooseLeft | ChooseRight
            | BindTo ID
```

With this definition the type constraint to support unification is simply:

6.8. ADDING CONSTRAINTS

```
data Constraint = ID :=: Choice
```

In order to compute the correct constraints for a given term and also to treat the locally solvable part of unification we introduce a new type class.

```
class (NonDet a)    Unifiable a where
  bind :: ID    a    Constraint
  (=.=) :: a    a    Success
```

Instances for this class are straight forward to formulate.

```
instance Unifiable Bool where
  bind i False = i :=: ChooseLeft
  bind i True  = i :=: ChooseRight

  True  =.= True  = Success
  False =.= False = Success
  _     =.= _     = failCons
```

With this, we can define the operation (=:=). In a case distinction of the dierent constructors of type Try the operation directly solves the case which require only local information and defers the ones needing global information by introducing a guardCons constructor.

```
(=:=) :: Unifiable a    a    a    Success
x =:= y = unify (try x) (try y)
  where
    ...
    unify (Val vx) (Val vy) = vx =.= vy

    unify (Val v) (Free j _ _)
      = guardCons (bind j v) success

    unify (Free i _ _) (Val v)
      = guardCons (bind i v) success

    unify (Free i _ _) (Free j _ _)
      = guardCons (i :=: BindTo j) success
```

The cases omitted above are the schematic cases to lift the guard and choice constructors and to propagate failure.

Global information is only available at the top level of evaluation, i.e., in one of the search operations examined in Section 6.2. Here, we reconsider the required extension of depth-first search only. For this recall that at the heart of defining top level search operations we need not only to add the information to our current set of choices but we need also the ability to reset this information again. From the point of view of constraint programming, the sets of choices already represent a *constraint store*, i.e., a structure to collect propagated information about the solvability of currently valid constraints. Informatively speaking, the task of solving a constraint involves propagating new information when available as well as allowing to reset that information when a part of the search space has been exhausted. Consequently, an operation `solve` in our approach needs to propagate information contained in a given constraint to the store as well as yield an operation to reset the store to the previous state. A straight forward way to model this in the setting of `IORefs` for identifiers is to define an I/O-operation, which yields another I/O-operation (the "reset") as result if successful and `Nothing` for a failure.

```
type Solved = IO (Maybe (IO ()))

solved, unsolvable :: Solved
solved      = return (Just (return ()))
unsolvable  = return Nothing

solve :: Constraint     Solved
```

A typical auxiliary case for this function is an operation to set a given identifier reference to a given choice and yield a setting to `NoChoice` as result.

```
setUnsetChoice :: ID    Choice    Solved
```

We will define this operation below. First we define the `solve` which forms the context in which `setUnsetChoice` is employed.

```
solve :: Constraint     Solved
solve (i :=: cc) = lookupChoice i >>= choose cc
  where
    choose (BindTo j) ci      = lookupChoice j >>= check j ci
    choose c          NoChoice = setUnsetChoice i c
    choose c          x | c≡x = solved
    choose _          _       = unsolvable

    check j NoChoice NoChoice = setUnsetChoice i (BindTo j)
    check _ NoChoice y        = setUnsetChoice i y
    check j x        NoChoice = setUnsetChoice j x

    check _ x        y | x≡y = solved
    check _ _        _       = unsolvable
```

The astute reader might have pondered that unification can produce chains of variable bindings. For example, solving first `x1=:=x2` and some time after that `x2=:=x3` would lead to a chain `x1   x2   x3`. With this chain in place another unification `x2=:=x1` is problematic with the above definition. We would end up with the rule "`bind _ x y |x==y =solved`" substituted by `{x  BindTo x3,y  BindTo x2}` and the equality test would fail. The solution to this problem is not changing the definition of `solve` but making variable chains transparent by a redefinition of `lookupChoice`.

```
lookupChoiceRaw :: ID    IO Choice
lookupChoiceRaw i = readIORef (ref i)

lookupChoice :: ID    IO Choice
lookupChoice i = lookupChoiceRaw i >>= unchain
```

6.8. ADDING CONSTRAINTS

```
where
  unchain (BoundTo j) = lookupChoice j
  unchain c           = return c
```

Of course unchaining is also needed to set choices. But in order to correctly reset these choices later, we need to know the exact identifier associated with the given choice. For this purpose we add another operation which has the type signature `setChoiceGetID :: ID   Choice   IO ID` to the setting. This new operation calls the original `setChoice`.

```
setChoiceGetID :: ID    Choice     IO ID
setChoiceGetID i c = do j    lookupChoice i
                             setChoice j c
                             return j
```

With this we can declare the last missing operation `setUnsetChoice`.

```
setUnsetChoice :: ID     Choice      Solved
setUnsetChoice i c = do
  j    setChoiceGetID i c
  return (setChoice j NoChoice)
```

This completes the implementation of unification for simple data types.

6.8.2 Complex Data Types

Unification for complex data types can be developed by reconsidering the constructions of the previous section. There, we have introduced the type class `Unifiable` with the two operations `bind` and `(=.=)`. The latter should decide the unification on ground terms and the first should define what constraints should be added when a free variable is to be bound to a ground term. Let us reconsider these operations with regard to lists.

Example 6.8.5 *Reconsider the definition for* **generate** *for the list type (slightly polished):*

```
instance Generatable a    Generatable (List a) where
  generate i = List_Choice (freeID i)
                            Nil
                            (Cons (generate (leftID i))
                                  (generate (rightID i)))
```

The definition of operation `bind` *must correspond to this definition. Therefore, the identifier of a variable which is to be bound to* `Nil` *must be associated with* `ChooseLeft`. *But what should be the constraints to bind a variable to, e.g.,* `Cons True Nil`? *To correspond to the definition of* **generate**, *three associations must be established:*

- *the identifier of the given variable, e.g.,* `i`, *with* `ChooseRight`

  - *the identifier* `leftID i` *with* `ChooseRight` *(according to the definition for* `Bool`)

- *the identifier* `rightID i` *with* `ChooseLeft` *to represent* `Nil`

As illustrated in the example we need to communicate associations for several identifiers in the result of `bind`. For this we change our definition of class `Unifiable` such that more than one constraint can be yielded for a given binding.

```
class NonDet a     Unifiable a where
  bind :: ID    a    [Constraint]
  ...
```

Example 6.8.6 (Constraints for Complex Data) *As developed in the previous example the constraints computed for the call* `bind i (Cons True Nil)` *should be:*

`[i :=: ChooseRight, leftID i :=: ChooseRight, rightID i :=: ChooseLeft]`

The definition of `bind` *for lists is, accordingly:*

```
class (NonDet a)    Unifiable a where
  bind i C_Nil           = [i :=: ChooseLeft]
  bind i (C_Cons x xs)
    = i :=: ChooseRight : bind (leftID i) x ++ bind (rightID i) xs
```

There is, however, a further case left to define `bind` which does not appear when only simple types are considered. As we will see below, extending the setting to complex data implies that `bind` could also be called with a free variable as argument. In this case the result should be `BindTo`. For example, the definition for the `List` type class instance is completed by the following rule.

`bind i (List_Choice j _ _) = [i :=: BindTo j]`

The extension of $(=.=)$, the second operation of class `Unifiable`, is straight forward. For the arguments of complex constructors it needs to decent by calling the general operation $(=:=)$. When more than one argument is present the calls to $(=:=)$ are put together by (&) :: Success   Success   Success.

Example 6.8.7 (Defining Operation =.=)

```
instance Unifiable a    Unifiable (List a) where
  ...
  Nil       =.= Nil       = success
  Cons x xs =.= Cons y ys = x=:=y & xs=:=ys
  _         =.= _         = failCons
```

In order to reformulate the definition of $(=:=)$ for complex data types, we need a generic operation to compute the normal forms of a given expression. For convenience, this operation takes a continuation to be applied to the computed normal form. We only give the signature declarations and note where we include the corresponding type class context. The definitions of `Normalform` instances are fully schematic.

6.8. ADDING CONSTRAINTS

```
class (NonDet a, NormalForm a)    Unifiable a where ...

class Normalform a where
  ($!!) :: (a     b)     a     b
```

To adapt the operation (=:=) to the extended setting we need only to redefine those cases of auxiliary operation `unify` where a free variable is to be bound to an expression in head normal form. These cases have to be adapted such that the expression is evaluated to a complete normal form employing ($!!) and such that the result contains all the constraints in the list computed by `bind`.

```
unify (Val v)      (Free j _ _) =
  (foldr guardCons success  bind j) $!! v

unify (Free i _ _) (Val v)      =
  (foldr guardCons success  bind i) $!! v
```

The definition of operation `solve` is unchanged in the extended setting. There is, however, one last implication of the setting with complex data types to consider. When binding a variable of type, e.g., `List Bool`, there is also more than one association of identifiers and choices invloved. Indeed, potentially, infinitely many identifiers must be associated with each other. Clearly, we cannot solve this problem by simply adding all the necessary constraints at once. Rather, we *propagate* binding information *on demand*. In order to avoid duplicating work we need to distinguish whether bindings for an identifier i have already been propagated to `leftID i` and `rightID i` or not. For this, we let an entry `BindTo i` in the set of choices denote that no bindings have yet been added for the children `leftID i` and `rightID i`. To represent that such information has already been propagated we add a new constructor `BoundTo :: ID    Choice`.

```
data Choice = NoChoice  | ChooseLeft | ChooseRight
            | BindTo ID | BoundTo ID
```

Whenever `lookupChoice` encounters a choice `BindTo` it propagates the information.

```
lookupChoice :: ID    IO Choice
lookupChoice i = lookupChoiceRaw i >>= unchain
  where
    unchain (BoundTo j) = lookupChoice j

    unchain (BindTo j)  = do
      setChoice i (BoundTo j)
      setChoice (leftID i) (BindTo (leftID j))
      setChoice (rightID i) (BindTo (rightID j))
      lookupChoice j

    unchain c           = return c
```

Of course, we also need to include the propagated information when resetting a variable binding in the set of choices.

```
resetFreeVar :: ID    IO ()
resetFreeVar i = lookupChoiceRaw i >>= propagate
  where
    propagate (BindTo _)  = setChoice i NoChoice
    propagate (BoundTo _) = do
       setChoice i NoChoice
       resetFreeVar (leftID i)
       resetFreeVar (rightID i)
```

With this the redefinition of `setUnsetChoice` concludes the extension to complex data types.

```
setUnsetChoice :: ID    Choice    Solved
setUnsetChoice i c = do j    setChoiceGetID i c
                        case c of
                          BindTo _    return (Just (resetFreeVar j))
                          _           return (Just (setChoice j NoChoice))
```

For benchmark we have used the following standard example for unification in Curry.

```
last :: [a]    a
last l | xs ++ [x] =:= l = x where xs,x free
```

Figure 6.15 shows the result of computing the last element of a list with 10,000 and 100,000 elements.

systems	last (replicate 10000 True)	last (replicate 100000 True)
IDHO+	0.01	0.14
MCC	0.01	0.16
PAKCS	0.22	2.12

Figure 6.15: Benchmarks for unification

We have shown how to extend our setting by constraints to compute unification. The presented implementation should also su ce to give an idea how further possibilities like finite domain constraints, inequality constraints, constraints to implement function patterns and a concurrent implementation of operation (&) can be approached.

6.9 Drawbacks of the Presented Approach

As far as we have seen in this chapter the presented approach can be regarded as a serious alternative to current compilation techniques for functional logic programming languages. There is, however, one major drawback to our approach we would like to examine in this section.

It is a well known problem for lazy functional languages that Haskell expressions like `let (t1,t2)=e in f t1 t2` can induce memory leaks as examined by Wadler [1987], Sparud [1993]. The reason is that the standard way to treat

6.10. DEBUGGING

the expression is to simplify it to, e.g., `let x=e in f (fst x) (snd x)` before continuing with the compilation process. This simplified expression can be very bad for the memory behavior, e.g., in the following circumstances.

- `t1=fst x` evaluates to a very large term
- `f` consumes this term (its first argument) but touches its second argument only after this consumption is finished

In these circumstances the big data term `t1`, although consumed, is still referenced by the term `(snd x)` as we have `x=(t1,t2)`. *A single step* of evaluating `snd x` would free all the memory, but this step is done very late, although the evaluation of `(fst x)` already ensures that this single step would not lead to a failure. Modern compilation systems produce special code for these situations. This code ensures that whenever `fst x` is evaluated, `snd x` is also reduced one step and vice versa, cf. Sparud [1993]. Sometimes this task is also assigned to the garbage collector, cf. Wadler [1987]. The problem is, however, that neither the compiler nor the garbage collector are always able to reliably detect this kind of situations. Therefore, this problem is still an open question for the efficient compilation of functional languages.

There are situations in which the problem discussed above affects our approach with a multiplied impact. To give a concrete example reconsider the definition of `memberWithDelta :: [a]  (a,Int,a)` as introduced in Example 6.6.5. There we have defined the operation as:

```
membersWithDelta :: [a]  (a,Int,a)
membersWithDelta l = case memberWithRest l of
                      (x,xs)   case memberWithIndex xs of
                                (y,i)   (x,i,y)
```

If we redefine this operation to

```
membersWithDelta :: [a]  (a,Int,a)
membersWithDelta l = (x,i,y) where (x,xs) = memberWithRest l
                                   (y,i)  = memberWithIndex xs
```

the effects are quite notable. Instead of 0.81 seconds to compute queens 8 the new program fails to complete the evaluation because the 4 GB memory of the machine we used for benchmarking do not suffice. For the evaluation of queens 7 the program takes 11.48 seconds where the original program needs only 0.16.

In order to cope with this problem, some program analysis to detect such bad situations would be needed. In the mean time, a programmer employing our approach is well advised to prefer `case` expressions or auxiliary functions over complex `let`/`where` expressions when deconstructing *non-deterministic* expressions.

6.10 Debugging

Designing debugging tools for lazy functional programming languages is a complex task which is often solved by expensive tracing of lazy computations. In

[Braßel et al., 2007] we have presented an approach in which the information collected as a trace is reduced considerably (kilobytes instead of megabytes). The basic idea, which we will present in this section, is to collect a kind of step information for a call-by-value interpreter, which can then e ciently reconstruct the computation for debugging/viewing tools, like declarative debugging. In the original paper we have shown the correctness of the approach. That approach covered purely functional programs only. With the development of the present work, the results by Braßel et al. [2007] directly carry over to the setting of functional *logic* programs.

6.10.1 Debugging Functional Programs with Oracle

The demand-driven nature of lazy evaluation is one of the most appealing features of modern functional languages like Haskell [Peyton Jones, 2003]. Unfortunately, it is also one of the most complex features one should face in order to design a debugging tool for these languages. In particular, printing the step-by-step trace of a lazy computation is generally useless from a programmer's point of view, mainly because arguments of function calls are often shown unevaluated and because the order of evaluation is counterintuitive.

There are several approaches that improve this situation by hiding the details of lazy evaluation from the programmer. The main such approaches are: Freja [Nilsson and Sparud, 1997a] and Buddha [Pope and Naish, 2003], which are based on the declarative debugging technique from logic programming by Shapiro [1983], Hat [Sparud and Runciman, 1997a], which enables the exploration of a computation backwards starting at the program output or error message, and Hood [Gill, 2001], which allows the programmer to observe the data structures at given program points.

Many of these approaches are based on recording a tree or graph structure representing the whole computation, like the Evaluation Dependence Tree (EDT) for declarative debugging or the *redex trail* in Hat. For finding bugs, this recorded structure is represented in a user-friendly (usually innermost-style) way to the programmer in a separate viewing phase. Unfortunately, this structure dramatically grows for larger computations and can contain several mega-, even gigabytes of information.

In our paper [Braßel et al., 2007], we have introduced an alternative approach to debugging lazy functional programs. Instead of storing a complete redex trail or EDT, we memorize only the information necessary to guide a call-by-value interpreter to produce the same results. To avoid unnecessary reductions, similarly to the lazy semantics, the call-by-value interpreter is controlled by a list of step numbers determining which redexes should not be evaluated. If every redex is evaluated even by a lazy strategy, the list of step numbers reduces to a single number – the total number of reduction steps in the complete computation – which demonstrates the compactness of our representation. Furthermore, Braßel et al. [2007] give a proof of correctness for the approach, in contrast to other existing approaches in which the compression of stored information is only motivated as an implementation issue.

6.10. DEBUGGING

We illustrate our approach by a small example.

Example 6.10.1 *Consider the following program.*
```
from :: Int      [Int]
from n = n : from (n+1)

head :: [a]      a
head (x:_) = x

tail :: [a]      [a]
tail (_:xs) = xs
```

The lazy evaluation of the expression (head (tail (from 0))) *in the context of that program can be depicted as:*
```
head (tail (from 0))
head (tail (0:from (0+1)))
head (from (0+1))
head (0+1:from ((0+1)+1))      0+1      1
```

This evaluation can be described as: "Do three steps innermost then discard the next two left-most innermost expressions and do two more eager steps." In short the information can be comprised to the list of eager steps [3,0,2]. *For each step in replaying the evaluation the first number is decreased and a leading zero means a discard step. The example derivation can then be mapped to the left-most innermost (eager) evaluation:*

```
[3,0,2]  head (tail (from 0))
[2,0,2]  head (tail (0:from (0+1)))
[1,0,2]  head (tail (0:from 1))
[0,0,2]  head (tail (0:1:from (1+1)))
[0,2]    head (tail (0:1:from _))
[2]      head (tail (0:1:_))
[1]      head (1:_)
[0]      1
```

In our paper [Braßel et al., 2007] we have formalized a technique to automatically record and replay such step information. Apart from showing the soundness of the approach we were able to prove interesting properties about the magnitude of resources needed to compute the step information. Here and in the following the step information is nicknamed an "oracle".

The example demonstrates the compactness of our representation that usually only requires a fairly limited amount of memory (kilobytes instead of megabytes). The step list is used in the subsequent tracing/debugging session to control the call-by-value evaluation that replays the original evaluation in a more comprehensible order. In a nutshell, we trade time for space in our approach.

In a further work [Braßel and Siegel, 2008] we have shown how to implement a debugging tool with the technique described above. The following example describes the usage of the debugger.

Example 6.10.2 *Consider the following simple (but erroneous) program (where the concrete code for* `fib`*, which computes the corresponding Fibonacci number, is omitted):*

```
length []      = 0
length (_:xs) = length xs

exp = length (take 2 (fiblist 0))

fiblist x = fib x : fiblist (x+1)

fib :: Int    Int
fib _ = error "this will not be evaluated"
```

With the transformation described in the original paper *[Braßel et al., 2007]* the program is transformed such that the step information is recorded via side eects. Then a second transformation generates code which uses this step information to run the program in a lazy call-by-value manner. Upon completion of the second transformation the actual debugging session starts. The debugging tool described in *[Braßel and Siegel, 2008]* supports two modes. The first is an implementation of the well known declarative debugging method, also known as algorithmic debugging *[Shapiro, 1983]*. The second is a step-by-step tracer allowing to follow a program's execution as if the underlying semantics was strict, allowing to skip uninteresting sub computations. In addition, the tool gives some support for finding bugs in programs employing I/O, which is not easily integrated in related approaches.

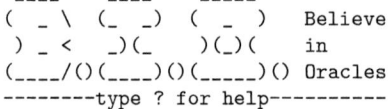

```
exp
```

Initially, we only see a call to function `exp` *which was the main expression in our example. Pressing* `i` *turns on* inspect *mode. In inspect mode, the result of every sub computation is directly shown and can be "inspected" by the user, i.e., rated as correct or wrong. Inspect mode therefore corresponds to the declarative debugging method. The display of results of sub computations can be turned on and o at any time, switching between declarative and step-wise debugging.*

After pressing `i`*, the debugger evaluates the expression and displays the result.*

```
exp ~> 0
```

We expected main to have value 2*, but the program returned value* 0*. Thus, we enter* `w` *(wrong) in order to tell the debugger that the result was wrong. The debugging tool stores this choice as explained in the paper [Braßel and Siegel,*

6.10. DEBUGGING

2008]. As the value of exp *depends on several function calls on the right hand side of its definition, the tool now displays the first of these calls in a leftmost, innermost order:*

```
fiblist 0 ~> _ : (_ : _)
```

The line above shows that the expression fiblist 0 *has been evaluated to a list that has at least two elements. This might be correct, but we are not too sure, since this result depends strongly on the evaluation context. A "don't know" in declarative debugging actually corresponds to the skipping of sub computations in the step-by-step mode. We therefore press* s *(skip).*

```
take 2 (_ : (_ : _)) ~> [_,_]
```

Actually, this looks quite good. By entering c *(correct) we declare that this sub computation meets our expectation. Now the following calculation is displayed:*

```
length [_,_] ~> 0
```

The function length *is supposed to count the elements in a list. Since the argument is a two-element list, the result should be* 2, *but it is actually* 0. *By pressing* w *we therefore state that this calculation is erroneous. Now the debugger asks for the first sub computation leading to this result:*

```
length [_] ~> 0
```

This is also wrong, but for the sake of demonstration we delay our decision. By pressing the space bar (step into) we move to the sub expressions of length [_]. *We now get to the final question:*

```
length [] ~> 0
```

The length of an empty list [] *is zero, so by pressing* c *(correct) we state that this evaluation step is correct. Now we have reached the end of the program execution, but a bug has not been isolated yet. We have narrowed down the error to the function call* length [_,_], *but still there are unrated sub computations which might have contributed to the erroneous result. The tool asks if the user wants to restart the debugging session re-using previously given ratings:*

```
end reached. press 'q' to abort or any other key to restart.
```

After pressing < SPACE >, *the debugger restarts and asks for the remaining function calls. There is only one unrated call left within the erroneous sub computation:*

```
length [_] ~> 0
```

Now we provide the rating we previously skipped. After entering w *(wrong) it is evident which definition contains the error:*

```
found bug in rule:
  lhs = length [_]
  rhs = 0
```

A further interesting advantage of our approach to reexecute the program with a strict evaluation strategy is the possibility to include "virtual I/O". During the execution of the original program, all externally defined I/O-actions with non-trivial results, i.e., other than IO (), are stored in a special file. These values are retrieved during the debugging session. In addition, selected externally defined I/O-actions, e.g., getChar, are provided with a "virtual implementation". To show what this means, we demonstrate how the main action of the following program is treated by our debugging tool.

```
getLine :: IO String
getLine = getChar >>= testEOL

testEOL :: Char    IO String
testEOL c = if isNewLine c then return []
                           else getLine >>= λ cs    return (c:cs)

main = getLine >>= writeFile "userInput"
```

As described above the program is executed to obtain the oracle in a file. As this program additionally contains user interaction, we have to enter a line during execution. We type, for example, "abc". Meanwhile, along with the file containing the oracle, a second file is written that contains the sequence of values for getChar and the number of bytes for their representation in the file:

3,'a'3,'b'3,'c'4,'\n'

There is no need to identify the dierent calls to external functions, since I/O-actions will be executed in the strict version in exactly the same order as in the original program. This is of course essential for correctness.

When using the debugging tool presented in [Braßel and Siegel, 2008] in stepwise mode, a GUI called B.I.O.tope is started, which represents the virtual I/O environment. In our example, B.I.O.tope is told that someone has typed an a on the console, which is the "virtual I/O-action" we connected with getChar. The corresponding B.I.O.tope window is shown in Figure 6.16. The result of executing the writeFile action is shown in the B.I.O.tope as depicted in Figure 6.17. There we can see that the GUI has switched to the file dialog. It contains a list of files which have been read (R:) or written (W:) during the debugging session and clicking a file in this list makes the file contents visible as they are at the current point of the debugging session.

Following the work by Braßel and Siegel [2008], we have supervised a master thesis Siegel [2008] with the aim to bring the approach to Haskell (the original work was done for the Curry compilation system KiCS [Braßel and Huch, 2009]).

6.10. DEBUGGING

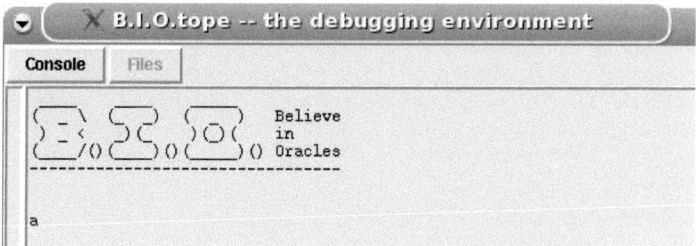

Figure 6.16: The B.I.O.tope Virtual I/O Environment

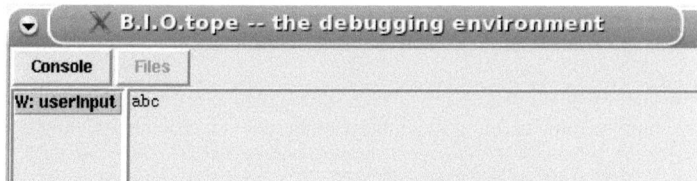

Figure 6.17: Files in the B.I.O.tope Virtual I/O Environment

6.10.2 Debugging Functional Logic Programs with Oracle

The original approach to debugging with oracle information [Braßel et al., 2007] was devised for functional programs only. We have presented the approach here because with the development of this work the extension for functional logic languages comes (nearly) for free. As we have developed a technique to translate functional logic programs to purely functional ones, the approach to record step information [Braßel et al., 2007] directly carries over to correctly record the information about the evaluation of the resulting programs.

Example 6.10.3 *Reconsider the definition of* insert *from example 1.1.12.*

```
insert x []     = [x]
insert x (y:ys) = x:y:ys ? y:insert x ys
```

The lazy evaluation of the expression head (insert 3 [1,2] 7) *can be depicted as follows, where* 7 *is an identifier arbitrarily chosen to be different from* 1,2,3:

```
head (insert 3 [1,2] 7)
head (Choice_List 7 [3,1,2] (1:insert 3 [2] (leftID 7))
Choice_Int 7 (head [3,1,2]) (head (1:insert 3 [2] (leftID 7)))
Choice_Int 7 3 (head (1:insert 3 [2] (leftID 7)))
Choice_Int 7 3 1
```

In order to describe the innermost derivation with oracle, all we need to do is describe the derivation of the purely functional program resulting from our

178 CHAPTER 6. ADVANCED TOPICS AND BENCHMARKS

transformation. This means, we state that we do the first leftmost innermost step because the corresponding redex (insert 3 [1,2] 7) *was unfolded and in the result, which is* (Choice_List 7 [3,1,2] (1:insert 3 [2] (leftID 7))), *the next leftmost innermost redex, which is* (leftID 7), *is not evaluated as well as the one after that* (insert 3 [2] (leftID 7)). *Then all remaining redexes are unfolded. The resulting oracle is therefore* [1,0,3] *and we can replay the derivation as:*

```
[1,0,3]   head (insert 3 [1,2] 7)
[0,0,3]   head (Choice_List 7 [3,1,2] (1:insert 3 [2] (leftID 7)))
[0,3]     head (Choice_List 7 [3,1,2] (1:insert 3 [2] _))
[3]       head (Choice_List 7 [3,1,2] (1:_))
[2]       Choice_Int 7 (head [3,1,2]) (head (1:_))
[1]       Choice_Int 7 3 (head (1:_))
[0]       Choice_Int 7 3 1
```

Note that it is essential for correctness that our approach features sharing across non-determinism, cf. Section 6.4. Otherwise, arbitrary parts of the step file, which is written via side-eects, would be repeatedly recorded and the resulting information would not be reliable.

As we have seen, the recording and interpretation of step files seamlessly carries over from the original work [Braßel et al., 2007]. The only adaption of the approach required to debug functional logic programs concerns the debugging tools. These tools need to be extended by the ability to represent information about non-determinism which is comprehensible for the user. Here we describe how debugging tools were extended as developed by Braßel [2008].

The derivations with Choice constructors and identifiers as well as the more technical details of the completed reductions are not suited for the programmer who is looking for a bug in his Curry program. Therefore several conventions help to get a more simple view on derivations.

- Unfolding of generator functions is never seen (trusted functions).

- The references of Choice constructors are hidden. For example, a value like (Choice 2 True False) is represented as (True ? False).

- Invalid parts of the search space due to the modelling of call-time choice are always omitted, cf. Section 5.2.1.

- When a Choice node has only a single valid alternative this alternative is shown rather than any failures.

Accordingly, the following output is generated by a step by step examination for permSort [2,1] in the debugging tool presented in Braßel [2008]:

```
permSort [2,1]
  permute [2,1]
    permute [1]
      permute []    []
```

```
      insert 1 []       [1]
    permute [1]         [1]
    insert 2 [1]
       insert 2 []       [2]
       insert 2 [1]      [2,1] ? [1,2]
    permute [2,1]       [2,1] ? [1,2]
    sorted ([2,1] ? [1,2])
      2 < 1     False
      1 < 2     True
      sorted [2]
      sorted [2]         True
    sorted ([2,1] ? [1,2])    True
permSort [2,1]      [1,2]
```

In order to omit the representation of references in Choice constructors without loosing semantically important information, we have adopted *bubbling* as first presented in Antoy et al. [2006a]. Bubbling is related to the approach developed in this work in the sense that non-deterministic branching is treated (almost) like a constructor. The Choice constructors of our approach are "lifted up" one step at a time by the rules added by our transformation like:

```
head (Choice_List r x y) = choiceCons r (head x) (head y)
```

In bubbling, in contrast, when a (?) is at a needed position it is moved up in the term structure until a "proper dominator" has been copied, i.e., a symbol which is above all references to that (?). The exact definition of bubbling [Antoy et al., 2006a, Definition 5] employs term graphs and the basic idea is quite intuitive. In order to exemplify it we will use the style of let-rewriting López-Fraguas et al. [2007].

Example 6.10.4 (Bubbling) *Consider the following evaluation:*

```
            let l=insert 1 [2] 7 in (head l,1)
    ...     let l=Choice_List 7 [1,2] [2,1] in (head l,1)
```

In the approach of this work the (inlined) end result of this derivation would be (Choice_Int 7 1 2,Choice_List 7 [1,2] [2,1]). *The identifier 7 is needed to reconstruct the fact that both parts of the tuple share the same choice, i.e., that* (1,[2,1]) *is not a valid projection of the result. In bubbling, in contrast, the next step is to copy the whole* let *expression. (If there was an outer context of this expression, that context would not be copied.) In the notions of Antoy et al. [2006a], the tuple constructor is the dominator.*

```
            let l=insert 1 [2] in (head l,1)
    ...     let l=[1,2] ? [2,1] in (head l,1)
            let l=[1,2] in (head l,1) ? let l=[2,1] in (head l,1)
            (1,[1,2]) ? (2,[2,1])
```

The advantage of this technique is that (?) is never duplicated and, thus, no identifiers are needed. This is why we can use the technique to omit the references when presenting values. In our tool, the derivation is presented as:

```
main
  insert 1 [2]
    insert 1 []      [1]
  insert 1 [2]       [1,2] ? [2,1]
head ([1,2] ? [2,1])    1 ? 2
main    (1,[1,2]) ? (2,[2,1])
```

The operation head is applied to the non-deterministic argument ([1,2] ? [2,1]) but the representation at the end is the result of a bubbling procedure in the pretty printer.

6.10.3 Related Work for Debugging

We have already given a detailed accord of related work with regard to debugging tools in Section 1.3.1. Here we would like to discuss the attempts to decrease the memory requirements of related approaches. As already mentioned, many of the approaches to debug lazy functional programs are based on recording the computation in a *redex trail* Sparud and Runciman [1997a] or an EDT Nilsson and Sparud [1997a]. The size of these structures crucially grows with the length of the computation to be debugged. As a solution to this problem, some dierent approaches were proposed.

Sparud and Runciman [1997b] present one of the first approaches to reduce the size of redex trails. It is based on not recording *trusted* computations (e.g., the evaluation of Prelude functions) and on pruning trails. Unfortunately, considering trusted functions does not reduce memory consumption as expected, since trusted functions are applied to expressions for which debug information has to be recorded, cf. Pope and Naish [2003]. Pruning trails was not considered further since the resulting trail is incomplete and the buggy computation can be cut from the recorded information.

In the further development of Hat [Wallace et al., 2001], the problem of recording large *redex trails* was not really tackled. All information is written to a large file which results in a slowdown when generating this file and analyzing it in viewer components.

The piecemeal tracing approach of Nilsson [1999, 2001] and Pope and Naish [2003] was defined for declarative debugging by means of an *Evaluation Dependence Tree* (EDT) used in Freja [Nilsson and Sparud, 1997a] or Buddha Pope [2005]. In this approach, only a piece of the entire EDT is initially generated, and new pieces are computed only if they are needed by re-executing the entire program. Hence, the saving of space is purchased by additional run-time during debugging. In contrast, our approach is directly space e cient and only stores a minimal amount of information at execution time. Furthermore, their approach is basically oriented to declarative debugging in contrast to our step lists.

Pope and Naish [2003] propose an optimization of the piecemeal EDT construction in which it is not necessary to restart the whole computation to compute new pieces of the EDT. Instead computations are stored which allow the generation of the missing parts of the EDT. However, there exists no evaluation on how much memory is needed for storing these computations. Furthermore,

6.10. DEBUGGING

the implementation highly depends on the internal structure of the Glasgow Haskell Compiler (ghc) and the underlying C heap in which structures are stored to prevent them from garbage collection. This makes it non-portable to other Haskell systems. The whole approach is motivated from the implementation perspective, without any correctness proofs.

Finally, we would like to mention that a practical course was held at the Christian-Albrechts-University of Kiel to implement a framework with which new debugging tools based on the presented work can be easily implemented. Some results of this course were published by Wulf [2009].

Chapter 7

Conclusion

In this work we have presented an approach to translate lazy functional logic programs to purely functional ones. The translation fully preserves the laziness of the original declarations and makes use of the sharing provided by the target language. We have given a proof of soundness for the core concepts and we have demonstrated the practical relevance of the approach.

More concretely, we have connected to previous work in the field of functional logic programming by basing our work on an operational semantics proposed by Albert et al. [2005]. We have shown that this semantics suers from an anomaly with regard to the evaluation of certain expressions. We have proposed a fix for this problem, extensively justifying our modification in Chapter 2 and Section 6.5.

After that, we have transferred a recent result about the relation of free variables with so called "generators" to the resulting operational semantics. With our transfer this theorem was obtained for the first time for a setting in which the important property of sharing is modeled on the formal level (Chapter 3).

In Chapter 4 we have shown that the calculus to model functional logic programs can be simplified further. The resulting formalism features several advantages. Firstly, the calculus has less and simpler rules, featuring less purely technical details. Secondly, the programs interpreted by the calculus are, at least in our opinion, more readable. Last but not least, we have argued that the relation to another important approach to model the operational semantics of functional logic programs, namely term-graph rewriting, is now considerably closer.

The main theoretic result of our work is contained in Chapter 5. There, we have motivated and formalized our approach to eliminate the non-determinism inherent to functional logic programs by a simple program transformation. The basic ideas are a) to compute on a treelike representation of the logic search space and b) to associate dependent choices by labeling them with identifiers.

Chapter 6 is dedicated to the demonstration of the practical relevance of our approach. Several benchmarks for various functional logic programs witness that the programs resulting from our transformation can be compiled to machine code that is more efficient than that generated by existing compilation systems. Especially, we have given account that the simplicity of our transformation enables a better optimization of the target language's compiler than comparable approaches. Furthermore, we have presented how several features of functional logic languages, like free variables, recursive let bindings, different search strategies and constraints, can be implemented in our setting. In addition, we have implemented several features which go beyond the possibilities of systems currently in use. One such feature is that the presented search strategies include a parallel search. Another unique feature of our approach is the sharing of deterministic results across the border of non-deterministic choice. The latter feature is, as we have argued, not only advantageous for run-time efficiency but also of key importance for a seamless integration of the functional and logic paradigms in a unified language. Furthermore, the presented implementation of encapsulated search is the first to feature both strong and weak encapsulation in a declarative way, i.e., independent of the order of evaluation. For the integration of weak encapsulation we have shown how to support "set functions" in our settings, which have recently been proposed as a syntactic extension for functional logic languages. Finally, we have introduced a technique for debugging purely functional programming languages which we have developed recently. The reason to discuss the approach in this work is that our translation makes it possible to transfer it to the more general setting of functional logic languages. As we have demonstrated, this transfer is only possible because of the features uniquely present in our implementation, as it depends on sharing across non-determinism.

Bibliography

E. Albert, M. Hanus, F. Huch, J. Oliver, and G. Vidal. Operational semantics for declarative multi-paradigm languages. *Journal of Symbolic Computation*, 40(1):795–829, 2005.

S. Antoy. Evaluation strategies for functional logic programming. *Journal of Symbolic Computation*, 40(1):875–903, 2005.

S. Antoy and B. Braßel. Computing with subspaces. In *Proceedings of the 9th ACM SIGPLAN International Conference on Principles and Practice of Declarative Programming (PPDP'07)*, pages 121–130. ACM Press, 2007.

S. Antoy and M. Hanus. Functional logic design patterns. In *Proc. of the 6th International Symposium on Functional and Logic Programming (FLOPS 2002)*, pages 67–87. Springer LNCS 2441, 2002.

S. Antoy and M. Hanus. Declarative programming with function patterns. In *Proceedings of the International Symposium on Logic-based Program Synthesis and Transformation (LOPSTR'05)*, pages 6–22. Springer LNCS 3901, 2005.

S. Antoy and M. Hanus. Overlapping rules and logic variables in functional logic programs. In *Proceedings of the 22nd International Conference on Logic Programming (ICLP 2006)*, pages 87–101. Springer LNCS 4079, 2006.

S. Antoy and M. Hanus. Set functions for functional logic programming. In *Proceedings of the 11th ACM SIGPLAN International Conference on Principles and Practice of Declarative Programming (PPDP'09)*, pages 73–82. ACM Press, 2009.

S. Antoy and S. Johnson. Teabag: A functional logic language debugger. In *Proc. 13th International Workshop on Functional and (Constraint) Logic Programming (WFLP 2004)*, pages 4–18, Aachen (Germany), 2004. Technical Report AIB-2004-05, RWTH Aachen.

S. Antoy, R. Echahed, and M. Hanus. A needed narrowing strategy. In *Proc. 21st ACM Symposium on Principles of Programming Languages*, pages 268–279, Portland, 1994.

S. Antoy, M. Hanus, J. Liu, and A. Tolmach. A virtual machine for functional logic computations. In *Proc. of the 16th International Workshop on Implementation and Application of Functional Languages (IFL 2004)*, pages 108–125. Springer LNCS 3474, 2005.

S. Antoy, D. Brown, and S.-H. Chiang. On the correctness of bubbling. In F. Pfenning, editor, *17th International Conference on Rewriting Techniques and Applications*, pages 35–49, Seattle, WA, Aug. 2006a. Springer LNCS 4098.

S. Antoy, D.W. Brown, and S.-H. Chiang. Lazy context cloning for nondeterministic graph rewriting. In *Proc. of the 3rd International Workshop on Term Graph Rewriting (Termgraph'06)*, pages 61–70, Vienna, Austria, 2006b.

J. Armstrong, M. Williams, C. Wikstrom, and R. Virding. *Concurrent Programming in Erlang*. Prentice Hall, 1996.

L. Augustsson, M. Rittri, and D. Synek. On generating unique names. *Journal of Functional Programming*, 4(1):117–123, 1994.

H.P. Barendregt. *The Lambda Calculus: Its Syntax and Semantics*, volume 103 of *Studies in Logic and the Foundations of Mathematics*. North-Holland, Amsterdam, 1984. Revised edition.

R. Berghammer. *Ordnungen, Verbände und Relationen mit Anwendungen*. Vieweg+Teubner, 2008.

S. P. Booth and S. B. Jones. Walk backwards to happiness - debugging by time travel. In *Proceedings of the Third International Workshop on Automatic Debugging (AADEBUG)*, pages 171–183, 1997.

B. Braßel. A framework for interpreting traces of functional logic computations. *Electronic Notes in Theoretical Computer Science*, 177:91–106, 2007.

B. Braßel. A Technique to build Debugging Tools for Lazy Functional Logic Languages. In M. Falschi, editor, *Proceedings of the 17th Workshop on Functional and (Constraint) Logic Programming (WFLP 2008)*, pages 63–76, 2008.

B. Braßel and J. Christiansen. Denotation by transformation: Towards obtaining a denotational semantics by transformation to point-free style. In A. King, editor, *Proceedings of the 17th International Symposium on Logic-Based Program Synthesis and Transformation (LOPSTR 2007)*, volume 4915 of *LNCS*, pages 90–105. Springer, 2008.

B. Braßel and J. Christiansen. A relation algebraic semantics for a lazy functional logic language. In R. Berghammer, B. Möller, and G. Struth, editors, *RelMiCS*, volume 4988 of *Lecture Notes in Computer Science*, pages 37–53. Springer, 2008.

B. Braßel and S. Fischer. From Functional Logic Programs to Purely Functional Programs Preserving Laziness. In *Proc. 20th Workshop on Implementation and Application of Functional Languages (IFL 2008)*, pages 214–215, 2008.

B. Braßel and M. Hanus. Nondeterminism analysis of functional logic programs. In *Proceedings of the International Conference on Logic Programming (ICLP 2005)*, pages 265–279. Springer LNCS 3668, 2005.

B. Braßel and F. Huch. On a tighter integration of functional and logic programming. In *Proc. APLAS 2007*, pages 122–138. Springer LNCS 4807, 2007a.

B. Braßel and F. Huch. On a tighter integration of functional and logic programming. In Zhong Shao, editor, *APLAS*, volume 4807 of *Lecture Notes in Computer Science*, pages 122–138. Springer, 2007b.

B. Braßel and F. Huch. The Kiel Curry system KiCS. In D. Seipel, M. Hanus, and A. Wolf, editors, *Applications of Declarative Programming and Knowledge Management*, volume 5437 of *Lecture Notes in Artificial Intelligence*, pages 195–205. Springer, 2009.

B. Braßel and H. Siegel. Debugging Lazy Functional Programs by Asking the Oracle. In O. Chitil, editor, *Proc. Implementation of Functional Languages (IFL 2007)*, volume 5083 of *Lecture Notes in Computer Science*, pages 183–200. Springer, 2008.

B. Braßel, O. Chitil, M. Hanus, and F. Huch. Observing functional logic computations. In *Proc. of the Sixth International Symposium on Practical Aspects of Declarative Languages (PADL'04)*, pages 193–208. Springer LNCS 3057, 2004a.

B. Braßel, M. Hanus, and F. Huch. Encapsulating non-determinism in functional logic computations. *Journal of Functional and Logic Programming*, 2004(6), 2004b.

B. Braßel, M. Hanus, F. Huch, and G. Vidal. A semantics for tracing declarative multi-paradigm programs. In *Proceedings of the 6th ACM SIGPLAN International Conference on Principles and Practice of Declarative Programming (PPDP'04)*, pages 179–190. ACM Press, 2004c.

B. Braßel, M. Hanus, F. Huch, J. Silva, and G. Vidal. Run-time profiling of functional logic programs. In *Proceedings of the International Symposium on Logic-based Program Synthesis and Transformation (LOPSTR'04)*, pages 182–197. Springer LNCS 3573, 2005.

B. Braßel, S. Fischer, and F. Huch. A program transformation for tracing functional logic computations. In *Pre-Proceedings of the International Symposium on Logic-based Program Synthesis and Transformation (LOPSTR'06)*, pages 141–157. Technical Report CS-2006-5, Università ca' Foscari di Venezia, 2006.

B. Braßel, S. Fischer, M. Hanus, F. Huch, and G. Vidal. Lazy call-by-value evaluation. In *Proc. of the 12th ACM SIGPLAN International Conference on Functional Programming (ICFP 2007)*, pages 265–276. ACM Press, 2007.

B. Braßel, S. Fischer, and F. Huch. Declaring numbers. *Electronic Notes in Theoretical Computer Science*, 216:111–124, 2008.

B. Braßel, S. Fischer, M. Hanus, and F. Reck. Transforming functional logic programs into monadic functional programs. In *Proc. of the 19th International Workshop on Functional and (Constraint) Logic Programming (WFLP 2010)*, pages 2–18. Universidad Politécnica de Madrid, 2010.

R. Caballero and M. Rodríguez-Artalejo. DDT: a declarative debugging tool for functional-logic languages. In *Proceedings of the 7th International Symposium on Functional and Logic Programming (FLOPS 2004)*, pages 70–84. Springer LNCS 2998, 2004.

M. Cameron, M. García de la Banda, K. Marriott, and P. Moulder. Vimer: A visual debugger for mercury. In *Proceedings of the 8th ACM SIGPLAN International Conference on Principles and Practice of Declarative Programming (PPDP'03)*, pages 56–66. ACM Press, 2003.

A. Casas, D. Cabeza, and M.V. Hermenegildo. A syntactic approach to combining functional notation, lazy evaluation, and higher-order in lp systems. In *Proc. of the 8th International Symposium on Functional and Logic Programming (FLOPS 2006)*, pages 146–162. Springer LNCS 3945, 2006.

O. Chitil and F. Huch. Monadic, prompt lazy assertions in Haskell. In *Proc. APLAS 2007*, pages 38–53. Springer LNCS 4807, 2007.

O. Chitil, C. Runciman, and M. Wallace. Freja, Hat and Hood – a comparative evaluation of three systems for tracing and debugging lazy functional programs. In *Proc. of the 12th International Workshop on Implementation of Functional Languages (IFL 2000)*, pages 176–193. Springer LNCS 2011, 2001.

A. Church. *The Calculi of Lambda Conversion*. Princeton University Press, 1941.

K. Claessen and J. Hughes. Quickcheck: A lightweight tool for random testing of haskell programs. In *International Conference on Functional Programming (ICFP'00)*, pages 268–279. ACM Press, 2000.

M. Clavel, F. Durán, S. Eker, P. Lincoln, N. Martí-Oliet, J. Meseguer, and C. L. Talcott, editors. *All About Maude - A High-Performance Logical Framework, How to Specify, Program and Verify Systems in Rewriting Logic*, volume 4350 of *Lecture Notes in Computer Science*, 2007. Springer.

O. Danvy and L. R. Nielsen. Defunctionalization at work. In *PPDP '01: Proceedings of the 3rd ACM SIGPLAN international conference on Principles and practice of declarative programming*, pages 162–174, New York, NY, USA, 2001. ACM.

J. Dios and F.J. López-Fraguas. Elimination of extra variables from functional logic programs. In P. Lucio and F. Orejas, editors, *VI Jornadas sobre Programación y Lenguajes (PROLE 2006)*, pages 121–135. CINME, 2006.

R. Kent Dybvig. *The Scheme Programming Language*. MIT Press, third edition, 2002.

R. Echahed. Inductively sequential term-graph rewrite systems. In H. Ehrig, R. Heckel, G. Rozenberg, and G. Taentzer, editors, *ICGT*, volume 5214 of *Lecture Notes in Computer Science*, pages 84–98. Springer, 2008.

R. Ennals and S. Peyton Jones. Hsdebug : Debugging lazy programs by not being lazy, 2003.

L. Erkök. Value recursion in monadic computations. Technical report, OGI School of Science and Engineering, OHSU, 2002.

S. Fischer and H. Kuchen. Data-flow testing of declarative programs. In *Proc. of the 13th ACM SIGPLAN International Conference on Functional Programming (ICFP 2008)*, pages 201–212. ACM Press, 2008.

S. Fischer, O. Kiselyov, and C. Shan. Purely functional lazy non-deterministic programming. In *Proceeding of the 14th ACM SIGPLAN International Conference on Functional Programming (ICFP 2009)*, pages 11–22. ACM, 2009.

M.J. García de la Banda, B. Demoen, K. Marriott, and P.J. Stuckey. To the gates of hal: A hal tutorial. In *Proc. of the 6th International Symposium on Functional and Logic Programming (FLOPS 2002)*, pages 47–66. Springer LNCS 2441, 2002.

A. Gill. Debugging Haskell by observing intermediate datastructures. *Electronic Notes in Theoretical Computer Science*, 41(1), 2001.

J.C. González-Moreno, M.T. Hortalá-González, F.J. López-Fraguas, and M. Rodríguez-Artalejo. An approach to declarative programming based on a rewriting logic. *Journal of Logic Programming*, 40:47–87, 1999a.

J.C. González-Moreno, M.T. Hortalá-González, F.J. López-Fraguas, and M. Rodríguez-Artalejo. An approach to declarative programming based on a rewriting logic. *Journal of Logic Programming*, 40:47–87, 1999b.

M. Hanus. Reporting failures in functional logic programs. *Electronic Notes in Theoretical Computer Science*, 177:59–73, 2007a.

M. Hanus. Multi-paradigm declarative languages. In *Proceedings of the International Conference on Logic Programming (ICLP 2007)*, pages 45–75. Springer LNCS 4670, 2007b.

M. Hanus and C. Prehofer. Higher-order narrowing with definitional trees. *Journal of Functional Programming*, 9(1):33–75, 1999.

M. Hanus and P. Réty. Demand-driven search in functional logic programs. Research report rr-lifo-98-08, Univ. Orléans, 1998.

M. Hanus and R. Sadre. A concurrent implementation of curry in java. In *Proc. ILPS'97 Workshop on Parallelism and Implementation Technology for (Constraint) Logic Programming Languages*, Port Jeerson (New York), 1997.

M. Hanus and F. Steiner. Controlling search in declarative programs. In *Principles of Declarative Programming (Proc. Joint International Symposium PLILP/ALP'98)*, pages 374–390. Springer LNCS 1490, 1998.

M. Hanus, S. Antoy, B. Braßel, M. Engelke, K. Höppner, J. Koj, P. Niederau, R. Sadre, and F. Steiner. PAKCS: The Portland Aachen Kiel Curry System. Available at http://www.informatik.uni-kiel.de/~pakcs/, 2010.

M. Hanus (ed). Curry: An integrated functional logic language (vers. 0.8.2). Available at http://www.curry-language.org, 2006.

R. Hinze. Deriving backtracking monad transformers. In P. Wadler, editor, *Proceedings of the 2000 International Conference on Functional Programming, Montreal, Canada, September 18-20, 2000*, pages 186–197, sep 2000.

P. Hofstedt and A. Wolf. *Einführung in die Constraint-Programmierung*. Springer, 2007.

F. Huch and P. H. Sadeghi. The interactive Curry observation debugger COOiSY. In *Proceedings of the 15th Workshop on Functional and (Constraint) Logic Programming (WFLP 2006)*. ENTCS, 2006.

H. Hußmann. *Nondeterministic Algebraic Specifications and Algebraic Programs*. Birkhäuser Verlag, 1993.

T. Johnsson. Lambda lifting: Transforming programs to recursive functions. In *Functional Programming Languages and Computer Architecture*, pages 190–203. Springer LNCS 201, 1985.

S. Peyton Jones, D. Vytiniotis, S. Weirich, and G. Washburn. Simple unification-based type inference for gadts. In *ICFP '06: Proceedings of the eleventh ACM SIGPLAN international conference on Functional programming*, pages 50–61. ACM, 2006.

S. Peyton Jones, D. Vytiniotis, S. Weirich, and M. Shields. Practical type inference for arbitrary-rank types. *J. Funct. Program.*, 17(1):1–82, 2007.

O. Kiselyov. Simple fair and terminating backtracking monad transformer. http://okmij.org/ftp/Computation/monads.html#fair-bt-stream, October 2005.

P. Koopman, R. Plasmeijer, M. van Eekelen, and S. Smetsers. Functional programming in clean. http://www.cs.ru.nl/~clean/contents/Clean_Book/clean_book.html, 2001.

J. Launchbury. A natural semantics for lazy evaluation. In *Proc. 20th ACM Symposium on Principles of Programming Languages (POPL'93)*, pages 144–154. ACM Press, 1993.

F. López-Fraguas and J. Sánchez-Hernández. TOY: A multiparadigm declarative system. In *Proc. of RTA'99*, pages 244–247. Springer LNCS 1631, 1999.

F. J. López-Fraguas and J. Sánchez-Hernández. Narrowing failure in functional logic programming. In Zhenjiang Hu and M. Rodríguez-Artalejo, editors, *FLOPS*, volume 2441 of *Lecture Notes in Computer Science*, pages 212–227. Springer, 2002.

F.J. López-Fraguas and J. Sánchez-Hernández. Proving failure in functional logic programs. In *Proc. First International Conference on Computational Logic (CL 2000)*, pages 179–183. Springer LNAI 1861, 2000.

F.J. López-Fraguas and J. Sánchez-Hernández. A proof theoretic approach to failure in functional logic programming. *Theory and Practice of Logic Programming*, 4(1):41–74, 2004.

F.J. López-Fraguas, J. Rodríguez-Hortalá, and J. Sánchez-Hernández. A simple rewrite notion for call-time choice semantics. In *Proceedings of the 9th ACM SIGPLAN International Conference on Principles and Practice of Declarative Programming (PPDP'07)*, pages 197–208. ACM Press, 2007.

B. Lorenz. Ein Debugger für Oz. Master's thesis, Fachbereich Informatik, Universität des Saarlandes, April 1999.

W. Lux. Comparing copying and trailing implementations for encapsulated search. In *Proc. 13th International Workshop on Functional and (Constraint) Logic Programming (WFLP 2004)*, pages 91–103, Aachen (Germany), 2004. Technical Report AIB-2004-05, RWTH Aachen.

W. Lux. Implementing encapsulated search for a lazy functional logic language. In *Proc. 4th Fuji International Symposium on Functional and Logic Programming (FLOPS'99)*, pages 100–113. Springer LNCS 1722, 1999.

W. Lux and H. Kuchen. An e cient abstract machine for Curry. In K. Beiersdörfer, G. Engels, and W. Schäfer, editors, *Informatik '99 — Annual meeting of the German Computer Science Society (GI)*, pages 390–399. Springer, 1999.

J. Maraist, M. Odersky, and P. Wadler. The call-by-need lambda calculus. *J. Funct. Program.*, 8(3):275–317, 1998.

J. McCarthy. History of LISP. In R. L. Wexelblat, editor, *History of Programming Languages: Proceedings of the ACM SIGPLAN Conference*, pages 173–197. Academic Press, June 1–3 1978.

R. Milner, M. Tofte, and R. Harper. *The Definition of Standard ML*. MIT Press, 1990.

M. Naylor, E. Axelsson, and C. Runciman. A functional-logic library for wired. In *Haskell '07: Proceedings of the ACM SIGPLAN workshop on Haskell workshop*, pages 37–48, New York, NY, USA, 2007. ACM.

H. Nilsson. Tracing piece by piece: aordable debugging for lazy functional languages. In *Proceedings of the 1999 ACM SIGPLAN international conference on Functional programming*, pages 36–47, Paris, France, September 1999. ACM Press.

H. Nilsson. How to look busy while being as lazy as ever: The implementation of a lazy functional debugger. *Journal of Functional Programming*, 11(6): 629–671, November 2001.

H. Nilsson and P. Fritzson. Algorithmic debugging for lazy functional languages. *Journal of Functional Programming*, 4(3):337–370, 1994.

H. Nilsson and J. Sparud. The Evaluation Dependence Tree as a Basis for Lazy Functional Debugging. *Automated Software Engineering*, 4(2):121–150, 1997a.

H. Nilsson and J. Sparud. The Evaluation Dependence Tree as a Basis for Lazy Functional Debugging. *Automated Software Engineering*, 4(2):121–150, 1997b.

W. Partain. The nofib benchmark suite of haskell programs. In J. Launchbury and P. M. Sansom, editors, *Functional Programming*, Workshops in Computing, pages 195–202. Springer, 1992.

S. Peyton Jones, editor. *Haskell 98 Language and Libraries—The Revised Report*. Cambridge University Press, 2003.

S.L. Peyton Jones. *The Implementation of Functional Programming Languages*. Prentice Hall, 1987.

B. C. Pierce. *Types and Programming Languages*. MIT Press, Cambridge, MA, USA, 2002.

B. Pope. Declarative Debugging with Buddha. In V. Vene and T. Uustalu, editors, *Advanced Functional Programming, 5th International School, AFP 2004*, volume 3622 of *Lecture Notes in Computer Science*, pages 273–308. Springer Verlag, September 2005. ISBN 3-540-28540-7.

B. Pope and L. Naish. Practical aspects of declarative debugging in Haskell-98. In *Fifth ACM SIGPLAN Conference on Principles and Practice of Declarative Programming*, pages 230–240, 2003.

F. Pottier and N. Gauthier. Polymorphic typed defunctionalization. In N. D. Jones and X. Leroy, editors, *POPL*, pages 89–98. ACM, 2004.

J. C. Reynolds. Definitional interpreters for higher-order programming languages. In *Reprinted from the proceedings of the 25th ACM National Conference*, pages 717–740. ACM, 1972.

C. Runciman, M. Naylor, and F. Lindblad. SmallCheck and Lazy SmallCheck: Automatic exhaustive testing for small values. In *Haskell '08: Proceedings of the first ACM SIGPLAN symposium on Haskell*, pages 37–48. ACM, 2008.

J. Sánchez-Hernández. Constructive failure in functional-logic programming: From theory to implementation. *Journal of Universal Computer Science*, 12 (11):1574–1593, 2006.

P.M. Sansom and S.L. Peyton Jones. Formally based profiling for higher-order functional languages. *ACM Transactions on Programming Languages and Systems*, 19(2):334–385, 1997.

M. Schmidt-Schauß, E. Machkasova, and D. Sabel. Counterexamples to simulation in non-deterministic call-by-need lambda-calculi with letrec. Frank report 38, Institut für Informatik. Fachbereich Informatik und Mathematik. J. W. Goethe- Universität Frankfurt am Main, August 2009.

M. Schönfinkel. Über die Bausteine der mathematischen Logik. *Mathematische Annalen*, 92:305–316, 1924.

P. Sestoft. Deriving a lazy abstract machine. *Journal of Functional Programming*, 7(3):231–264, 1997.

E. Shapiro. *Algorithmic Program Debugging*. MIT Press, Cambridge, Massachusetts, 1983.

H. Siegel. Debugging non-strict programs by strict evaluation. Diplomarbeit, Institut für Informatik, Christian-Albrechts-Universität zu Kiel, October 2008.

J. Silva. A comparative study of algorithmic debugging strategies. In G. Puebla, editor, *LOPSTR*, volume 4407 of *Lecture Notes in Computer Science*, pages 143–159. Springer, 2006.

J.R. Slagle. Automated theorem-proving for theories with simplifiers, commutativity, and associativity. *Journal of the ACM*, 21(4):622–642, 1974.

G. Smolka. The oz programming model. In J. van Leeuwen, editor, *Computer Science Today: Recent Trends and Developments*, pages 324–343. Springer LNCS 1000, 1995a.

G. Smolka. The Oz programming model. In J. van Leeuwen, editor, *Computer Science Today: Recent Trends and Developments*, pages 324–343. Springer LNCS 1000, 1995b.

Z. Somogyi and F. Henderson. The design and implementation of mercury. Slides of a tutorial at JICSLP'96, 1996.

J. Sparud. Fixing some space leaks without a garbage collector. In *Proceedings of the conference on Functional programming languages and computer architecture*, FPCA '93, pages 117–122, New York, NY, USA, 1993. ACM.

J. Sparud and C. Runciman. Tracing Lazy Functional Computations Using Redex Trails. In *Proc. of the 9th Int'l Symp. on Programming Languages, Implementations, Logics and Programs (PLILP'97)*, pages 291–308. Springer LNCS 1292, 1997a.

J. Sparud and C. Runciman. Complete and partial redex trails of functional computations. In *Selected papers from 9th Intl. Workshop on the Implementation of Functional Languages (IFL'97*, pages 160–177. Springer LNCS, 1997b.

J. Sparud and C. Runciman. Tracing Lazy Functional Computations Using Redex Trails. In *Proc. of the 9th Int'l Symp. on Programming Languages, Implementations, Logics and Programs (PLILP'97)*, pages 291–308. Springer LNCS 1292, 1997c.

P. Wadler. Fixing some space leaks with a garbage collector. *Softw. Pract. Exper.*, 17:595–608, September 1987.

P. Wadler. How to replace failure by a list of successes. In *Functional Programming and Computer Architecture*, pages 113–128. Springer LNCS 201, 1985.

P. Wadler and S. Blott. How to make ad-hoc polymorphism less ad hoc. In *Proc. POPL'89*, pages 60–76, 1989.

M. Wallace, O. Chitil, T. Brehm, and C. Runciman. Multiple-View Tracing for Haskell: a New Hat. In *Proc. of the 2001 ACM SIGPLAN Haskell Workshop*. Universiteit Utrecht UU-CS-2001-23, 2001.

M. Wirsing. Algebraic specification. In J. van Leeuwen, editor, *Handbook of Theoretical Computer Science*. North-Holland, 1990.

C. Wulf. Code-Erzeugung zur Unterstützung der Fehlersuche. Bachelorarbeit, Institut für Informatik, Christian-Albrechts-Universität zu Kiel, april 2009.

i want morebooks!

Buy your books fast and straightforward online - at one of world's fastest growing online book stores! Environmentally sound due to Print-on-Demand technologies.

Buy your books online at
www.get-morebooks.com

Kaufen Sie Ihre Bücher schnell und unkompliziert online – auf einer der am schnellsten wachsenden Buchhandelsplattformen weltweit! Dank Print-On-Demand umwelt- und ressourcenschonend produziert.

Bücher schneller online kaufen
www.morebooks.de

 VDM Verlagsservicegesellschaft mbH
Heinrich-Böcking-Str. 6-8   Telefon: +49 681 3720 174   info@vdm-vsg.de
D - 66121 Saarbrücken   Telefax: +49 681 3720 1749   www.vdm-vsg.de

Printed by Books on Demand GmbH, Norderstedt / Germany